THE TRIAL

A Procedural Description
and Case Study

THE TRIAL

A Procedural Description and Case Study

Howard Myers

FLORIDA A&M UNIVERSITY

Jan Pudlow

TALLAHASSEE DEMOCRAT

WEST PUBLISHING COMPANY

St. Paul • New York • Los Angeles • San Francisco

Copyeditor: Kim Kaliszewski
Design: Lois Stanfield
Cover Design: David Farr, Imagesmythe, Inc.
Typesetting: G & S Typesetters
Index: Virginia Hobbs

Library of Congress Cataloging-in-Publication Data
Myers, Howard.
    The trial : a procedural description and case study / Howard Myers, Jan Pudlow.
        p.   cm.
    ISBN 0-314-82441-3 (soft)
    1. Criminal procedure—United States.   2. Criminal courts—United States.   I. Pudlow, Jan.   II. Title.
KF9655.Z9M94   1991
345.73'05—dc20
[347.3055]
                                                            90-22059
                                                            CIP

Contents

Preface

Not much written on the undergraduate level explains in any detail how the criminal justice system disposes of a case in which a defendant is accused of committing a serious crime. Although trial practice textbooks deal with the trial aspect of the court process, they tend to emphasize courtroom strategy and preparation, topics better suited to law school. Introductory criminology and criminal justice textbooks often include a few chapters on a variety of court-related topics, such as plea bargaining, sentencing, bail reform, and the dual court system. The court process, however, is usually described only briefly. A few textbooks have been written for undergraduate courses in processes and procedures of the criminal courts. Current research is treated much more extensively in these specific texts than it is at the introductory level. Although the dispositional process is used typically to structure the temporal presentation of concepts (e.g., preparing for trial, trial, and sentencing), little attention is paid to actual procedures and their broader implications.

One author has attempted to deal with this problem by requiring students to go to trials. The courtroom visit is seen as a chance for students to become acquainted firsthand with court procedures. As a practical matter, however, the field trip is fraught with risks. One never knows whether a trial will be held because defendants often plead guilty or no contest at the last moment. Trials that do materialize, particularly those involving serious offenses, are frequently drawn out over days or weeks. The half day spent in the courtroom gives students only a fragmented view of the court process.

The Trial: A Procedural Description and Case Study affords students a risk-free chance to become acquainted with court procedures, explaining in some detail what actually happens to a defendant in a felony case at each stage of the court process. Although reading about a trial is not the same as being there, *The Trial* is unique because it combines description of court procedures with an account of an actual trial. It is intended as a supplementary text in undergraduate courses covering criminal courts, criminal procedure, and introductory criminal justice.

The procedural description depicts the settings in which hypothetical defendants might find themselves as their cases proceed through the criminal justice system—the station house, the jail, the lower court, the trial court, the appellate court, and, again, the trial court. It presents the actors likely to appear during the disposition of the case—the prosecutor, the defense attorney, the judge, the bondsman, the jurors, and others. Most significantly, it describes the procedures by which these actors implement the court process—indictment, arraignment, discovery, voir dire, and jury trial. In short, *The Trial* describes what happens when someone—anyone—is accused of a serious crime.

The case study is a narrative account. It describes what happened to a real defendant—John Wesley Peavy—when he was arrested and prosecuted in the courts at Tallahassee, Florida. Because Peavy flatly denied committing the murders, his case is a classic whodunit, lending a sense of real-life mystery to the lessons of the criminal justice process. His case study allows students to peer into the human side of the court process. It scrutinizes Peavy's fight for freedom through an elaborately prepared defense, details the prosecution's zeal to punish a brutal crime, and captures the emotions of a well-to-do family and a small-town community torn apart by those clashing positions. Quotations in the case study sections come from interviews, court testimony, and court transcripts.

The organization of the book is straightforward. With the exception of Chapter 1, each chapter consists of two parts: case study and procedural description. Chapter 1 includes an overview of the court process. Chapters 1–3 treat pretrial events, such as arrest, indictment, and trial preparation. Jury selection, the trial, and sentencing are the subject matter of Chapters 4–6. Chapter 7 deals with the aftermath of the trial. A number of study questions accompany each chapter. They, along with exhibits and excerpts from trial transcripts, are intended to help the student relate the events of the case study to the concepts of the procedural description.

The jurors' real names have been changed to protect their privacy.

A number of technical terms are used throughout this book. These terms are identified in boldface when first used. The reader who is unfamiliar with them is encouraged to refer to the glossary at the end of the text.

A number of people have been helpful in the production of this book, commenting on earlier drafts of chapters, explaining the ins and outs of courthouse routines, and assisting in the preparation of the manuscript. The authors thank Owusu-Ansah Agyapong, Joe Aloi, Liz Black, Edna Danielson, Thomas Duffy, the Florida Bar Association, Anthony Guarisco, Warren Goodwin, Robert Harper, Timothy Henry,

Leonard Holton, Emmit Hunt, Ray Marky, Hal McClamma, Randy Murrell, Philip Padovano, Roosevelt Randolph, George Reynolds, Herb Smith, Philip Smith, and Bill Wills. Special thanks go to Mark Pudlow, James Van Matre, and the reviewers of West Publishing for their useful criticism of an earlier draft of the entire manuscript.

1

Making an Arrest

The Law Grabs Johnny Peavy

Murder came knocking on a rainy Halloween night at Bobby Harrison's trailer on the Ochlockonee River.

Out of the North Florida country darkness, someone crept close to Harrison's home, put a gun to the window, pulled the trigger, and left behind broken glass, blood, and death (see Figures 1-1 and 1-2).

Mary Lee Driggers, Harrison's thirty-nine year old girlfriend, had just called her daughter on the phone and died clutching her eyeglasses in her hand. Three bullets, all fatal, ripped through her body. Harrison, a burly forty-year-old man, was hit with five bullets, one fatal. For both, death came within minutes.

Two days would pass before friends found the bodies sprawled on the kitchen floor. Fried chicken take-out dinners were left uneaten in their boxes (see Figures 1-3 and 1-4).

Who would want to kill Harrison? Was Driggers in the wrong place at the wrong time? Those questions drove investigators to a mammoth search door to door down backwoods dirt roads, to interviews with almost everyone in both families, to following drug leads at Gulf Coast ports, to scanning the whole country for 9mm guns. And, from salt shakers to Marlboro cigarette packs, detectives dusted dozens of items from Harrison's trailer for fingerprints. But they found none. Days and days of rain, dumped by a tropical storm swirling in the Gulf, erased any footprint or tire track in the sandy soil.

"I readily concede I've seen cases that were a lot stronger," said Mickey Watson, agent-in-charge at the Tallahassee Region Office of the Florida Department of Law Enforcement (FDLE). "There were no tire tracks, fingerprints, hairs or fibers that can say, 'It's that man.'"

It was a classic whodunit involving the death of a man with a share of enemies and a married woman with a boyfriend on the side. When people talked about Harrison, they described him as "macho," "tough," "rough-

1

Figure 1-1 The kitchen window of Harrison's trailer. This photo was taken near the spot where the killer stood.

Figure 1-2 Close-up of Harrison's shattered kitchen window.

Figure 1-3 Interior of Harrison's trailer. The bodies of Harrison and Driggers lie on the floor.

Figure 1-4 Interior of Harrison's trailer.

Figure 1-5 The Shady Rest tavern.

and-tumble," "a cowboy born 100 years too late." He was a wheeler-dealer who worked hard and played hard. He grew tomatoes, roped cattle, and raised hell. As he had requested, Harrison was buried with a bottle of Early Times Kentucky straight bourbon, a pair of dice, and a little cash.

"Gambling. Drinking. Jukes. Bobby loved those three things, and that's why I left him," said Sandra Peavy Harrison about her ex-husband.

But whether Harrison's spirit ever spilled over into crime would remain in hot dispute and has never been proven.

One thing is certain: the day he died was looking like Harrison's lucky day. Rain drove his construction crew to the Shady Rest tavern, between the towns of Havana and Quincy, on the morning of October 31, 1985 (see Figure 1-5).

The idle workers got an early start on drinking beer and shooting craps in the back room. Harrison joined them later in the afternoon, bringing Driggers, an outdoorsy woman who always seemed to have dogs in the back of her pickup and who liked to hunt and hang out with the guys.

After several hours of rolling the dice, Harrison was a big winner, up at least $500. But he never lived long enough to spend it. Around 10:30 that night, gunfire rained through his kitchen window.

Johnny Peavy was at the Shady Rest that night, too. He was a member of a prominent Havana family one investigator called the "Ewings of Gadsden County," owners of thousands of acres of land and Peavy & Son Construction. Peavy, a former cop with a drinking problem, spent his days picking turnips and sometimes working with his big brother paving roads.

This Halloween evening, he'd already taken his two children and wife home, after a trick-or-treat outing. Peavy stopped at a country store down the road from his home, cashed a $100 check, and took another swig of vodka from the bottle he'd been sipping on most of the day. He strolled into the Shady Rest and exchanged greetings in the old country tavern, its weathered clapboard a decade shy of a paint job.

Sam Castle was tending bar when Peavy walked in around 9 P.M. and headed to the back room. Peavy returned to the bar a few minutes later. Castle remembered serving him a Miller draft. Peavy asked, "What's Bobby got on them that they won't play with me?" Next, Castle said, Peavy told him that Harrison was his "ex-brother-in-law" and that Harrison had "lost my sister's house."

Words now frozen in time, that quick exchange between a tavern owner and a customer would become important information to investigators searching for a murderer.

For weeks and weeks, agents were busy sniffing out cocaine connections. Deputies dug into drug leads.

"They had to," said Major Larry Campbell, at the helm of a joint investigation between the Leon County Sheriff's Department and the FDLE.

Harrison was a good buddy of Martha Munroe, a flamboyant cheesecake baker who married into a rich family. She had been arrested for cocaine trafficking a few months before the killings, and was later convicted and sentenced to eighteen years in prison.

"And," Campbell said, "they poked around in the jealous lovers department. Harrison had former girlfriends, and Driggers, his current girlfriend, had a husband."

Leads were followed. Alibis were checked. Of all the people questioned, investigators kept coming back to Johnny Peavy. Bit after bit of evidence began stacking up against him, Campbell said.

- Peavy's sister Sandra had divorced Harrison three years earlier.

- Peavy owned a 9mm gun, and Driggers and Harrison were killed with 9mm bullets.

- Peavy became so distraught and drunk on the day of Harrison's funeral that he couldn't attend.

- The day after the funeral, Peavy, a long-time alcoholic, checked into an out-of-town treatment center.

- Peavy saw Harrison and Driggers at the Shady Rest tavern about an hour before the killing.

- He mentioned to the bartender that night that Harrison wouldn't let him place bets in the crap game. Then Peavy volunteered that Harrison was divorced from his sister, had gone bankrupt, and had caused his sister to lose her house.

- He gave inconsistent accounts of what time he got home.

- Peavy was a gun enthusiast and was never without his Intratec 9. When investigators visited him at the treatment center, Peavy gave them permission to look for the gun, sparing them the hassle of obtaining a search warrant. But the gun couldn't be found.

- Peavy failed a polygraph test, which constituted evidence inadmissible in court but important to the police.

Investigators asked Peavy's nephew, Little Delacy Peavy, to take them to several locations where he and his uncle practiced shooting, helping them collect shell casings.

The clincher, Campbell said, was FDLE ballistics expert Don Champagne's conclusion that 9mm shell casings at the crime scene matched those recovered from three other places Peavy shot his gun.

On December 20, 1985, Leon County Circuit Judge J. Lewis Hall signed the arrest warrant. Three days later, Peavy was brought to the sheriff's office for questioning. Campbell described it as "same song, verse three." It was the third time they'd questioned Peavy about the killings, and the two previous discussions had been amiable. Peavy was a former police officer in Georgia, and he acted like he was one of the guys at the Leon County Sheriff's Department.

This time, however, it wasn't so friendly. Sheriff's detective Bill Moody, FDLE agent Joe Mitchell, and Sheriff's Sergeant Keith Daws pulled up chairs in Campbell's office. But Campbell, sitting across from Peavy at a polished table, did the talking.

"Your gun killed them," Campbell said, his blue eyes piercing into Peavy's.

"There ain't, there ain't no doubt?" Peavy asked.

"There is no doubt," Campbell said. "I am telling you for a flat fact, your gun, with CCI Blazer ammunition, killed Bobby Harrison and Mary Lee Driggers. Flat-out, stone-cold dead, son. There ain't no question about it," Campbell said, taking a long drag from his cigarette. "You've been a cop for a long time, and you've played some good cop games with us."

"Larry," Peavy interrupted, "I ain't playing no games with you. I was not down there that night. I did not kill Bobby Harrison; I did not kill Mary Lee Driggers."

Daws spoke up. "So somebody stole your gun, went down there, and killed them, putting it all on you?"

"I don't know what the hell to think," Peavy said, fumbling for a cigarette.

"Yep," Campbell continued, "what it gets down to—and I tried to explain it to you the other day, Johnny—is it's your time. If you want to help yourself, now is the time. Because we're fixing to shoot or cut bait, bro'. Here we go. You ain't going to be no more Johnny Peavy sitting there talking to us friendly guys.

"You think we ain't been on you like flies on honey, son? We have been on your every damn step. We know what you say in your sleep at night, or damn near it.

"We're going to put it to you and it's going to be that Bobby Harrison pissed Johnny Peavy off because he wouldn't let him in the game. He done your sister wrong. He wasn't taking care of the children.

"That's the way it's going to go. You went outside and got your old Tec 9 and you came back and you settled the damn score. You was as drunk as a bear."

Peavy mustered up, "No, I wasn't."

"Yeah, you were," Campbell flung back.

"I did not get drunk that night. Not so drunk that I don't remember where I went," Peavy insisted.

"No, I think you remember. You know enough about psychology. You're trying to repress it because you don't want to remember. Because you know what it's going to do to your family."

"What have you all charged me with, Larry?" Peavy asked.

"It's up to you," Campbell said.

"Let's stop this interrogation then. Let me go ahead and get a lawyer," Peavy said.

"That's your shot, bro'," Campbell said.

"Well, Larry, I did not kill Bobby Harrison," Peavy inisted.

Campbell echoed: "That's your shot."

They could link him to the murder weapon, but they needed to prove he pulled the trigger. The plan was to get Peavy to confess.

Daws began the arrest paperwork while Campbell continued: "This is your day. You figure whether you want to tell your side of the story or not. Because if you don't tell it today, the next time you tell it will be on a witness stand. I hope that you got a better story than you got today."

Peavy kept muttering, "I did not kill Bobby Harrison and that girl."

Detective Moody turned to Peavy and said, "Everything we got shows Johnny Peavy as a cold-blooded, heartless murderer, OK? When a jury hears all that we have, Johnny Peavy's going to be headed for the electric chair. The only thing that can stop that, Johnny, is you. And you're the only one standing in between."

Again Peavy said, "I didn't kill Bobby Harrison. I didn't kill anyone."

They kept at him, trying to convince him a confession was the best way to help himself. But Peavy stuck to his innocence.

"I'm not going to admit to anything I didn't do," Peavy said.

He emptied his pockets. They counted the money in his wallet and wrote the amount on another form. Peavy asked if he could take his cigarettes on the ride to the jail.

"I don't know how in the hell I'm going to prove it," Peavy said. "But I'm not going to jail for this. And I don't know who did it."

"But Johnny," Moody said, "How can you explain about the polygraph? How can you explain about your gun?"

"Polygraph implicates, sometimes, the innocent and exonerates the guilty," Peavy answered. "I don't know about that gun. I can't figure where it came up missing. I can't. I have no idea."

In the booking room at the jail, Peavy posed for his mug shot, his eyes bloodshot, his nerves shattered. He traded in his garnet-and-gold Florida State University jacket for blue jail garb. Once he had worn a badge and had had the power to lock people up. Now, he was being locked in a cell.

They arrested Peavy on December 23 for a reason, Campbell admitted. They needed a confession. And what better time to get the blues and spill your guts than when you're sitting in the jail, charged with murder, at Christmastime?

OVERVIEW OF THE COURT PROCESS

A person is profoundly involved in the court process when accused of committing a serious offense. The accused and the state become adversaries in a two-sided dispute in which the accused is presumed innocent while the state has the burden of proving that the accused is guilty. The following is an overview of this process, including a discussion of the law, the criminal justice system, its adversary and accusatory features, and the court system.

Law

Law is a body of rules. If it is made by judges, it is called **common law.** If it is made by legislators, it is called **statutory law.** Historically, law in the United States was judge-made. Judges created law when they ruled on specific cases. These rulings formed precedents to be followed in deciding later cases in which the facts were similar. Although American courts still follow the principle of **stare decisis,** the doctrine that judges should be bound by precedents, most laws today are statutory. Judges usually consult legislatively enacted criminal codes to determine how crime is defined and what sanctions are appropriate.

The purpose of law is to prevent or minimize conflict. Failing that, law provides a means for resolving disputes when conflicts do arise. In any discussion of law, it is customary to distinguish between **civil law** and **criminal law.** Civil law involves disputes between *private* parties. These disputes are settled on the basis of civil law, a body of laws concerned with private rights and **remedies.** Typically, in a civil case the **plaintiff** sues the **defendant** for monetary damages. Criminal law differs from civil law in that a crime is a *public* wrong. While the plaintiff initiates action in a civil case, the government brings charges in a criminal case on the basis of criminal law, a body of rules that deal with crime and its punishment.

Criminal law consists of **substantive law** and **procedural law.** Substantive law defines conduct that is legally prohibited and subject to punishment. A typical criminal statute defines murder as the unlawful killing of a human being when perpetrated from a premeditated design to effect the death of the person killed. The **elements of the crime** define it as murder. The conduct is unlawful killing. The harm is the death of a human being. There is a guilty state of mind which precedes the guilty act. Intent, the guilty act, and harm are causally related.

Procedural law consists of rules by which substantive law is administered, rules pertaining to matters such as **double jeopardy,** self-incrimination, search and seizure, assistance of counsel, and speedy trial. These are the rules governing the procedures by which crimes are investigated, prosecuted, and adjudicated. The cornerstone of procedural law is **due process.** Due process refers to the exercise of government power. In the United States, certain limits are put on the use of government power. Those limits are determined by legal principles designed to protect the rights of individuals and established in the federal and state constitutions and rules of criminal procedure.

Criminal Justice System

Criminal justice refers to the system established to apprehend, **adjudicate,** and punish those who break the law. The components of this system are law enforcement, court, and correction agencies organized on municipal, county, state, and federal levels of government.

Criminal justice also refers to the process by which agencies dispose of criminal cases. The stages of this process include investigation, **arrest, booking, first appearance, preliminary hearing, charging, arraignment,** trial, sentencing, appeal, and punishment (see Figure 1-6).

Each agency in the system has responsibilities for only certain stages of the process. Investigation, arrest, and booking are the responsibilities of law enforcement. The **lower courts** usually handle pretrial proceedings, such as first appearances and preliminary hearings. The prosecution's duty is to bring charges against the accused and to prosecute cases. The defense is responsible for representing its clients at trial and in **plea negotiations.** The judge in the **major trial court** presides over trials and hearings, including sentencing and plea conferences. At the appellate level, judges hear appeals concerning convictions and other requests for legal **relief.** Correction agencies are responsible for the punishment of convicted offenders; such

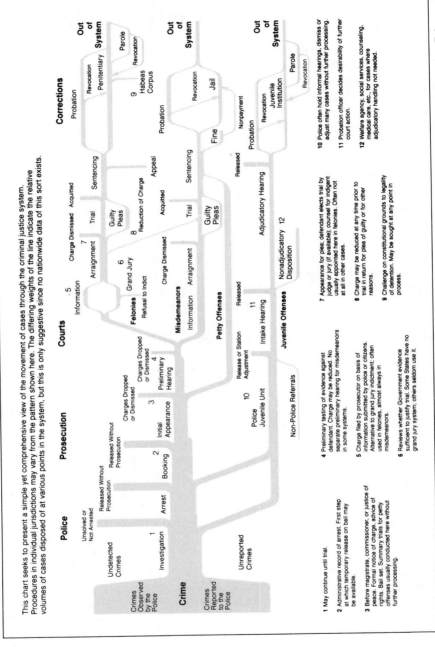

Figure 1-6 Overview of the criminal justice process. Adapted from *The Challenge of Crime in a Free Society*, Presidents Commission on Law Enforcement and Administration of Justice, 1967.

agencies oversee the administration of facilities such as classification centers, penitentiaries, and halfway houses.

Adversary and Accusatory Features

American criminal justice is a system that is both adversary and accusatory. It is an **adversary system** in that every criminal case is a dispute between two sides: the government and the accused. Represented by law enforcement and the prosecutor, the government makes arrests, marshals evidence, and prosecutes cases. The energies of defense attorneys are engaged in presenting their clients' cases in a most favorable light. In the middle are the judges, who rule on matters of law and keep the dispute from becoming disorderly. Finally, juries consider questions of fact and issue the verdict. The system of justice is predicated on the idea that only through adversary proceedings is the truth likely to prevail.

As an adversary system, criminal justice has certain safeguards. One is that each side may examine the truthfulness of witnesses and probe for possible bias. Another safeguard is the diffusion of power among the participants. A jury, for example, could reach a fair verdict even if the judge were biased. That would not be possible if the judge had all the power. Finally, protecting the rights of the accused is built into the system. It is the job of one of the principal actors in the adversary system—the defense attorney—to assert the rights of clients and to look for possible violations of those rights.

American criminal justice is an accusatory system in that the **burden of proof** is on the government, which must establish its claim that the accused is guilty. In many countries, guilt is presumed and innocence must be proved. The **presumption of innocence** is an integral part of American criminal justice. A defendant is presumed, at least in principle, to be innocent until proven guilty. **Reasonable doubt** is the standard of proof required in a criminal case. The state must prove that the defendant is guilty beyond, and to the exclusion of, every reasonable doubt.

Court System

The modern organization of American courts reflects our English heritage. In form, the early colonial courts were copies of English courts. Each colony modified its courts over the years to meet variations in local customs. As a result, each colony's courts developed differently. These differences persisted. That is why so much variation exists today among courts in the United States.

The huge increase in litigation that accompanied the growth of cities and commerce in the nineteenth century also contributed to the variation. New courts were formed to handle this litigation. Most of them were located in urban areas, and many of them were specialized. The end result of this sporadic and unplanned growth was the complex court structure of twentieth century America. What follows is a description of some of the basic principles underlying that structure: **jurisdiction,** fact finding, and the dual nature of courts.

Jurisdiction can be classified as geographical, subject matter, and hierarchical.[1] Geographical jurisdiction refers to specific political boundaries of a court's power. The jurisdiction of a major trial court in California, for example, is the county. Subject-matter jurisdiction refers to the type of issues a court can hear. For example, while lower courts hear **misdemeanor** cases, major trial courts hear **felony** cases. Hierarchical jurisdiction refers to whether a court has authority to try a case or to hear it on appeal. The major trial court has original jurisdiction, the authority to try a case. Appellate courts have appellate jurisdiction, the authority to review and revise the judicial action of lower courts.

Another basic principle is that appellate courts review the law, not the facts. They are not supposed to second-guess the jury as to the weight of the evidence. This does not mean, however, that appellate courts never examine facts. Suppose, for example, that a prosecutor presented a case based solely on circumstantial evidence. If that evidence was legally insufficient, the appellate court could conclude that the case should never have been submitted to the jury. It must review the factual evidence, though, before it can draw such a conclusion.[2] Appellate courts mostly review the legal aspects of a case, examining, for example, whether the defendant was provided with effective representation, whether a confession introduced as evidence was legally obtained, or whether the court correctly instructed the jury.

An important characteristic of the American court system is its dual nature. Federal courts and state courts are separate. There are, in fact, fifty-one court systems in the United States—one for every state and one for the federal government. Basically, federal courts have jurisdiction over violations of federal laws. State courts have jurisdiction over violations of state laws. Defendants convicted in state courts may appeal to the federal courts under certain circumstances. An inmate in a state prison, for example, might file a writ of **habeas corpus** in a federal district court. Habeas corpus refers to court proceedings to discharge a prisoner from unlawful custody.

The federal court system consists of three layers: district courts, circuit courts of appeals, and the Supreme Court. The district court is the court of original jurisdiction in most cases in the federal system. District court judges preside over felony cases. Magistrates, who are appointed by district court judges, hear petty cases and conduct preliminary hearings.

A circuit court of appeals is an intermediate court, standing between the district court and the Supreme Court. There are twelve circuit courts, organized into regional divisions. Georgia, for example, is in the Eleventh Circuit. The number of judges in each circuit varies from six to twenty-eight. Circuit courts normally use three-judge panels in deciding cases. In each case, the judges read **briefs** (written arguments submitted on appeal), hear oral arguments, and render a written **opinion.**

The Supreme Court is composed of nine justices. The main avenue by which criminal cases proceed to the Supreme Court is through a writ of **certiorari.** This is an order to the lower court to send up the records of a case so that the Supreme Court can determine if the law has been properly applied. The justices vote to decide whether they will hear a case, and it takes at least four votes before the Supreme Court will hear a case. This is called the **Rule of Four.** Before the Supreme Court will hear a case on appeal, two things usually must happen: (1) the **appellant** must have exhausted other avenues of appeal, and (2) the legal issue must involve a substantial federal question.

Like the federal system, state courts are organized on several levels. In all states there are trial courts and appellate courts. At the lowest level are the lower courts or courts of limited jurisdiction, often referred to as municipal courts or as courts of the justice of the peace. They hold first appearances, preliminary hearings, and conduct trials in minor cases. They can impose a sentence of no more than one year in jail or a small fine. These courts are not usually courts of record, meaning that an appealed case must be heard again in its entirety in the major trial court. This is called **trial de novo.**

Major trial courts, or courts of general jurisdiction, are referred to as circuit courts, superior courts, and district courts. Major trial courts hear felonies and can impose sentences ranging from probation to death.

About half of the states have intermediate courts of appeal. Their purpose is to relieve the state supreme courts of having to hear all appeals. Typically, they use a three-judge panel. Most criminal appeals stop at this level in states having a three-tiered system of courts.

State supreme courts have from three to nine justices. Such courts are usually the ultimate review board for matters involving interpretation of state constitutions, statutes, and rules of procedure. Like the federal Supreme Court, these state supreme courts read briefs, hear oral arguments, and render opinions.

==== PROCEDURAL DESCRIPTION ====

The law enforcement officer files a **complaint** with the court, indicating that there is **probable cause** to believe that the accused committed a crime. The judge reviews the complaint and issues an arrest warrant. An alternate scenario is that the officer makes a warrantless arrest and writes up the probable cause in a complaint/arrest affidavit, reviewed and approved later by the judge at first appearance. Arrestees are taken to the jail to be booked and admitted. The pretrial release officer interviews them, deciding whether they should be released into a pretrial release program or whether they are eligible for release on monetary **bail.**

Arrest

The court process in a criminal case begins with the filing of the complaint (see Exhibit 1-1), a task usually performed by law enforcement officers. If the suspect has not been arrested, the complaint serves as the basis for the judge to decide whether probable cause exists to justify issuing an arrest warrant (see Exhibit 1-2). In making this decision, the judge may also consider information from witnesses other than the **complainant.** Such information is presented in the form of a sworn written statement, referred to as an **affidavit.** In a warrantless arrest, the complaint/arrest affidavit is completed by the arresting officer and filed at the suspect's first appearance before the judge. It then becomes the basis for the judge's decision regarding probable cause.

Once a warrant is issued, law enforcement officers must execute it by arresting the alleged offender without unnecessary delay. "Without unnecessary delay" does not mean that they always make an arrest immediately upon receipt of the warrant. Planning is often a prerequisite, and a complicated case might require elaborate preparation. In a warrantless arrest, officers make an arrest if there is probable cause to believe that the suspect has committed a felony. With certain exceptions, officers may not enter a suspect's home without consent to make an arrest.[3] An exception occurs when arresting officers are about to arrest someone in a public place, and that person retreats to the privacy of his home. A warrantless entry of that person's home in **hot pursuit** is permissible.[4] For the most part, a warrant does not authorize them to enter a third person's home without consent to make an arrest. They are obliged to obtain a search warrant to justify entry into the home of a person other than the suspect named on the arrest warrant.[5] In the case of a misdemeanor, law enforcement officers may make an arrest without a warrant usually only if the crime was committed in their presence.

Arrest occurs when the suspect is "taken into custody or otherwise deprived of his freedom in any significant way."[6] It is important to distinguish between arrest and lesser forms of detention. Asking a suspect to appear at the station for questioning or stopping a vehicle to inspect the driver's license are examples of lesser forms of detention. There is no intention of taking the person into custody, but if the encounter would cause a reasonable person to believe that the de-

In the County Court

County, Florida

STATE OF FLORIDA

vs.

JOHN WESLEY PEAVY
W/M DOB: 11/15/46   Defendant.

Address.

COMPLAINT FIRST DEGREE MURDER

LCSO Case #85-44808

IN THE NAME AND BY THE AUTHORITY OF THE STATE OF FLORIDA:

Before me, the undersigned authority, personally appeared ___S/A Joe Mitchell - FDLE and Det. W. B. Moody -___
LCSO
who, being first duly sworn says that on the ___31st___ day of ___October___ A.D. 19__85__
in   Leon   County, Florida, the aforesaid defendant

did unlawfully kill a human being, ROBERT LESTER HARRISON, by shooting him with a
firearm, and the killing was perpetrated from or with a premeditated design or intent
to effect the death of ROBERT LESTER HARRISON, contrary to Section 782.04, Florida
Statutes.

12-26-85

contrary to Sec., ___ F.S.

contrary to the statute, rule, regulation or other provision of law in such case made and provided, and against the
peace and dignity of the State of Florida.

SA Joe mitchell   / W. B. Moody
Complainant

___Florida Department of Law Enforcement & Leon County Sheriff's Department___
Address

Sworn to and subscribed before me this ___27th___ day of ___December___, 19__85__.

Linda L Smith
Judge, Assistant State Attorney or Notary Public
Notary Public, State of Florida
My Commission Expires
Bonded

S E A L

STATE WITNESSES
NAME   ADDRESS

1.
2.
3.
4.
5.   21
6.

Exhibit 1-1 Complaint filed against John Wesley Peavy.

tainee was not free to leave, it could be considered a seizure tanta-
mount to arrest. Unless supported by probable cause, such an encounter would be illegal.

The intention to take someone into custody is an element of the
arrest. The communication of that intention and its understanding by

IN THE COUNTY COURT

COUNTY, FLORIDA

THE STATE OF FLORIDA, PLAINTIFF

vs.

John Wesley Peavy _____
Defendant

_____
Address

WARRANT

Received this Warrant on the ___20___

day of ___Dec.___, 19 85 ,

and served same on the ___23___ day of

___Dec.___, 19 85, by deliver-

ing a true copy of same to the within named

defendant,

John Wesley Peavy

Eddie Boone _____
Sheriff, _____ County, Florida.

By: ___W.B. Wood___
Deputy Sheriff.

**THE AMOUNT OF BAIL IN THIS CASE
IS HEREBY SET IN THE SUM OF**

$ _____

Exhibit 1-2 Warrant issued for John Wesley Peavy's arrest.

the person to be arrested are additional elements. Arrest is complete when seizure or detention occurs; such an action may be actual or constructive. An actual seizure is one in which there is physical contact between officers and the accused. For example, officers may handcuff the suspect. A constructive seizure occurs when the suspect submits to control without the application of physical force.

Stop and frisk is a lesser form of detention based on a reasonable standard similar to that of probable cause. The difference is that, in stop and frisk, no crime has been committed. Believing that a crime is about to be committed, law enforcement officers detain the suspect. A hunch is insufficient for making such a stop. Officers must be able to point to specific facts that indicate the distinct possibility of an impending crime. If there is reason to believe that the suspect is armed and dangerous, they may conduct a pat-down search for weapons. The purpose of the search is to protect the officers and others. For example, in *Terry v. Ohio*, an experienced officer observed men pacing back and forth in front of a store window.[7] Suspecting that the men were casing the store, he detained them. A search revealed that two of the three men were armed.

Probable Cause

Both the law enforcement officer who makes a warrantless arrest and the judge who issues an arrest warrant are concerned with whether probable cause justifies an arrest. Technically, probable cause exists when the facts and circumstances would warrant a person of reasonable caution to believe that an offense had been or is being committed by the person to be arrested.

Before making an arrest, law enforcement officers usually develop probable cause from a set of facts that fall short of actually seeing the crime being committed. What they do see, however, may be highly suggestive. Did the suspect attempt to flee when approached by an officer? Did the suspect behave furtively, as if trying to hide something? Did the suspect fail to provide a satisfactory explanation for suspicious conduct? Did the suspect make revealing admissions? Was the suspect observed at the scene of the crime? Does the suspect resemble the alleged offender? Does the evidence permit the inference that the suspect committed the crime? Although no fact or circumstance alone may be sufficient to establish probable cause, several facts together can be quite convincing.

Third-person information, such as that obtained from witnesses or informants, is **hearsay.** It may be used in developing probable cause, but law enforcement officers must determine whether the basis of such information is sufficient to warrant an arrest. Information based on suspicion or rumor, for example, is not sufficient. It is also necessary to determine whether these persons are basically honest. Informants who have supplied truthful information in the past are more likely to be trusted. Neither the basis of the information nor the reliability of the informant is more important, but when one is weaker, that deficit may be countered by the strength of the other. The totality of circumstances counts.[8]

Through surveillance or investigation, law enforcement officers may strengthen probable cause by corroborating information supplied by a third person. The corroborative information may be added to or may actually verify the informant's hearsay information. It may even become the basis for probable cause, independent of the informant's tip, if it provides a strong indication of criminal activity.

Booking

Booking is the administrative procedure that follows arrest and precedes detention. After usually giving the **Miranda** (self-incrimination) **warnings,** law enforcement officers may take the accused to the station house, where fingerprints and photographs are procured for in-house files; or they may transport the accused directly to the jail. Admission to the jail usually requires either a complaint/arrest affidavit or warrant, plus a **rap sheet.** Computerized data concerning an accused's criminal history· are readily available to arresting officers from various sources, such as the Federal Bureau of Investigation's National Crime Information Center.

The Miranda warnings are a product of *Miranda v. Arizona*, a case that the Supreme Court decided in 1966.[9] Before *Miranda* and its immediate predecessor, *Escobedo v. Illinois,* the test for the admissibility of a suspect's statement to a law enforcement officer was the statement's voluntary nature.[10] If it was coerced, it was involuntary and, consequently, inadmissible. In *Escobedo,* the Supreme Court held that when an investigator focuses on a particular suspect, the accused must be permitted to consult with a lawyer, a Sixth Amendment right. In *Miranda,* the area of inquiry shifted to the Fifth Amendment privilege against self-incrimination. Intending to remove coercion from custodial interrogation, the Supreme Court held that the prosecution may not use statements that a suspect has made during custodial interrogation unless it can be demonstrated that procedural safeguards were observed during the interrogation. Before an interrogation, officers usually read suspects their rights (see Exhibit 1-3). After the warnings have been given, officers ask if the accused understand their rights and are willing to talk without consulting a lawyer. Affirmative responses are noted, preferably in a written waiver of rights.

The first thing that arrestees do when admitted to jail is to surrender the property on their person. If not eligible for immediate release, they change from street clothes to jail garb. Their clothes and personal items are recorded on an inmate property report and stored in a secure place.

The arrestees next undergo a preliminary screening in order to determine if they have any medical problems or need medical treatment. They are taken to the emergency ward of a hospital if they need medical treatment.

When screening is complete, the inmate is assigned a jail number, photographed, and fingerprinted. The correctional officer may take major case prints in addition to prints of the fingers. Major case prints are prints of the palms of the hands, the tips of the fingers, and the sides of the hands.

Pretrial Release

Pretrial release procedures vary widely.[11] In one jurisdiction, for example, the pretrial release officer interviews detainees after they have been booked, asking them about their prior record, employment history, length of residence, and family ties. The purpose of the interview is to gather information that pretrial release officers or the court may use in determining bail status. Generally, detainees are eligible for release into the pretrial release program if they meet certain criteria, such as having an address in the court's jurisdiction, being charged with less than a second-degree felony, and scoring high on a

FLORIDA DEPARTMENT OF LAW ENFORCEMENT

YOUR CONSTITUTIONAL RIGHTS

Before you make any statement you must fully understand your rights.

1.   You have the right to remain silent.

2.   Anything you say can and will be used as evidence against you in court.

3.   You have the right to call or obtain an attorney at this time and have one present now or at any time during questioning.

4.   If you cannot afford to hire an attorney, the court will appoint one for you without cost, and you have the right to have this attorney present at any time during questioning.

5.   If you decide to answer questions now, you have the right to stop answering at any time during questioning.

I have read the above statements and fully understand what my rights are.

(Signed) _____

(Date) _12 - 23 - 85_

WAIVER OF RIGHTS

I have carefully read the above statements. I fully understand what my rights are. Knowing these rights, I do not want an attorney at this time. I am willing to make a statement and answer questions concerning this investigation. I fully understand and know what I am doing. No promises, threats, or inducements have been made to me. No pressure or coercion of any kind has been used against me.

(Signed) _____

(Date) _12 - 23 - 85_

WITNESS: _Joe Mitchell_

WITNESS: _W. Blwood_

TIME & DATE: _9:50   12-23-85_

PLACE: _Leon Co. Sheriff Office_

Exhibit 1-3 Miranda warnings and waiver of rights.

community-ties index (see Exhibit 1-4). In some jurisdictions, pretrial release officers may have the authority to release detainees into the pretrial release program even if a judge has set bond. Eligible detainees are released before first appearance if what they have said on the community-ties index can be verified. (The column marked VER on the form in Exhibit 1-4 is for this purpose.) Usually, verification can be done within a few hours. It involves checking computerized data on the accused's criminal history as well as contacting such persons as an employer, landlord, and relatives. Once released, they are not expected to appear in court until arraignment. Release into the pretrial release program is conditional. In addition to agreeing to appear at court proceedings, releasees may be required to participate regularly in activities such as drug counseling or urinalysis. Pretrial release officers monitor releasees to see that they comply with these conditions.

```
                        COMMUNITY-TIES INDEX

                                              DATE:_____
NAME:_____
          (Defendant)
CASE NO.(s):_____
INTERVIEW (INT) SCORE:_____    VERIFIED (VER) SCORE:_____
NAME:_____
          (Pre-Trial Officer completing interview score)
NAME:_____
          (Pre-Trial Officer completing verified score, if different)


   INT   VER   PRIOR CRIMINAL RECORD
    3     3    No Convictions.
    0     0    No Convictions in the Past Year.
   -1    -1    Misdeameanor Conviction(s) in the Past Year.
   -2    -2    Felony Conviction(s) in the Past 3 Years.
   -2    -2    Incarceration in a Penal Institution in the Past 5 years.
         NOTE: One (1) point may be deducted for any pending criminal charge.
   INT   VER   EMPLOYMENT/SCHOOLING
    4     4    Present job one (1) year or more.
    3     3    Present job four (4) months, or
              Present and Prior job six (6) months.
    2     2    Present job one (1) month.
    1     1    Current job, or
              Unemployed three (3) months or less with nine (9) months
              or more on prior job, or
              Receiving unemployment compensation or welfare, or
              Supported by family.
   NOTE: Deduct one (1) point from the first three categories IF:
         The job is not steady, or
         The job is not salaried, or
         The defendant has no investment in it.

   INT   VER   RESIDENCE
    3     3    Present residence one (1) year or more.
    2     2    Present residence six (6) months, or
              Present and prior residence one (1) year.
    1     1    Present residence four (4) months, or
              Present and prior residence six (6) months.
   INT   VER   FAMILY TIES
    3     3    Lives with spouse, and
              Has had contact with other family members.
    2     2    Lives with spouse and/or parents, OR alone with family contact.
    1     1    Lives with family person whom he gives with reference.
   DEFINITIONS:  "Spouse" - If unmarried, must have lived together for
                           two (2) years.

               "Contact"- Must see the person at least once a week.
   INT   VER   TIME IN THE SECOND JUDICIAL CIRCUIT
    2     2    Five (5) years or more.
```

Exhibit 1-4 Community-ties index.

Those detainees not released into the pretrial release program may be eligible for release on monetary bail. **Bond** is often set by the judge issuing the arrest warrant. Where it is not, pretrial release officers or other officials consult a **bond schedule** to determine the appropriate amount (see Exhibit 1-5).

CAUTION: If bond is not posted, subject must be brought before the judge within twenty-four (24) hours of being taken into custody.

Criminal

Assault	250
Beer—Selling after hours	200
Beer—Selling to minors	500
Bolita	300
Camping on other than designated campsite	100
Carrying a concealed weapon	500
Contributing to the delinquency of minors	500
Criminal Mischief—under $200	100
Criminal Mischief—over $200	500
Cruelty to an Animal (not serious)	250
Cruelty to an Animal (serious)	1,000
Culpable Negligence (No Injury)	500
Culpable Negligence (with personal injury)	1,000
Dance Hall—operating on Sunday	100
Discharging a Firearm in Public	250
Disorderly conduct	175
Disorderly intoxication	100
Drugs (See Narcotics)	
Failure to Compel School Attendance	100
False Report to Law Enforcement Officer	250
Gambling	50
Harassing Phone Calls	300
Improper Exhibition of Dangerous Weapon	500
Indecent Exposure (sex organ)	1,000
Indecent Exposure (urinating in public)	100
Interference with custody	1,000
Littering	100
Loitering and Prowling	250
Narcotics:	
Marijuana, less than twenty grams	250
Possession of paraphernalia**	
**see felony bond schedule if possession charge is in connection with felony	
Obscene Phone Calls	2,500
Obstructing officer without violence	500
Obstruction by a disguised person	500
Obtaining lodging or food with intent to defraud	250
Passing Worthless Bank Checks (per check)	50
Petit Theft (including shoplifting);	
1st offense	100
2nd offense	1,000
3rd offense	none
Prostitution	250
Public Assistance Fraud	250
Public Nuisance	500
Removing property under lien	250
Resisting arrest without violence	500
Trespassing	100
Trespassing after warning	500
Whiskey violations	1,000
Withholding support from minor child	250
Unnatural and lascivious Act	500
OTHER MISDEMEANORS:	
Minor	100
Major	500

Exhibit 1-5 Bond schedule of Leon County, Florida.

```
                                                    FOR FURTHER ACTION ON THIS BOND NOTIFY:

    INTERNATIONAL FIDELITY INSURANCE COMPANY
              24 Commerce Street
           Newark, New Jersey 07102
                                              ALOI - WILLIAMS Bonding Co.
   GENERAL SURETY APPEARANCE BOND            524 Appleyard Drive
                                             Tallahassee, Florida 32304

   POWER #_____   (904) 575-9173

   ARREST #_____                    In The
           STATE OF FLORIDA
               vs.                           _____ Cour

   _____                                         _Count
                                                        STATE OF FLORIDA
```

KNOW ALL MEN BY THESE PRESENT: That we, _____ same as above _____ as principal, an INTERNATIONAL FIDELITY INSURANCE COMPANY, a New Jersey Corporation, surety are held and firmly bound unto the Governor o the State of Florida, and his successors in office, the said principal, in the sum of $ _____ and the said surety for a like amount for the payment whereof well and truly to be made we bind ourselves, our heirs, executors, administrators and assigns firmly by these presents

Signed and sealed this _____ day of _____ A.D., 19 _____.

The condition of this obligation is such that if the said principal shall appear on _____ 19 ____ at the next Regular or Special term of the _____ same as above _____ and shall sumbit to the said Court to answer. charge of_____ and shall submit to orders and process of said Cour and not depart the same without leave, then this obligation to be void, else to remain in full force and virtue.

TAKEN BEFORE ME AND APPROVED BY ME:

_____ (L.S.
                                              (PRINCIPAL)

_____ Sheriff

By _____ D.S.   INTERNATIONAL FIDELITY INSURANCE COMPANY

                                        By _____
                                            (ATTORNEY-IN-FACT) (SURETY)

| This bond not valid for pre-sentence investigation or fines. |

CERTIFICATE OF DISCHARGE OF BOND

                                        I.F.I.C. POWER # _____
DEFENDANT: _____
                                        BOND AMT. $ _____
COURT: _____

This is to certify that on or about _____ , I examined the records of this Court and I found that the bond with the corresponding number has been discharged of record.   DISPOSITION: _____

PERSON RENDERING DECISION: _____ DATE OF DISCHARGE: _____

Witness my hand and official seal this day of _____ .

SIGNED: _____ TITLE: _____

RETURN COMPLETED DISCHARGE TO:
                            ALOI - WILLIAMS Bonding Co.
                            524 Appleyard Drive
                            Tallahassee, Florida 32304
                            (904) 575-9173
FORM 533

Exhibit 1-6 Surety appearance bond.

A purpose of bail is to ensure the appearance of the accused at court proceedings. Reflecting a competing concern, the protection of society from those who are perceived dangerous, bail sometimes is set so high that the accused cannot afford to post it. Certain offenses, such as first-degree murder, armed robbery, or kidnapping, may not even be bondable. If the offense is bondable, the accused may have several options. They may deposit cash equal to the amount of the bond. They may pledge property equal to or greater than the amount of the bond. Or they may secure a surety appearance bond from a bondsman (see Exhibit 1-6).

Detainees who use the services of a bondsman usually pay a non-refundable fee of ten percent. As principal to an agreement, the accused must agree to meet certain conditions. Failure to appear in court, for example, would be a breach of contract. Never certain that the accused will abide by the agreement, the bondsman usually insists on adequate monetary security. In addition to a fee, the bondsman frequently requires collateral, such as a mortgage on the accused's home or car, and may require that a relative promise to pay a certain amount of money if the bond is forfeited. A bondsman must be selective in choosing clients. It would be risky, for example, to take on as clients individuals who are totally lacking in community ties.

The bondsman can assist clients who are out on bond by guiding them around the judicial bureaucracy. Telling the accused when and where to go enables bondsmen to monitor the movements of their clients and decreases the likelihood of their nonappearance. Many times clients fail to appear simply because they are unfamiliar with the court process and do not know their way around the courthouse.

If clients fail to appear, the bond is **estreated** (forfeited), and the bondsman is required to pay the court the face amount of the bond within a certain period of time. The choice is either to pay or to apprehend the errant clients and have the estreature (forfeiture) set aside. Bondsmen who do neither run the risk of the civil division of the court entering a judgment against them and the companies that insure them.

Study Questions

1. Find the times Johnny Peavy gave up his rights. What rights were they?

2. Circuit Judge J. Lewis Hall signed a warrant on December 20 for Peavy's arrest. On what basis did the judge have probable cause to think that Peavy had committed murder?

3. What do you think investigator Campbell meant when he said to Peavy, "You've been a cop for a long time, and you've played some good cop games with us," and "If you want to help yourself, now is the time."? With an arrest warrant with his name on it already signed by the judge, how could Peavy have helped himself? How could confessing have helped him? What did Campbell mean by "cop games"? Did Campbell play any during this case?

Endnotes

1. David W. Neubauer, *America's Courts and the Criminal Justice System.* 3d ed. (Pacific Grove, CA: Brooks/Cole Publishing Co., 1988), 40–41.

2. Thomas Duffy, law clerk, Florida Supreme Court, personal communication, Tallahassee, FL, 9 July 1990.

3. *Payton v. New York*, 445 U.S. 573 (1980).

4. *United States v. Santana*, 427 U.S. 38 (1976).

5. *Steagald v. United States*, 451 U.S. 204 (1981).

6. *Miranda v. Arizona*, 384 U.S. 436, 444 (1966).

7. *Terry v. Ohio*, 392 U.S. 1 (1968).

8. *Illinois v. Gates*, 462 U.S. 213 (1983). For a discussion of cases pertaining to information obtained through informants, see John N. Ferdico, *Criminal Procedure for the Criminal Justice Professional*, 3d ed. (St. Paul, MN: West Publishing Co., 1985), 153–74.

9. *Miranda v. Arizona*, 384 U.S. 436 (1966). Supreme Court is used throughout this textbook to refer to the Supreme Court of the United States.

10. *Escobedo v. Illinois*, 378 U.S. 478 (1964).

11. See Stevens H. Clarke, "Pretrial Release: Concepts, Issues, and Strategies for Improvement," in *Research in Corrections*, ed. Stevens H. Clarke (Santa Monica, CA: The Rand Corporation, 1988), 1–40.

2

Bringing Charges

The Defense Search for an Alibi

John Wesley Peavy's roots reached back to one of Gadsden County's pioneer families. He served in the Marines. He had worn a police badge in Bainbridge, Georgia. He had been married to the same woman for nineteen years, and they had two children. He was a member of the Lion's Club, the Masons, and the Baptist church. Letters of support from community leaders became a part of his court file. Defense attorney Tony Bajoczky gathered together those biographical details and, like a scrapbook of respectability, carried them into a bond hearing on January 7, 1986.

Making his best pitch to get thirty-nine-year-old Johnny out of the Leon County Jail, Bajoczky stressed Peavy's ties to the community, calling them "great and extensive."

Bajoczky brought on Gadsden County Sheriff W. A. Woodham. The popular law-and-order politician shifted in his seat, looking a bit uncomfortable in his role as a defense witness. Woodham testified that Peavy had had no run-ins with the law in the twenty or so years that Woodham had known the Peavy family.

Not only should Peavy be allowed out of jail awaiting trial, Bajoczky argued, he shouldn't have to post bail at all.

But Deputy State Attorney Tony Guarisco blasted that idea as "outrageous" and set out to detail Peavy's far-from-pristine life. Guarisco told the judge about Peavy's drinking, a problem so bad that Peavy was seeking treatment at the time of his arrest. And the prosecutor said there was evidence that Peavy was violent when he drank.

Leon County Circuit Judge Charles McClure agreed with the prosecutor and said there would be no bond whatsoever. The judge said he believed the state had proven that the presumption of guilt was great, and he thought the chances of Peavy fleeing were "very great," considering that he was charged with murder.

Two weeks later, on January 23, a Leon County grand jury returned indictments against Peavy for two counts of first-degree murder, for shooting a firearm into a dwelling, and for the use of a firearm in the commission of a felony.

Peavy clung to the only hope he had of ever getting out of jail. He would have to wait until his trial. Then, he prayed, the jury would find him not guilty; and he would be free.

But the wait until his trial would be a long one. For more than a year, his home remained the four walls of a windowless cell. Peavy had become just another inmate awaiting trial in a jail so crowded it was under court order to correct the conditions. Warehoused there, month after month, Peavy had plenty of time to think with a clear head—to try to remember just where he was when bullets sprayed through Harrison's kitchen window.

In jail, time was marked when guards shoved chow through the steel bars. It was easier to remember back when the rising and setting sun measured the day. It was comforting to picture home.

Weathered tobacco barns still stand on the Peavy land, vintage reminders of the days this pioneer family worked the soil for its wealth. The shade-tobacco days are long gone from this rural North Florida countryside—but not the Peavys and not their field hands. Paintless wood tenement shacks leaning under rusty tin roofs still dot the landscape, blotches of poverty on the way to the several handsome brick homes where the Peavys live.

Winessa "Queen" Jackson is one of the more comfortable tenants, living in a white trailer at the beginning of a long, winding drive up to Johnny Peavy's place. Her father, who "farmed for Johnny's granddad," she says, was a sharecropper who raised his family on Peavy land.

Now Queen is in her fifties, and her field days are pretty much over. When it was time to pick greens, Johnny would come by Queen's looking for field hands who lived nearby, to remind them to get up early the next morning. Even when the crops weren't ready for picking, Johnny liked to stop by Queen's place. Her trailer was near a place Johnny called "my tree."

Under its branches, Johnny would swig his liquor, the stuff he needed as much as the air he breathed to keep going. He would toss the empty bottles in the bushes before going home to "Boo," a nickname for Gloria, his wife.

She knew her husband was an alcoholic. When people asked her how she could live with him, she would say he suffered from a disease. "Would you leave your husband just because he had cancer?" she would ask in return. She was willing to stick by Johnny in sickness and in health.

At least, Johnny rationalized, he didn't drink at home, in front of his wife and two kids. He sucked mints to mask the booze on his breath. And Johnny had his tree, where he could drink in peace and where folks like Queen would join him to chew the fat without a hassle.

The Peavy family had paid for expensive private treatment for Johnny more than once. They could afford it. The big business in the Peavy family is a road-paving company called Peavy & Son Construction, its headquarters a short way down the highway from the Peavy home. The booming business is run by Johnny's older brother, "Big Delacy." Johnny's constant company with a liquor bottle didn't make him the most reliable worker. But Big Delacy hired him anyway. Gloria said the only job her husband was ever fired from was working for Big Delacy.

So Johnny spent much of his time on the farm: beautiful pasture-land dotted with cattle, curving into scuplted edges of hardwood forest.

Now, Johnny's only room to roam was in a jail cell. The company he was forced to keep consisted of other men charged with murder. If friends could be made in a place like that, Peavy's friends were a man charged with shooting his girlfriend while she sat at her office desk and a jealous husband who shot his estranged wife in the head when she returned from a date.

Like his roommates behind bars, Peavy was charged with killing someone he said he loved. Like most defendants awaiting trial, Peavy insisted he was innocent.

"I loved Bobby," Peavy told a newspaper reporter while locked in his cell. "No one on the face of the earth can say we had any trouble. I believe in my heart the truth will favor me. The evidence is going to be on my side. If they came to me and said, 'Plead guilty to time served,' I wouldn't do it. The idea to confess to something I didn't do. . . ."

He stopped to look down and shake his head. "No, I'm not going to do it. I can't stand the thought that people would think I'd kill someone."

Peavy's family didn't believe he was capable of killing. And they had the money to support their belief with a feisty defense team. The Peavys wasted no time in hiring Bajoczky, a sometimes-cocky, always-confident bulldog of a defense lawyer, and Ronnie Boyce, a former sheriff's deputy who was now a private eye for the defense.

"I told Johnny Peavy when I met him that I didn't go along with him or anybody sneaking up and bushwhacking anybody," Boyce recalled of his first talk with Peavy at the jail.

"I'll tell you exactly why I felt so strongly that Peavy [was] innocent. I looked Johnny right in the eye and I told him, 'I'm going to work as hard as I can on your behalf. But I'm going to work just as hard to prove you did this. Bear in mind, now, if I find out you did this murder, I'm going to testify against you. If I find the damn gun, I'll take it to the FDLE, and I'll either clear your ass or you're in deep shit.' And he had no problem with it . . . He didn't blink an eye and he said, 'You go work it.' That right there, in my heart, told me [he was] an absolute nut—or he didn't do it. And the more I talked to him, I knew he wasn't a nut."

Believing in someone's innocence and proving it are as different as Johnny when he was drinking and Johnny when he was sober. Boyce set out on a mission to find Johnny's alibi. It wouldn't be easy.

Johnny had been drinking the day of the killings, and blocks of time were sucked from his memory. There were gaps that Peavy couldn't fill. Boyce had to find the people who could.

This much Johnny remembered about the day of the murder: it was Halloween, and he drove his kids and wife into Tallahassee. While the kids were picking out their costumes and his wife was in a salon having her nails done, Johnny was sneaking sips from a pint of vodka.

It was a rainy night, so rather than door-to-door trick-or-treating, Johnny and Gloria drove the kids to several country stores to show off their costumes and get candy. Back home around 8 P.M., Johnny carved a big pumpkin and made a fire in the woodstove. Gloria remembered that Johnny "made like the Good Witch" and passed out candy to the kids.

Later, Johnny left his family, drove to a country store just down the road, cashed a $100 check, bought a pair of dice, and headed for the Shady Rest.

"I thought about going to the Shady Rest because I knew there was always a card game or crap game in progress," Johnny said to a newspaper reporter.

But the argument at the Shady Rest that the police clung to, Johnny insisted, had been greatly exaggerated. Nothing bad crept between Bobby and him, he swore. He talked about how much he loved Bobby. Sandra, Peavy's sister, and Bobby got married in 1966, the same year Gloria and Johnny married. They had double-dated and were in each other's weddings. They were tight.

After one beer at the Shady Rest, Johnny said, he took the back roads home. Once he pulled onto the Peavy land, he rolled up under his tree. He remembered asking where "Jabo" was, to remind the field hand that they would be picking collard greens in the morning.

But whatever happened after that sank into a bog of blankness. As hard as Johnny tried, he could conjure up nothing more than black, empty chunks of unfilled time where each minute was critical to proving his innocence.

Investigators at Bobby Harrison's trailer found a receipt for the uneaten chicken showing that it was purchased at a Havana Inland gas station at 9:22 P.M. From there, it was six miles to Bobby's place across the river in Leon County. The long-distance bill showed that Driggers called her daughter at 9:56 P.M. and that they talked for only three minutes. Harrison's next-door neighbor would tell sheriff's investigators that he heard shots coming from Bobby's trailer "somewhere between ten-thirty and eleven."

Considering all that, the investigators placed the time of death somewhere between ten-thirty and eleven.

Where was Johnny? If Peavy couldn't remember where he was, perhaps others could. The Peavys trusted Boyce to find someone who could potentially place Johnny on Halloween night.

"At first, I didn't know when the murder happened," Boyce told a newspaper reporter in his private eye office with a view of Little Lake Jackson. "All they told me was that it was between Wednesday and Saturday."

He leaned back in his chair and put his cowboy boots up on his desk, talking about his theory that the killer hid in the woods until Bobby returned home, much like a deer hunter waiting for his prey.

Even before anyone pinpointed the time of the killing, Boyce said, Queen told him Johnny was at her house on Halloween night.

"But it wasn't that important to me at [the] time," Boyce said.

Then, one winter weekend, he was taking a breakfast break at a Quincy restaurant during a hunting outing when he heard someone at the next table talking about a man who had heard shots coming from Bobby's trailer on Halloween night.

Boyce gulped down his eggs and sped over to the house of Bobby's next-door neighbor, Jamie Fuller. Boyce said that Fuller told him the shots went off "just after ten."

Queen had told Boyce that Johnny had been by her place "around ten" and had stayed about twenty-five minutes. How, then, Boyce wondered, could Johnny have been at the murder scene?

"My head is spinning. The next Monday, I shoot over and tape Queen this time. She said 'Ten to 10 P.M.' They drank a beer and Queen says, 'I saw his taillights disappear over the hill,' on the way to his house.

"I thought, 'We've got it made now. We're cooking with grease now. And there'll be this big apology: "I'm sorry, John." And they'll go and find out who really did it.'"

But Fuller would eventually change the time he heard the shots by nearly an hour later. And the case against Johnny would stick.

Who willing to testify for the defense could pinpoint where Johnny was between the time he left the Shady Rest and the time he walked in his front door?

Queen was one. Gloria was another. And a woman who would keep it her dark secret for more than a year was a third.

The jury at Johnny Peavy's trial would hear from none of them.

But Queen was willing to tell what she remembered about that Halloween night to a newspaper reporter. Inviting the reporter into her humble trailer, Queen thought back to Halloween night. Yes, she said, Johnny came by around 10 P.M., gave her kids little bags of candy, complimented their costumes, downed an Old Milwaukee and headed home after twenty-five minutes or so.

"He really didn't seem drunk to me," Queen said. "Just as sober as I ever see him . . . Yeah, he was here. He was here. Like I told the law, I have no reason to lie. I know I'm telling the truth." Her hands rose from her ample lap, and she slapped them together for emphasis. "I have no reason to lie."

But the law made Queen feel like a liar, she said, asking her all sorts of questions about whether the Peavys gave her money, free rent, furniture, or food. Was there any reason at all why she would lie to help Johnny?

They took Queen from her trailer in the Havana countryside to the state attorney's office twelve miles away in Quincy. With two men firing questions while a tape recorder rolled, they tried to break her story. But Queen stuck by her guns.

FDLE Agent Joe Mitchell asked Queen how she could be so sure of the time Johnny stopped by her house that night.

And Queen answered, "You know why I knowed? 'Cause when he give the kids the candy, I said, 'Ya'll not going to eat all this candy,' and I took it and I walked right in there to my little bar. I have a clock right up there. I happened to look up, and it was ten minutes to ten o'clock. And I laid the candy up there. That's how I know."

Over and over, they questioned whether she was lying or telling the truth.

"All I want to understand is if there is anything you've said tonight that ain't true," the prosecutor said, "that now's the time to put it straight. Right now, while we still got this tape machine on, rather than waiting until it's too late, until the harm's done."

The humble country black woman was outnumbered by a bunch of city white men with badges. Still, Queen folded her arms and said, "Well, I'm telling you what I know. Now, I'm not going to tell no lie for nobody. I don't have no reason to lie, and there ain't no use in nobody trying to make me lie."

"Well, there are other judges besides me," the prosecutor continued, "to decide who tells the truth, and that big judge up in the sky will make the final decision."

Queen nodded and said, "That's right."

When Gloria Peavy sized up the case, the truth was that her husband was innocent. She spent every spare minute trying to turn her faith into proof.

Gloria took a long, last drag on a dark brown More cigarette, crushed it out, and got up to find another confidential FDLE report she kept in a box above the refrigerator.

Somewhere in that box, she believed, rested the key to Johnny's cell door, if only she could piece together enough fragments of facts and make it add up to her husband's exoneration.

"I know as much about this as any policeman," Gloria said. "And I think it was drug-related. There's just too many coincidences. But if I point my finger at any one person, my life wouldn't be worth a plugged nickel. They're bad people."

The phone rang. It was Johnny calling from the jail. They talked in hushed, loving tones, a couple forced to celebrate their wedding anniversary in a courtroom with a quick hug and kiss while a bailiff kept guard.

Through the years, Gloria had had to forgive Johnny many things. When it came to forbidden bouts with drinking and other women, she knew Johnny cheated. She knew her husband had used cocaine, back when he was feeding drug tips to his high-school friend, a Gadsden County deputy who died, some said suspiciously, in a one-car crash the year of the killings. And when it was time to give her deposition, she had to tell, under oath, about the times Johnny had hit her.

But for this latest episode of big trouble, Gloria said there was nothing to forgive. She was sure her husband did not have it in him to kill. She knew he was innocent.

There was an FDLE report with her name on it in her box. On December 4, 1985, while Johnny was at the alcohol treatment hospital,

Gloria was questioned by Leon County Sheriff's Captain Dale Wise and FDLE Agent Joe Mitchell. A synopsis of what she told them, before she had the faintest idea her husband was a key murder suspect, was typed: she had heard street talk that Bobby Harrison was involved in drugs and kept a lot of guns at his place and that, as far as she knew, Bobby and Johnny got along. The report also chronicled what Gloria remembered of the night of the killings: that her family returned from trick-or-treating around 8 P.M.

"She emphasized that she was almost certain that they all bedded down, no one left the residence," the report said.

Gloria exhaled a cloud of smoke and said with disgust, "Bedded down! It's like I threw the straw out. I never used those words."

And she insisted she did not tell the investigators that Johnny never left the house again. As she testified at her deposition, Johnny came home about halfway through "Knots Landing," at approximately 10:30 P.M.

She tried to carry on as well as she could without him. There was strength in knowing a lot of people were supporting her. Even Harrison's children were willing to testify for Uncle Johnny.

It was hard to do, but, for the children's sake, she tried to keep hope alive at their brick house overlooking a peaceful pond.

Gloria stood on the front steps of her house and told a newspaper reporter about all the stray dogs Johnny had fed, about the kindness she knew lived in her husband's heart.

"I know to the bottom of my soul that he didn't do this," Gloria said. "I know killing is not in him."

She said that she survived by thinking about the day Johnny would finally come home, and the day the truth would come out.

"I'm putting the killer on notice," Gloria said. "I'm not going to rest until I find him. I may be 100 years old in my wheelchair, but I'll still be looking."

PROCEDURAL DESCRIPTION

The accused are brought before a lower-court judge at first appearance to determine whether there is probable cause to detain them. If there is, the judge informs them of the charges, sets bail, and assigns counsel to those who cannot afford to hire a lawyer. Those who are detained after first appearance are classified and assigned a cell at the jail. Defendants are charged formally by the prosecutor in an information or by the grand jury in an indictment. The decision to bind them over for trial is usually made by the lower-court judge at a preliminary hearing or by the majority of the grand jury. The accused enter a plea at arraignment: guilty, not guilty, or no contest. Those pleading not guilty begin their preparation for trial by having their attorney issue subpoenas and depose witnesses.

First Appearance

Defendants who have not been released from jail within a day or so are brought before a judge of the lower court at first appearance. First appearance is a non-adversary proceeding in which the judge determines probable cause and decides whether to release the accused, based on information contained in documents such as the complaint, the pretrial intake interview, and the summary of offense and probable-cause affidavit (see Exhibit 2-1). When probable cause is found, as it usually is, the judge informs the accused of the charges, provides

```
TO:  FIRST APPEARANCE MAGISTRATE
DEFENDANT: JOHN WESLEY PEAVY  W/M 11/15/46    DATE ARRESTED: 12-23-85
CHARGES: 1st DEGREE MURDER (2 Counts); Use of Firearm in Felony;
         Shooting Firearm into Dwelling
         SUMMARY OF OFFENSE AND PROBABLE CAUSE AFFIDAVIT

    THE ABOVE NAMED DEFENDANT WAS ARRESTED FOR THE FOLLOWING REASONS:

      Victim ROBERT LESTER HARRISON was divorced from defendant's sister
several years ago & defendant admits this resulted in financial hardships for
her, that she had discussed marital problems with him, & he remains very close
to her & her children.  On the evening of 10/31/85 we can establish that PEAVY
cashed a check for $100 near Havana, Florida, & said he was then going to the
Shady Rest (a tavern West of Havana on SR 12) to gamble.  This was between
7:00-8:00 P.M.  We have interviewed witnesses who place PEAVY arriving that
evening at the Shady Rest & attempting to gamble with a group which included
victim HARRISON, his former brother-in-law, as victim MARY LEE DRIGGERS was
watching the activity & accompanying HARRISON.  Witnesses also state that
when PEAVY spoke to the group upon arriving that HARRISON did not acknowledge
his greetings & PEAVY was rejected in his attempts to join their game by
placing side bets.  Shortly afterwards the game broke up & HARRISON & DRIGGERS
left together in DRIGGERS' vehicle.  Then a witness tells us that PEAVY was
"pissed" about being rebuffed by HARRISON & made disparaging statements about
HARRISON & how badly HARRISON had treated PEAVY's sister & some specifics of
the financial hardships he had caused her.  PEAVY said he did not understand
why HARRISON did not want him to play in their game.  By about 9:30 PM PEAVY
also left the Shady Rest apparently leaving by himself.
      Between 9:00-10:00PM HARRISON & DRIGGERS purchased chicken dinner boxes
at an Inland Station/Deli in Havana, Florida & apparently proceeded with the
                    (USE REVERSE SIDE IF NECESSARY)

    THE PRECEDING IS TRUE TO THE BEST OF MY PRESENT KNOWLEDGE OR BELIEF.
    SIGNATURE                          AGENCY: F.D.L.E.

    NOTARIZATION:  SWORN AND SUBSCRIBED BEFORE ME THIS     DAY OF
                         , 19      .

                                  NOTARY PUBLIC /ASSISTANT STATE ATTORNEY
    MY COMMISSION EXPIRES


                              ORDER
    THIS CAUSE coming before me as a First Appearance Magistrate,
and having reviewed the preceding Affidavit, this Court finds:
         Probable cause is sufficient.
         Probable cause is not sufficient and unless corrected
within seventy-two hours the defendant shall be released on his
own recognizance.
                                                        JUDGE
```

Exhibit 2-1 Summary of offense and probable cause affidavit.

boxes on to HARRISON'S residence off SR 12 east of Havana on the Leon County side of the Ocklocknee River. According to victim DRIGGERS' daughter in Wakulla County as supported by telephone company long distance records, victim MARY LEE DRIGGERS telephoned her daughter at about 9:56 p.m. Defendant PEAVY has stated that after leaving the Shady Rest he proceeded straight home which is located north of Havana, and arrived about 11:00 p.m. & the news was on the television. A neighbor of HARRISON has told an LCSO deputy that on the night of 10/31/85 he was awakened by a burst of gunfire sometime between 9:00–11:30 p.m. coming from the HARRISON residence and he estimated 10 to 15 shots were fired.

Officers have not located anyone who saw HARRISON or DRIGGERS after her 9:56 p.m. phone call on 10/31/85 until friends of HARRISON drive to his residence around 5:30 p.m. on Saturday, 11/2/85 and found their bodies laying near the dinette table adjacent to broken windows. Crime scene officers have collected 12 fired 9MM caliber cartridge cases from outside the window area from where it appears the fatal shots were fired into HARRISON & DRIGGERS as they were seated at the table eating their fried chicken. In our investigation we learned that PEAVY and his nephew each owned 9MM caliber firearms. The nephew has allowed us to borrow his 9MM firearm and it has been eliminated by FDLE Crime Lab Technician as a source of the fired cartridge cases at the murder scene.

We have found documentation from Kevin's Gun Shop that PEAVY purchased an Intratec brand 9MM semiautomatic firearm which is capable of holding up to 32 cartridges in a clip and firing same in rapid semiautomatic succession. PEAVY admits to these investigators purchasing this firearm on 12/20/84. Bullets removed from the victims have been identified as 9MM hollow point type and PEAVY admits to purchasing a case of CCI/BLAZER brand 9MM hollow point bullets and officers retrieved this type of bullets from his residence with his consent (unfired cartridges still in the factory box). PEAVY has stated that he has previously fired his Intratec 9MM on the grounds of his residence and officers have collected fired 9MM cases from that location. Witnesses have told officers of seeing PEAVY fire his 9MM Intratec at a pond on property of a relative of PEAVY and we have gathered fired 9MM cases from this location. He is identified firing at this pond location within two weeks preceding the homicides. Soon after he purchased the Intratec, PEAVY is identified as showing it at his place of employment, allowing a coworker relative to test fire it, and one of the bullets hit a radiator and has been recovered as have two fired cases. Also one expended bullet was recovered from the water of the pond where shots had been fired within two weeks preceding the homicides.

Don Champagne, firearms examiner, qualified numerous times in courts as an expert, has examined multiple fired submitted cartridge cases and/or fired bullets from the homicide scene, the pond, PEAVY'S residence property and the radiator at PEAVY'S place of employment. As to the fired bullets, none have any conventional rifling marks, none can be eliminated as coming from separate firearms and therefore could have come from the same firearm. However, as to his examination of the fired cartridge cases, they are identified as 9MM CCI/BLAZER brand and from the totality of breech/extractor/ejector/firing pin markings it is his opinion that they were fired in the same firearm. This includes fired cases retrieved at the homicide scene outside the window, from PEAVY'S residence grounds, from his relative's pond location, and from his place of employment.

On 12/5/85 FDLE Agent Joe Mitchell and LCSO Sgt. Keith Daws interviewed PEAVY while he was staying at a facility in Mary Esther, Florida. On that occasion he said his 9MM Intratec firearm was either in his truck or if not, secured inside his house near Havana, Florida. He also said he had no knowledge of his Intratec being missing. He gave a consent to search and his Intratec could not be found. In a subsequent interview on 12/11/85 PEAVY said he could not find his firearm, assumed it had been stolen, and he had been making inquiries offering a reward to recover it. Also on 12/11/85 he told Major Larry Campbell of LCSO that he last remembers seeing the firearm either one or two weeks prior to the murders and someone must have stolen it from his vehicle. Witnesses report that PEAVY took the 9MM with him in vehicles on a daily basis, seemed fond of it, showed it off, yet there is no report of any theft to area law enforcement and PEAVY admits not making any theft report but did not provide us any specific basis for failing to make a theft report.

Exhibit 2-1 Continued.

them with a copy of the complaint, assigns counsel to those who are **indigent** (too poor to hire their own lawyer), and sets bail and other conditions of release. The judge sets a date for the preliminary hearing in states where the prosecution files an **information.** When probable cause is not found, defendants are held in custody, and the prosecution has a certain number of hours to cure the deficiency in the probable-cause statement. If the deficiency cannot be remedied, the accused are released.

The judge determines whether defendants are indigent by asking them if they have a job, how much money they make a week, if they own property or stocks, if they have any dependents, and if they are paying child support or alimony. Single persons with no dependents who earn less than $100 a week, for example, may be considered indigent if they do not own property or stocks. If they earn somewhat more but are married, support children, or pay alimony, they may still be considered indigent.

In determining whether to release defendants on bail, the judge considers a number of factors. They include the seriousness of the offense and the defendant's prior record, previous flight to avoid prosecution, failure to appear at previous proceedings, length of residence, family ties, employment history, financial resources, and source of funds. When the judge decides not to set bail, defendants may request a bail hearing later before a judge of the major trial court (see Exhibit 2-2).

When the decision is to release the defendant, the court has several options. It can release defendants on bond, on their own recognizance, or into a pretrial release program. In some jurisdictions defendants may deposit ten percent of the bond amount directly with the court. Release on recognizance differs from release into a pretrial release program in that release on recognizance is usually unsupervised and involves few conditions. Defendants released on personal recognizance are expected to appear at court proceedings and, when warranted, to have no contact with the victim.

Classification

Defendants who are detained after first appearance are interviewed at the jail by a classification officer. Based on such factors as the seriousness of the offense, prior record, past attempts to escape, health, age, and demeanor, detainees are placed in a cell that provides protection for them while maintaining security for the jail. For example, inmates who present a substantial risk of disruption are confined to a cell that provides what is commonly referred to as "intensive maximum custody." If they leave the cell, they may be escorted by two or more correctional officers.

Regulations in many jurisdictions separate men from women, juveniles from adults, felons from misdemeanants, and sentenced inmates from those awaiting trial. Unusual prisoners, such as the mentally ill, drug addicts, sexual deviates, suicide risks, informants, and inmates carrying communicable diseases are often segregated.

Grand Jury

Some states require that the grand jury formally charge defendants before they can be put on trial. The majority decides whether the prosecution has presented the quantum of proof necessary for **binding over** the accused. In other states, the prosecution can bring a charge solely on its own authority by means of an information. Where this approach is adopted, it is common to test the government's case at a preliminary hearing. It should be noted, however, that not all *information* states always use a preliminary hearing, that some *grand jury* states also use the preliminary hearing, and that capital cases are referred to the grand jury in a few states using the information.

The **grand jury** is chosen randomly from a qualified pool (see Chapter 4 for a description of the selection process). There are several ways to do this. One way is for the deputy court clerk to place slips of paper containing the names of the members of the jury pool in the bailiff's hat. The first eighteen names to be selected are the members of the grand jury. Anyone who plans not to be in town for the next six months, the term of the grand jury, is replaced. Of course, the term as well as the number of jurors required varies widely. Once the selection process is completed, the judge swears in the jurors and instructs them about various matters.

The judge instructs the jurors that their duty is to ascertain whether there is probable cause in a criminal case. If the evidence is sufficient to constitute probable cause, it is the jurors' duty to find a **true bill** (see Exhibit 2-3). When an indictment is not justified by the facts, it is the jurors' duty to clear the accused by returning a no bill. It should be noted that "indictment" and "true bill" are often used interchangeably. In some states, the grand jury is required to investigate all felonies. In other states, although it has the authority to examine any matter of public importance, the grand jury is required by law to investigate only in a **capital case.**

The court also instructs the jurors about procedural matters. It tells them that the prosecution will legally advise and counsel the grand jury. In some jurisdictions, the court appoints the foreperson and vice-foreperson; and the state attorney, clerk of the court, sheriff, or public defender may make recommendations regarding their appointment. The court next explains the duties of the officers of the grand jury. It informs the jurors, for example, that a certain number of members must be present if the grand jury is to function and that the foreperson signs all indictments approved by the jurors. Finally, the

IN THE CIRCUIT COURT OF THE
SECOND JUDICIAL CIRCUIT, IN
AND FOR LEON COUNTY, FLORIDA.

CASE NO. 85-4807

STATE OF FLORIDA,

    Plaintiff,

-vs-

JOHN WESLEY PEAVY,

    Defendant.

_____/

MOTION TO SET BOND

    COMES NOW the Defendant, JOHN WESLEY PEAVY, by and through his undersigned lawyer, Anthony L. Bajoczky, and pursuant to Florida Statute 903 and Rule 1.131, Florida Rules of Criminal Procedure, respectfully requests this Honorable Court to take jurisdiction of this cause and order that a reasonable bond be set in this case, and as a basis for this Motion would allege as follows:

    1. On Monday, December 23, 1985, the Defendant was arrested by deputies of the Leon County Sheriff's Office and was charged with two counts of Murder in the First Degree, capital offenses.

    Since being arrested on December 23, 1985, the Defendant has been incarcerated in the Leon County Jail and no bond has been set for his pre-trial release.

    2. The testimony and evidence upon which these charges have been filed against the Defendant have <u>not</u> been reviewed by any Grand Jury and no Indictment has been returned against the Defendant.

    5. The Defendant is presently 39 years of age and, other than his active service in the United States Army from 1968 to 1970 and his employment as a law enforcement officer with various law enforcement agencies in the South Georgia area from 1976 to 1982, has always resided in the Gadsden County area.

    The Peavy family is a "pioneer family" to this South Georgia/North Florida area and has always resided in the Decatur County, Georgia/Gadsden County, Florida area. The Defendant's father, Mr. M. D. Peavy, was born, raised and has continuously resided in the Gadsden County, Florida area his entire life. The Defendant's mother was born and raised in Decatur County, Georgia, and has now resided in Gadsden County, Florida, for in excess of 45 years.

Exhibit 2-2 Motion to set bond for John Wesley Peavy.

11. As a life-long resident of the Decatur County/Gadsden County area, the Defendant has been involved in many civic and other organizations and/or fraternities.

Some of the fraternities or organizations of which the Defendant is a member are as follows:

(a) Orion Lodge No. 8 of Free and Accepted Masons, 3rd Degree (Bainbridge, Georgia).

(b) Bainbridge Chapter No. 94 of Royal Arch Masons, 32nd Degree (Scottish Rite).

(c) Hasan Temple (Shriner's).

(d) Lion's Club (Bainbridge, Georgia).

(e) Other assorted organizations and/or fraternities.

12. The Defendant has further been a member of the First Baptist Church of Havana, Florida, for in excess of 15 years.

WHEREFORE, the Defendant, JOHN WESLEY PEAVY, respectfully requests this Honroable Court to take jurisdiction of this cause and order that a reasonable bond be set in this case for the Defendant's pre-trial release pending trial of all issues in this cause.

Anthony Bajoczky
ANTHONY L. BAJOCZKY

BARRETT AND BAJOCZKY
131 North Gadsden Street
Post Office Box 1501
Tallahassee, Florida 32302
(904) 222-9000

Lawyer for Defendant

Exhibit 2-2 Continued.

judge tells the jurors that as members of the grand jury they are bound to secrecy. Nothing that happens while they are in session is ever to be made known, except by order of the court. The punishment for violating this prohibition, a first-degree misdemeanor in some jurisdictions, can be up to one year in jail.

The grand jury meets in a conference room closed to the public. One or more prosecutors are present at the hearing, questioning witnesses who are called one at a time. Jurors themselves frequently ask questions. Each witness is obliged to swear an oath of truthfulness and secrecy. Although the accused are rarely subpoenaed, they are

In the Circuit Court of the Second Judicial Circuit of the State of Florida in and for Leon County

Fall Term, 1985

THE STATE OF FLORIDA
vs.
JOHN WESLEY PEAVY

INDICTMENT FOR
FIRST DEGREE MURDER (2 Counts);
SHOOTING INTO DWELLING
USE OF FIREARM IN COMMISSION OF A FELONY

A TRUE BILL

Foreman of the Grand Jury

WITNESSES FOR THE STATE

This to certify that the undersigned, as Assistant State Attorney, as authorized and required by law, has advised the Grand Jury returning this Indictment.

AS ASSISTANT STATE ATTORNEY, SECOND JUDICIAL CIRCUIT, IN AND FOR LEON COUNTY, FLORIDA.

Presented in open Court by the Grand Jury and filed this 23rd day of January, 1986

Paul F. Hartsfield
Clerk Circuit Court

By Jane G. Sauls
Deputy Clerk

WILLIAM N. MEGGS
~~DONALD E. MODESITT~~
STATE ATTORNEY

Exhibit 2-3 True bill returned by grand jury indicting John Wesley Peavy with murder.

usually heard if they request to give testimony. In some jurisdictions, the prosecution is expected to present **exculpatory** as well as indictable evidence to the grand jury.

The court reporter is always present during a federal grand jury hearing. Whether a stenographic record is made in some jurisdictions, though, is a matter of prosecutorial discretion. There are two situations in which it is desirable to record testimony. One is when the state anticipates blatant perjury. For example, if a drunken driver switches places with a sober friend after an accident in order to avoid DWI prosecution and witnesses have observed the switch, the state might want to record the compelled testimony of the defendant in light of the conflict between the defendant's story and that of the witnesses. Another situation is when the state anticipates that personal loyalty will override commitment to the truth as the case becomes old. It may be important to perpetuate testimony early, while the event is fresh. For example, it is not unusual for victims of domestic violence to change their story as the trial approaches. Loyalty to one's spouse may take priority over the truth.

Although most witnesses who testify before a grand jury are also likely to do so at trial, hearsay evidence is sometimes permitted at the grand jury hearing. For example, in a homicide case, the medical examiner testifies at trial as to the cause of a victim's death. In order to save the government from paying a consulting fee twice, officers investigating the crime may testify at the hearing that they attended the autopsy and were advised by the medical examiner that the cause of death was, for instance, a stab wound to the heart or a lethal dose of arsenic.

At the completion of the testimony, the prosecution discusses the elements of the crime that the accused allegedly committed. It may instruct the jurors that before returning a true bill the state must prove a **prima facie case**. A prima facie case is one in which the prosecution has presented evidence sufficient to produce a guilty verdict if uncontradicted by any defense during a trial. Notice that the amount of evidence required for an indictment may be greater than that required for a probable-cause determination at first appearance. Not all jurisdictions, however, require this greater degree of proof.

The grand jury deliberates alone. Its deliberations usually only take a few minutes or, at most, an hour.[1] A favorable vote of not less than a majority is necessary to the finding of any true bill. Some states, though, require more than just a majority to indict.

Information

An information is a written accusation by the state charging the accused with committing a crime. It is filed with the clerk of the court.

In addition to name, place, and time, the charging document cites the law supposedly violated and includes the allegation of essential facts.

The grand jury's power to find a true bill and the prosecution's power to file an information are independent of one another in some jurisdictions. For example, a grand jury's failure to indict the accused may not affect the prosecution's ability to charge the accused by information.

The decision to file an information is based on the admissibility and weight of the evidence. First, the prosecution must decide whether it can prove the case. For example, if a confession is likely to be challenged successfully by the defense because suspects were not given their Miranda warnings, the prosecution probably cannot prove the case if the outcome hinges on that confession. Second, the prosecution must decide whether it has a prima facie case. It must determine whether the evidence is sufficient to convince a jury of the accused's guilt. If the evidence is such that the state cannot prove its case or the jury is likely not to be convinced, no information is filed.

The prosecution in some jurisdictions does not go to the scene of the crime when the police are called. Therefore, the prosecution must rely on the complaint, the offense report, various affidavits, physical evidence, and crime-scene photographs in piecing together the elements of a crime. In addition, the prosecution reviews the results of laboratory tests and interviews with the investigating officers.

The offense report is a document with blanks for details concerning a crime, such as incident, victim, witnesses, suspect, and modus operandi. It is filled out by law enforcement officers investigating a crime. Those who first appear at the scene of a crime briefly interview those involved, such as the victim and witnesses. Based on this information and on what the officers themselves observe, they complete the form and write a narrative summary of the events surrounding the offense. Supplemental attachments are provided later by detectives conducting the follow-up investigation.

Preliminary Hearing —Probable cause hearing.

In Los Angeles, a preliminary hearing can be like a mini-trial without a jury.[2] The prosecution presents evidence in an attempt to convince the judge that there is probable cause to hold the accused for trial. Witnesses for the state are examined and cross-examined at a public hearing. At the conclusion of the testimony for the prosecution, the defense may present evidence in order to persuade the judge that the accused should not be bound over for trial. Witnesses brought on behalf of the accused may be cross-examined in the same manner as witnesses for the prosecution. Although the accused may waive the preliminary hearing, such a hearing is often to the accused's advantage because they can discover evidence held by the prosecution. Knowledge of the state's case can only help the accused better prepare their defense.

In other jurisdictions, the preliminary hearing can be a routine proceeding, occupying no more than a few minutes of the court's time. The state makes its case, and the judge rules. It is rare for the defense to contest the state's presentation. Frequently, it even waives the proceeding.

The preliminary hearing is not used in all states. For example, in one jurisdiction the accused are entitled to an adversary preliminary hearing if they have not been charged in an information or indictment within twenty-one days from the time they were arrested.[3] It is rare, however, that they are not charged within that time. For all practical purposes, the adversary preliminary hearing has been replaced by a first appearance that has become the probable-cause determination and a liberalized policy toward **discovery,** the exchange of information between prosecution and defense. Charges in a capital case, however, must be brought by the grand jury.

Arraignment

Arraignment is the first time felony defendants are called upon to enter a plea. It is conducted in the major trial court. Most, if not all, of the courthouse regulars are in attendance: judge, prosecutor, defense attorney, deputy court clerk, court reporter, and bailiff. Defendants approach the bench singly as the prosecutor or deputy court clerk calls their names. When defendants are not present, the judge may instruct the bailiff to sound the call. For example, if John Doe fails to appear when his name is called, the bailiff will say, "John Doe, present yourself before the court or your bond will be revoked." The bailiff calls out the judge's instructions three times. Then, if no response is forthcoming, it is presumed that Doe's absence is a willful failure to appear. The judge orders the bailiff to execute a **capias** for the arrest of John Doe. His bond is estreated (forfeited). (Recall that the bondsman may avoid having to pay the face amount of the bond by bringing the errant client to the jail.)

The prosecutor or judge reads the accused the charges, and the judge informs those not yet represented by an attorney of their right to counsel. Indigent defendants who were not appointed an attorney earlier are appointed one now, and a plea of not guilty is entered. Theoretically, the pleas available at arraignment to defendants who are represented by counsel are not guilty, guilty, and **nolo contendere** (no contest).

A plea of not guilty puts at issue the facts alleged in the information or indictment. A plea of nolo contendere is not an admission of guilt and may not be used against defendants in civil action. It means

IN THE CIRCUIT COURT OF THE
SECOND JUDICIAL CIRCUIT, IN
AND FOR LEON COUNTY, FLORIDA.

CASE NO. 85-4810

STATE OF FLOIRDA,

    Plaintiff,

-vs-

JOHN WESLEY PEAVY,

    Defendant.
_____/

1-31-86

FILED

PLEA OF NOT GUILTY

AND

DEMAND FOR JURY TRIAL

    COMES NOW the Defendant, JOHN WESLEY PEAVY, by and
through his undersigned lawyer, Anthony L. Bajoczky, and
pursuant to Florida Rules of Criminal Procedure 3.160(a)
enters this his PLEA OF NOT GUILTY to the charges alleged
in the above-styled cause, subject to all motions, and

    FURTHERMORE, demands a TRIAL BY JURY.

ANTHONY L. BAJOCZKY

BARRETT AND BAJOCZKY
131 North Gadsden Street
Post Office Box 1501
Tallahassee, Florida   32302
(904) 222-9000

Lawyer for Defendant

CERTIFICATE OF SERVICE

    I HEREBY CERTIFY that a true and correct copy of the
foregoing Plea of Not Guilty and Demand for Jury Trial has
been furnished this 31st day of January, 1986, to Mr. C.
Warren Goodwin, Assistant State Attorney, Suite 500, First
Florida Bank Building, Tallahassee, Florida 32301.

ANTHONY L. BAJOCZKY

Exhibit 2-4 John Wesley Peavy's plea of not guilty and demand for jury trial.

that they simply do not want to contest the charge. A plea of guilty or
nolo contendere requires the court's consent. When defendants refuse to plead, the court enters a plea of not guilty. Generally, defendants commonly waive arraignment by having their attorney file a
written plea of not guilty (see Exhibit 2-4).

Once a plea of not guilty is entered, the judge may assign the case a trial date. Sometime before that date, the judge and attorneys confer at a **docket sounding** to decide whether the defendant will go to trial or negotiate a plea. Most cases are plea-bargained, usually sometime between arraignment and the trial date.

Discovery

The right of pretrial discovery is the right of defendants to inspect and copy certain materials held by the prosecution. Knowledge of these materials eliminates surprises and is helpful in pretrial preparation. Not all states recognize the right of pretrial discovery in a criminal case. In those that do, rarely is it granted to the prosecution.

Florida is one jurisdiction that extends to the prosecution many of the same rights of pretrial discovery that are granted to the defendant. After written demand by the defendant, following the filing of the information or indictment, the prosecutor must allow the defense attorney to inspect, copy, test, and photograph the following:

- Names, addresses, and statements of persons known to the prosecution to have information that may be relevant to the offense charged;

- Written or recorded statements made by the accused and co-defendants;

- Segments of recorded grand jury minutes containing testimony of the accused;

- Papers or objects obtained from the accused;

- Reports or statements of experts that relate to the case;

- Papers or objects that the prosecutor intends to use at trial but that were not obtained from the accused.

In addition, the defense attorney may inquire:

- Whether the state has information or material provided by a confidential informant;

- Whether there has been any electronic surveillance of the premises of the accused or of conversations to which the accused was a party;

- Whether there was any search or seizure (see Exhibit 2-5).[4]

IN THE CIRCUIT COURT OF THE
SECOND JUDICIAL CIRCUIT, IN
AND FOR LEON COUNTY, FLORIDA.

CASE NO. 85-4810

STATE OF FLORIDA,

     Plaintiff,

-vs-

JOHN WESLEY PEAVY,

     Defendant.

_____/

DEMAND FOR DISCOVERY

    COMES NOW the Defendant, JOHN WESLEY PEAVY, by and through
his undersigned lawyer, Anthony L. Bajoczky, and hereby demands
the prosecutor to disclose to defense counsel and permit defense
counsel to inspect, copy, test, and photograph the information
and material within the State's possession or control as specified
in Florida Rules of Criminal Procedure 3.220(a), (i), (ii), (iii), (iv),
(v), (vi), (vii), (viii), (ix), (x), (xi), and 3.220(2), including but not limited to the following:

    1. The names and addresses of all persons known to the
prosecutor to have information which may be relevant to the
offense charged, and to any defense with respect thereto.

    2. The statement of any person whose name is furnished in
compliance with the preceding paragraph, including but not
limited to, written statements made by said person(s) and signed
and otherwise adopted or approved by them or a stenographic,
mechanical, electrical or other recording, or a transcript
thereof, or which is a substantial verbatim recital of an oral

    11. Any tangible papers, or objects which the State
intends to use in the hearing or trial and which were not
obtained or belonging to the Defendant.

ANTHONY L. BAJOCZKY

BARRETT AND BAJOCZKY
131 North Gadsden Street
Post Office Box 1501
Tallahassee, Florida 32302
(904) 222-9000

Lawyer For Defendant

Exhibit 2-5 Demand for discovery, filed by Anthony Bajoczky.

The prosecution is also entitled to disclosure of certain information. A judge may require that the accused perform the following:

- Appear in a lineup;

- Speak for identification by witnesses;

- Be fingerprinted;

- Pose for certain photographs;

- Try on articles of clothing;

- Permit the taking of specimens of material from under the fingernails;

- Permit the taking of samples of blood, hair, and other materials of the body;

- Provide specimens of handwriting;

- Submit to reasonable physical and medical inspection.[5]

In addition, if the prosecution has provided a list of witnesses, the defense must reciprocate. If the defense demands discovery of statements of persons whom the state expects to call as witnesses, of reports or statements of experts, and of papers or objects that the prosecution intends to use at trial, the defense must disclose similar information.[6] Furthermore, if the defense claims that the defendant was not at the scene of the crime at the time the crime was committed, the defense must provide the prosecutor with the names and addresses of witnesses by whom the defense intends to establish the defendant's alibi (see Exhibit 2-6).

Matters often not subject to disclosure are work product and the identity of informants.[8] Neither prosecution nor defense is required to disclose the product of its work to the extent that the product contains opinions, theories, or conclusions. Examples of such work include legal research, correspondences, and the narrative summary of the offense report. Disclosure of confidential informants is not required unless they will be present at trial or unless failure to disclose their identity somehow infringes on the constitutional rights of defendants.

In practice, what is discoverable is largely a matter of individual discretion. Many attorneys do not follow the rules strictly, reasoning that the more information is exchanged, the better it is for both parties. To promote cooperation, for example, the prosecutor might show the defense the narrative summary of an offense report, even though the summary could be considered a work product. Of course, cooperation

IN THE CIRCUIT COURT OF THE
SECOND JUDICIAL CIRCUIT, IN
AND FOR LEON COUNTY, FLORIDA

CASE NO. 85-4810

STATE OF FLORIDA

vs.

JOHN WESLEY PEAVY,

    Defendant.

_____/

2-27-86

DEMAND FOR NOTICE OF ALIBI

The State of Florida, pursuant to Rule 3.200, Florida
Criminal Procedure Rules, demands that the Defendant, in the
event he intends to offer an alibi in his defense, file and
serve upon the State a notice in writing of his intention to
claim an alibi, including specifically the place where the
Defendant claims to have been at the time of the alleged
offenses and, as particularly as is known to the Defendant or
his attorney, the names and addresses of the witnesses by whom
he proposes to establish such alibi.

In making this written demand upon the Defendant, the State
alleges as particularly as is known, that the offenses appearing
on the Indictment occurred between 8:00 p.m. and 11:59 p.m. on
October 31, 1985, at or around the residence or dwelling occupied
at the time by Robert Lester Harrison and Mary Lee Driggers,
located at Fairbanks Ferry Court, Leon County, Florida or elsewhere in Leon County, Florida to the prosecutor unknown.

                                  WILLIAM N. MEGGS
                                  STATE ATTORNEY

                                  ANTHONY S. GUARISCO, JR.
                                  Deputy State Attorney

Exhibit 2-6 Demand for notice of alibi, made to John Wesley Peavy.

is not always the chosen route. For example, in a big drug case where the opposition is an out-of-town lawyer who takes pride in ambushing the other side, the prosecutor is not likely to be open. When defendants demand discovery, if one party holds back the name of a "surprise" witness whose testimony could possibly alter the outcome of the trial, the court may prohibit the party from calling that witness or grant a mistrial. It can also grant a **continuance** so that the other party has time to **depose** the witness.

Discovery Deposition and Subpoena

The discovery deposition is the taking of oral testimony, ordinarily attended by the defense attorney, prosecutor, court reporter, and the **deponents** (persons who testify to the truth of certain facts). Although the deposition is usually taken at the courthouse, the parties may agree to its being taken anywhere. The court reporter usually records testimony stenographically (see Exhibit 2-7).

The discovery deposition differs from a deposition to perpetuate testimony. The latter is used when one party anticipates the likely unavailability of a witness and wants to preserve that witness's testimony for later use at trial. In contrast, the discovery deposition gives the deposing party an opportunity to ask questions that might reveal facts potentially useful in pretrial preparation. Of course, these same questions—or the way in which they are asked—may be revealing to the other side. Like a deposition to perpetuate testimony, the discovery deposition also memorializes testimony so that the deposing party is not at the mercy of the deponent if, during trial, the deponent's story changes. The deposition may be used to **impeach** the courtroom testimony of a witness. Unlike the deposition to perpetuate testimony, the discovery deposition cannot be used as evidence against the accused if the deponent is unavailable at trial because the discovery deposition lacks certain procedural safeguards.[9]

There are two kinds of subpoenas: **subpoena ad testificandum** and **subpoena duces tecum.** The former, known simply as a witness subpoena, notifies the witnesses to appear at a certain time and place to give testimony. The latter commands persons who have some paper, document, or other physical evidence in their possession to produce it at a certain time and place (see Exhibit 2-8). The subpoena is prepared by an attorney, stamped and signed by the court clerk, and usually served by a deputy sheriff. Private attorneys frequently use **process servers,** usually private investigators who are bonded by the sheriff's department. When process servers deliver a subpoena, they file a certificate of service with the court clerk. When they are unable to deliver the subpoena, they file a certificate of no service. Deputy sheriffs follow a procedure that is quite similar to that employed by

IN THE CIRCUIT COURT OF THE
SECOND JUDICIAL CIRCUIT, IN
AND FOR LEON COUNTY, FLORIDA.

CASE NO. 85-4810

STATE OF FLORIDA,

      Plaintiff,

-vs-

JOHN WESLEY PEAVY,

      Defendant.

_____/

(FLA. BAR NO. 0160351)

12360

IN COMPUTER SCT

NOTICE OF TAKING DEPOSITION

TO: Mr. Anthony S. Guarisco
       Assistant State Attorney
       Suite 500
       First Florida Bank Building
       Tallahassee, Florida 32301

     PLEASE TAKE NOTICE that the undersigned lawyer will take
the deposition upon oral examination before an Official Court
Reporter, or some other officer duly authorized to take depositions,
of the persons listed below and at the date, time and place stated
herein.

DEPOSITION OF:	See Attached Subpoenas
DATE and TIME:	June 5, 1986 (Thursday) 2:00 to 5:00 p.m.
	June 6, 1986 (Friday) 9:00 a.m. to 5:00 p.m.
	June 10, 1986 (Tuesday) 9:00 a.m. to 5:00 p.m.
PLACE:	Room 308 Leon County Courthouse Tallahassee, Florida

ANTHONY L. BAJOCZKY

BARRETT AND BAJOCZKY
131 North Gadsden Street
Post Office Box 1501
Tallahassee, Florida 32302
(904) 222-9000

Lawyer for Defendant

Exhibit 2-7 Notice of taking deposition, showing the date, time, and place.

IN THE CIRCUIT COURT OF THE
SECOND JUDICIAL CIRCUIT IN
AND FOR LEON COUNTY, FLORIDA

CASE NO. 85-4810

STATE OF FLORIDA,

                Plaintiff,

vs.

JOHN WESLEY PEAVY,

                Defendant.

Received this _Subpoena_
on the _8th_ day of _July_
19_86_ and Served the same on
Ann White on the _8th_ day
of _July_ 19_86_, at _12:05_ p.M.

Richard E. Campbell

SUBPOENA DUCES TECUM FOR DEPOSITION

THE STATE OF FLORIDA:

To: Capt. Dale Wise
     Leon County Sheriff's Office
     Tallahassee, Florida

YOU ARE HEREBY COMMANDED to appear at _Leon County_ _Courthouse, Room 308, Tallahassee, Florida_ _____ at _1:30 p.m._ on _Wednesday_ the _9th_ day of _July_, _1986_, upon oral examination, before an official court reporter duly authorized by law to take depositions. You are required to have with you at said time and place the following:

> Any and all lead sheets and other information
> regarding which officers were assigned to what
> specific portion of this investigation and
> which officer(s) interviewed which witness(es).

You are subpoenaed to appear by the following attorneys and unless excused from this subpoena by these attorneys of the Court, you shall respond to this subpoena as directed.

WITNESS my hand and seal of said Court this _7th_ day of _July_ _____, 19_86_.

(seal)

Anthony Bajoczky
     Attorney
ANTHONY L. BAJOCZKY

PAUL F. HARTSFIELD,
Clerk of the Circuit Court,

BY: _____
               Deputy Clerk

Exhibit 2-8 Subpoena duces tecum served to Captain Dale Wise.

process servers. Those who refuse to obey a subpoena can be held in contempt of court.

Study Questions

1. Peavy was arrested on December 23 and indicted on January 23. Why did the state not expedite the bringing of charges by filing an information earlier than January 23?

2. In the early stages of the case, what was the apparent strategy for Peavy's defense? How did the prosecution prepare for this strategy?

3. Collecting evidence is central to pretrial preparation. Did one side in the Peavy case have an inherent advantage over the other in collecting evidence?

Endnotes

1. Alan Sprowls, assistant U.S. attorney, Northern District of Florida, Tallahassee, Florida, personal communication, 11 June 1990; Warren Goodwin, assistant state attorney, Second Judicial Circuit, Tallahassee, Florida, personal communication, 5 August 1988. See Robert A. Carp, "The Behavior of Grand Juries: Acquiescence or Justice?" *Social Science Quarterly* 1(1975), 853–70.

2. For a concise discussion of the various forms the preliminary hearing takes in practice, see David W. Neubauer, *America's Courts and the Criminal Justice System*, 3d ed. (Pacific Grove, CA: Brooks/Cole Publishing Co., 1988), 205–6.

3. *Florida Rules of Criminal Procedure*, rule 3.133 (1987).

4. *Florida Rules of Criminal Procedure*, rule 3.220 (1987).

5. *Florida Rules of Criminal Procedure*, rule 3.220 (1987).

6. *Florida Rules of Criminal Procedure*, rule 3.220 (1987).

7. *Florida Rules of Criminal Procedure*, rule 3.200 (1987).

8. *Florida Rules of Criminal Procedure*, rule 3.220 (1987).

9. Jerome C. Latimer, "Depositions in Criminal Cases," *Florida Pretrial Practice in Criminal Cases*, ed. William R. Eleazer (Tallahassee, FL: Florida Bar, 1987), 211–82.

3

Preparing for Trial

The Prosecution Links
a Missing Gun to Murder

No living soul could put Johnny at the murder scene. If anyone did see him point a semiautomatic weapon at his brother-in-law's window and spray fatal lead into the rainstorm, they weren't talking.

Deputies trudged for miles up and down Fairbanks Ferry Road, a paved country road crossing the Ochlockonee River. They knocked on doors, as well, along adjoining Fairbanks Ferry Court, the sandy lane that twined down to the river and Bobby's place.

No one had seen Johnny's light blue Ford Ranger pickup on Halloween night. But eyewitnesses are a luxury for prosecutors. The *State of Florida v. John Wesley Peavy* was another circumstantial-evidence case, and far from open-and-shut.

"We didn't have the strongest case," said Major Larry Campbell. "No eyewitnesses, no gun, no good motive. But we did have inconsistencies after inconsistencies."

When it came to deep-down gut feelings shared by prosecutors and investigators, there were plenty.

No question about it: Johnny was their man. Not only was he a gun nut, he was a gun nut with alcohol coursing through his brain.

"The more Johnny was on a binge, the more gun-happy he was," Campbell said.

State Attorney Willie Meggs called Peavy "a guy who won't hesitate to get his gun and shoot at people."

Meggs was referring to information found by his investigators that Peavy allegedly shot at a man who had approached his house one night.

"We found out about a man who went to get his paycheck from John Peavy and was greeted with gunshot," said Tony Guarisco, the prosecutor assigned to the case.

Figure 3-1 Deputies search for evidence at the Harrison trailer, November 1985. Phil Coale.

Even if true, that incident, in which no arrest was made, would not be admissible evidence in this case. You can't show gut feelings to a jury. Prosecutors needed hard, physical evidence.

Usually, telltale signs are left behind at the crime scene. But rains from Tropical Storm Juan had washed away any possible tire tracks or footprints near Bobby Harrison's trailer (see Figure 3-1). And the murder weapon was never found.

The prosecutors' strongest evidence against Peavy boiled down to spent cartridge cases. However, before these cases—that part of the ammunition left behind when the bullet takes off—wound up as evidence in sealed paper bags, they were found scattered on the ground near Bobby's shattered kitchen window.

Although these were cases from CCI Blazer cartridges, the most common kind of 9mm ammo sold on the market, investigators had to convince the court that a gun Johnny owned left those very common ammo cases when the fatal shots were fired.

The big problem was that they needed the gun to make a certain match. With the gun, a crime lab expert could say whether or not those cases came from that particular weapon.

They had tailed Peavy before his arrest, hoping he would lead them to the place the murder weapon was stashed. No such luck. The gun was never found.

But they found the next-best thing: someone willing to take them to places where Johnny had fired his 9mm weapon. That someone was Magnum Delacy Peavy IV, better known as "Little Delacy," Johnny's blond-haired nephew in his twenties. When the police called on him for information, he obliged them, to the point of wearing a secret body "bug" when talking to his mother and Uncle Johnny.

Joe Mitchell wrote in his FDLE investigative report that a "confidential source," later identified as Little Delacy, went to Peavy's home on December 18, 1985, on a mission to "discuss the shooting deaths of Bobby Harrison and Mary Lee Driggers and the missing weapon." The twenty-five-minute conversation began on the front porch, but barking dogs forced Peavy and Little Delacy to take their talk inside. Two sheriff's deputies were recording the bugged conversation from down the road.

Mitchell typed this in his report, based on what Little Delacy told him when debriefed:

"From his observation of Johnny Peavy, Peavy did not appear nervous, and acted normal, as if nothing had happened. Further, Peavy commented to him that Peavy thought the weapon had been stolen by the Parkers (meaning a black family who lives in his nearby neighborhood). Peavy advised [him that] the Parkers go in his truck regularly, and have been known to take liquor from his vehicle. Further, Mr. Peavy advised he didn't know for a week after the shooting deaths of Harrison and Driggers that his weapon was missing."

So the secretly taped conversations turned up nothing incriminating against Johnny: mostly crackly, hard-to-hear conversations of no evidentiary value at all. But with Little Delacy's help in pointing out spent cartridge cases, investigators hit pay dirt.

On December 4, 1985, Little Delacy told Leon County Sheriff's Detective Bill Moody that he and his Uncle Johnny had been down to what he called the "river property," Peavy-owned land near Fairbanks Ferry Road, firing their guns one or two weeks before Halloween. Little Delacy was firing his Tec 9 Mini, and Uncle Johnny was firing his Tec 9 semiautomatic, the one that was missing.

Little Delacy took Moody and Florida Department of Law Enforcement Agent Joe Mitchell to the very spot at the river where he and Johnny had been firing their guns for fun. The investigators scooped up two dozen fired 9mm cartridge cases and one unfired 9mm cartridge. Little Delacy also let them take his Tec 9 Mini, along with fifty-eight rounds of 9mm CCI Blazer ammo his Uncle Johnny had given him.

Two days later, Moody and two other FDLE agents, Ronnie Cornelius and Jim Gettemmy, searched Johnny Peavy's house. They didn't need a search warrant because the Peavys gave them permission.

Moody, Cornelius, and Gettemmy found a box of 9mm CCI Blazer ammo in Peavy's gun closet. From the yard, where Johnny was known to target-practice, they collected seven fired 9mm cartridge cases.

The next day, Little Delacy called the investigators to say he had found two fired cartridge cases and one fired bullet at the shop of Peavy & Son Construction Company, where he had seen Uncle Johnny fire his gun soon after he bought it. Little Delacy turned the evidence over to Moody.

On December 10, 1985, Big Delacy permitted the police to send divers to the bottom of the pond on the Peavy river property that Little Delacy had shown them earlier. Campbell said they told Big Delacy that they needed to gather spent cartridge cases to eliminate Johnny Peavy as a suspect.

Moody collected another twenty-three fired 9mm cartridge cases from the ground around the pond, as well as one unfired cartridge. The divers brought up one fired projectile from the bottom of the pond, as well as one unfired cartridge. It was all packaged, labeled, and initialed, launching a chain-of-command chronology beginning with a sheriff's diver and eventually ending with the clerk of court.

"We helped them with the evidence, knowing it would clear Johnny," said Big Delacy, Little Delacy's father and Johnny's brother.

But as far as the prosecution was concerned, the evidence against Johnny was mounting. In late December, at FDLE headquarters, there was a meeting of all the chief officials on the case, incuding Campbell, Meggs, Guarisco, Mitchell, and Leon County Sheriff Eddie Boone.

Concern surfaced whether they had enough evidence to convince a jury beyond a reasonable doubt. They believed Johnny was the murderer, but would a jury believe it?

"We felt we had probable cause. We had a case on Johnny," Campbell said. "But we felt it'd be more open-and-shut if we had the weapon."

All of the ammunition packaged as evidence was hauled over to the FDLE crime lab and given to ballistics expert Don Champagne.

Champagne's findings became part of the probable-cause affidavit, which Chief Circuit Judge J. Lewis Hall signed on Dec. 20, 1985, saying there was enough evidence to arrest Peavy.

"We feel we have enough to get a case to a jury beyond a directed verdict," Campbell said. "But we sure could do better. We continued the investigation a few more days, looking for the proverbial break."

The plan was to bring Johnny in for one more talk and to see if he would break down and confess. When Peavy walked into Campbell's office on December 23, 1985, the place was wired.

"We're hoping he'll spill his guts," Campbell said.

Peavy never confessed to any murders. But he did admit that he owned a Tec 9mm gun and that he had fired it at his home and with his nephew at the pond. He also admitted that he had never reported the gun as stolen to law enforcement officers or to his insurance company. And Johnny told the police he didn't notice the gun was missing until after the murders. He told FDLE Agent Mitchell that he noticed the gun was missing when he went to lock up his truck, right before checking into the alcohol treatment hospital. He said he kept the gun behind the seat, planning to get it fixed.

"The gun is missing. Big deal," Campbell said, lowering his voice for emphasis. "This was Johnny's 'love-it' gun."

It seemed mighty suspicious, Campbell said, that the gun they suspected was the murder weapon was missing, and that Peavy had no explanation for not reporting it missing or stolen.

Meggs, the chief prosecutor of the six-county judicial circuit, agreed that Peavy's lack of concern was critical: "You lose your favorite gun and don't even know it's missing?"

Meanwhile, ballistics pro Champagne was busy in the crime lab, peering into a microscope and examining all the spent cartridge cases and bullets for revealing markings.

On January 2, 1986—more than a week after Peavy was already locked in jail on murder charges—Champagne wrote his report (see Exhibit 3-1).

His purpose was to determine if the bullets and cartridge cases found at the Peavy river property pond, at the Peavy construction company shop, and at Peavy's home were fired from the same weapon that left the bullets and spent cartridge cases at the murder scene.

When it came to the spent cartridge cases from the various locations, Champagne concluded, the same weapon could have been used. He couldn't say that the same weapon definitely had been used, but that it could have been used.

But that was enough to satisfy Campbell.

"Champagne made match after match," Campbell said, smiling as he explained the case to a newspaper reporter.

But when it came to matching bullets found at the murder scene with bullets found at the pond, there was a problem. The bullets found at Harrison's trailer and at the Peavy Pond had no telltale markings, called rifling, which can be matched with markings inside a particular gun's barrel. Champagne wrote in his report, "None of these bullets have conventional rifling marks on them. They could, therefore, have been fired from the same weapon. However, because of the absence of rifling, no correspondence of striated markings could be found. For that reason, a conclusive determination of relationship is not possible."

Without the missing gun, prosecutors could not prove the murder weapon had no rifling.

"I know my gun had rifling, as many times as I cleaned out the bore," Peavy insisted.

The semiautomatic weapon would have come from the factory with rifling. The only way the gun could lack rifling would be if someone had bored out its barrel in a machine shop making the barrel smooth. This would make whatever bullets it fired impossible to trace to the gun.

Peavy insisted that he was not mechanically inclined and that he never altered his gun. But prosecutors said all the tools necessary for boring out a gun's rifling were readily available at the Peavy & Son Construction Company machine shop.

The thing important to prosecutors was that they had Little Delacy, ready to swear under oath on the witness stand that he had watched his uncle fire that Tec 9 semiautomatic gun at the various locations and that the spent CCI Blazer cartridges, without marks from rifling, found at the murder scene were the same type his uncle used.

Besides rifling, there was another identifying mark. Found at the Peavy

Florida Department of
Law Enforcement

Robert R. Dempsey
Commissioner

Division of Staff Services
Tallahassee Regional
Crime Laboratory

420 N. Adams St.
P.O. Box 1489
Tallahassee, Florida 32302
(904) 488-7071
SUNCOM 278-7071

02 January 1986

TO: Honorable Eddie Boone
Sheriff, Leon County
P. O. Box 727
Tallahassee, Florida 32302

ATTN: Detective Bill Moody

RE: UNKNOWN SUBJECT
Death Investigation
Robert L. HARRISON
Mary Lee DRIGGERS
LEON COUNTY
11 02 85

FDLE LAB NO. 85 11 12038
AGENCY NO. 85-44808

SUBPOENAS PERTAINING TO THIS
CASE SHOULD REFER TO FDLE
LAB NO. 85 11 12038

Donald K. Champagne
Crime Laboratory Analyst,
Firearms

REFERENCE:

This report has reference to the following exhibits that were received at the laboratory from Detective Moody on December 5, 1985 (exhibits #1 (007), #2 (007) & #3 (007), on December 9, 1985 (exhibits #1 (008) & #2 (008) and on December 11, 1985 (exhibits #1 (010) and #2 (010) and from James Gettemy on December 11, 1985 (exhibits #1 (011) & #3a, 3b & 3c (011).

EXHIBITS:

#1 (007) Marked plastic bag and boxes containing five (5) expended 9MM Luger caliber (CCI) "Blazer" cartridge cases and one (1) unfired 9MM Luger caliber (CCI) "Blazer" JHP cartridge.

#2 (007) Marked plastic bag and boxes containing nineteen (19) expended 9MM Luger caliber (CCI) "Blazer" cartridge cases.

#3 (007) Ammunition box containing twenty-two (22) unfired 9MM Luger caliber (CCI) "Blazer" JHP cartridges.

#1 (008) Two (2) expended 9MM Luger caliber (CCI) "Blazer" cartridge cases.

#2 (008) One (1) fired 9MM caliber FMJ bullet.

#1 (010) Marked plastic jar containign twenty-three (23) expended 9MM Luger caliber (CCI) "Blazer" cartridge cases and one (1) unfired 9MM Luger caliber (CCI) "Blazer" JHP cartridge.

#2 (010) Marked plastic jar containing one (1) fired 9MM caliber JHP bullet and one (1) unfired 9MM Luger caliber (CCI) "Blazer" JHP cartridge.

#1 (011) Marked paper bag containing ammunition box and eight (8) unfired 9MM Luger caliber (CCI) "Blazer" JHP cartridges.

#3a (011) Marked paper bag containing three (3) expended 9MM Luger caliber (CCI) "Blazer" cartridge cases.

#3b (011) Marked paper bag containing three (3) expended 9MM Luger caliber (CCI) "Blazer" cartridge cases and one (1) expended .380 ACP caliber (Norma) cartridge case.

#3c (011) Marked paper bag containing one (1) expended 9MM Luger caliber (CCI) "Blazer" cartridge case.

PURPOSE:

Determine if any of the above bullets and cartridge cases were fired from and in the same (unidentified) weapon used to fire the previously submitted bullets and cartridge cases.

RESULTS:

Exhibit #1 (007)

One (1) of these cartridge cases has been identified as having been fired in the

Exhibit 3-1 The ballistics report filed by Don Champagne, comparing cartridge cases found at Harrison's trailer with cases known to have been fired from Peavy's gun.

same weapon used to fire the previously submitted cartridge cases, exhibits #1 thru #12, submission #001.

Exhibit #2 (007)

Five (5) of these cartridge cases have been identified as having been fired in the same weapon used to fire the previously submitted cartridge cases, exhibits #1 thru #12, submission #001.

Exhibit #1 (008)

One (1) of these cartridge cases has been identified as having been fired in the same weapon used to fire the previously submitted cartridge cases, exhibits #1 thru #12, submission #001. The remaining cartridge case is so badly damaged and distorted that it is of *no* identification value.

Exhibit #2 (008)

This bullet has been examined and compared microscopically with the previously submitted bullets, exhibits #13, #14, #15, #19, #20, #22, #23, #24 & #25 (001). None of these bullets have conventional rifling marks on them. They could, therefore, have been fired from the same weapon. However, because of the absence of rifling, no correspondence of striated markings could be found. For that reason a conclusive determination of relationship is not possible.

Exhibit #1 (010)

Thirteen (13) of these cartridge cases have been identified as having been fired in the same weapon used to fire the previously submitted cartridge cases, exhibits #1 thru #12, submission #001.

The unfired cartridge exhibits the following damage;—The bullet is pushed back into the case, the bullet is tipped in the case and the case walls are bulged.

Exhibit #2 (010)

This bullet does not have conventional rifling marks on it. See results under exhibit #2 (008).

The unfired cartridge has some striated damaged to one side of the case that is consistent with jamming in the action of a semi, or fully automatic firearm.

Exhibit #1 (011)

The cartridges in this box are the same as those found in exhibit #3 (007).

Exhibit #3a (011)

One (1) of these cartridge cases has been identified as having been fired in the same weapon used to fire the previously submitted cartridge cases, exhibits #1 thru #12, submission #001.

Exhibit #3b (011)

Two (2) of these cartridge cases have been identified as having been fired in the same weapon used to fire the previously submitted cartridge cases, exhibits #1 thru #12, submission #001.

Exhibit #3c (011)

This cartridge case has been identified as having been fired in the same weapon used to fire the previously submitted cartridge cases, exhibits #1 thru #12, submission #001.

Remarks:

The exhibits will be temporarily retained.

Exhibit 3-1 Continued.

& Son Construction Company shop, an unfired cartridge Champagne examined showed a type of damage in which the bullet was pushed back into the case, indicating a firing mechanism problem. The bullet was tipped in the case, and the case walls bulged.

An unfired cartridge found at the Peavy river property pond had some striated damage to one side of the case that Champagne concluded was "consistent with jamming in the action of a semi- or fully-automatic firearm."

By trusting Peavy's nephew's testimony, Meggs said, "We establish[ed] the fact [that it was] his gun. The only thing we didn't establish was that he was at the scene."

What the police had on Peavy was enough to legally lock him behind bars. But they wanted enough to convict him, then send him to death row to wait for his day to die. And, while Peavy's insufferable jailhouse wait for his trial dragged on, the investigation continued.

Little did Peavy realize that in the very jail where he sat locked up, prosecutors were talking to fellow inmates, striking deals and compiling incriminating testimony against him.

Prosecutors found two felons willing to testify that Peavy had confessed to the murders in their presence. And Guarisco wasn't about to apologize for using the testimony of convicts.

"What do you do, ignore them because they're slimy?," Guarisco asked. "Say, 'Get out of my face'?"

It was damning testimony. Peavy's defense blasted it as self-serving lies told by jailbirds out to save their own hides.

"The police have too much integrity to tell an outright, blatant lie," Bajoczky said. "But they knew if they put [Peavy] in jail and let the jailbirds know what they're looking for, they'll get a whole jail full of people to come forward and say he confessed. And they [did] get six or seven people to come forward. Some weren't real good. They [said], 'Keep an ear open, let us know.' I have no doubt that happened. Johnny kept his mouth shut in the jail, and he got set up."

But the prosecutors insisted that Peavy foolishly spilled his guts around a pair of opportunist inmates who were worthy of belief because they had passed polygraph tests. The prosecution wasn't about to use their testimony in court unless they were confident that Peavy's confessors were telling the truth.

Not only did prosecutors want to strengthen their case, they had to counterattack whatever the defense might present. Knowing Bajoczky to be a formidable opponent from past courtroom skirmishes, prosecutors braced for plenty of work.

Because the defense was tracking drug connections to Harrison and Driggers, the prosecution had to follow them every step of the way. The defense insisted they were finding threads that would eventually unravel drug connections and lead the way to the true killer. But the prosecution concluded it was no more than defense tactics to drag the victims through the mud and to muster up misguided doubt.

If Peavy decided to take the witness stand, prosecutors wanted as much negative evidence as possible to impeach his credibility. They planned to go full tilt for the death penalty, should they score a conviction. And the penalty phase of any potential death penalty case is a defendant's auto-biography compressed into a court docudrama in which the defense showcases the defendant's achievements and offers reasons for human frailties, in an attempt to save his life.

The prosecutor's job is to make sure no sin is overlooked. Each seedy detail a prosecutor can dredge up on any particular defendant comes in handy, even though every detail may not be used in court.

"I don't care who you are," Campbell said. "There's something you don't want anyone to know."

And Johnny Peavy had his share of flaws.

Even Bajoczky had to agree that "Johnny's biggest problem was that he was the family drunk." That problem, the prosecutors believed, was Peavy's fatal flaw. But it was no legal excuse for snuffing out two lives.

Before the trial, the defense had to tell the prosecution about any plans to present an alibi. Once law enforcement investigators learned that Queen was the alibi witness, they launched a mission to rip her testimony apart.

They didn't have to look far. At the office of the Florida Department of Law Enforcement worked a data-entry operator named Gloria Jackson Willis. She was Queen's daughter, and she lived right behind her mother along the lane to Peavy's house.

On February 17, 1987, just a few weeks before the trial, they took Willis's deposition testimony. She swore that she was at her mother's trailer on Halloween night, 1985, from 9 P.M. to 11 P.M. That would cover the time span during which prosecutors said the murder occurred.

In her deposition, Willis testified that she was sitting at her mother's kitchen table. She said she didn't remember that much about the night. But prosecutors clung to what she didn't see at her mother's place that night: Peavy or his truck. And all of the young children at the trailer, who agreed with Queen that they had seen Johnny that night, gave deposition testimony that the sheriff's investigators concluded sounded forced and rehearsed.

"They were desperate and they were trying to wrangle an alibi for Johnny," said Mickey Watson, agent-in-charge at the Tallahassee Region Office of the Florida Department of Law Enforcement. "I'm not saying it was 'bought testimony.' But it had the appearance of it, and we shot that alibi full of holes."

=========== PROCEDURAL DESCRIPTION ===========

Defendants have a right to legal representation. If they are too poor to hire a lawyer, the court will appoint one. Their right to counsel begins when formal charges have been brought against them. Once retained or appointed, their attorney interviews them, works to get them out on bail, investigates the facts, deposes witnesses, and decides on a defense strategy. Pretrial preparation also involves filing **motions** with the court, covering such matters as continuance, change of **venue**, suppression of evidence, severance of trials, severance of defendants, and **incompetency**. If pretrial publicity is a problem, the court may issue a **gag order**.

Right to Counsel

According to the Sixth Amendment, "[i]n all criminal prosecutions, the accused shall enjoy the right . . . to have the Assistance of Counsel for his defence." For years this right was interpreted to mean that if defendants could afford to hire an attorney to assist them in their defense at trial, they could not be denied that assistance. It certainly did not guarantee them such assistance if they could not afford an attorney.

This interpretation changed in 1963, when the Supreme Court decided *Gideon v. Wainwright*. Clarence Earl Gideon was charged with the felony of breaking and entering a poolroom in Panama City, Florida. Unable to afford an attorney, Gideon asked the trial court to appoint counsel for him. When the court denied his request, Gideon defended himself as best he could. He was convicted and sentenced to five years in the Florida State Prison at Raiford. In response to Gideon's petition, the Supreme Court held that "reason and reflection require us to recognize that in our adversary system of criminal justice, any person haled into court, who is too poor to hire a lawyer, cannot be assured a fair trial unless counsel is provided for him."[1]

In *Argersinger v. Hamlin*, the Supreme Court answered one of several questions left open by *Gideon:* What kind of criminal cases are covered by *Gideon?*[2] The charge in the *Gideon* case was a felony. Must counsel be appointed for a person brought to trial on a misdemeanor charge? In *Argersinger*, the Supreme Court held that nobody may be imprisoned for *any* crime unless represented by counsel.

Another question left open was how early in the criminal process the right to counsel should begin. The Supreme Court held that the accused have a right to legal representation once adversary judicial criminal proceedings have begun, "whether by way of formal charge, preliminary hearing, indictment, information, or arraignment."[3] That means, for example, that defendants have the right to have a lawyer present at a pretrial lineup once formal charges have been brought against them.[4] They have no such right, however, at a lineup conducted *prior* to that time.[5] While it is true that defendants are entitled to legal representation if taken into custody and questioned by law enforcement officers, that entitlement is not due to any "pure" right to counsel if formal charges have not been brought.[6] It owes its existence solely to the privilege against self-incrimination as interpreted by the Supreme Court in *Miranda v. Arizona*.[7]

Of course, what constitutes "formal charges" is open to interpretation. By statute, some states have determined that adversary judicial criminal proceedings begin once an arrest warrant is issued.[8] Furthermore, a state supreme court is not limited by decisions of the Supreme Court of the United States in interpreting its state constitution or rules of criminal procedure. There is no reason why a state cannot mandate broader safeguards than the minimum federal standards.[9]

If the Bill of Rights guarantees that defendants brought to trial must be afforded the right to assistance of counsel, can they waive the right and defend themselves? The Supreme Court decided this issue in 1972, in *Faretta v. California*. Although the trial court appointed a lawyer to represent him, Anthony Faretta asked if he could defend himself, saying that he did not want to be represented by a public defender. The judge accepted Faretta's waiver. Later, at a pretrial hearing, the judge asked Faretta questions about the hearsay rule and the California law governing the challenge of potential jurors. When Faretta did not know the answers, the judge reversed his ruling, saying that Faretta had not made an intelligent and knowing waiver of his right to assistance of counsel and that Faretta had no constitutional right to conduct his own defense. The judge again appointed a public defender to represent Faretta. The Supreme Court held that the right to self-representation is implied by the Sixth Amendment and that to "force a lawyer on a defendant can only lead him to believe that the law contrives against him."[10]

Hiring an Attorney or Having One Assigned

In practice, persons arrested for a serious crime usually make their first phone call to a close relative who attempts to hire an attorney if the family can afford it. That lawyer, as a criminal defense attorney, is expected to be an advocate for the accused, arguing for their legal innocence and making sure that their constitutional rights are respected.

The attorney calls the arresting law enforcement agency to inquire about the charges. When defendants are being questioned at the station house, the attorney may try to contact them there to instruct them not to say anything about the case to law enforcement officers or fellow cellmates. The attorney does not attempt to discuss the case with them then because of the lack of privacy.

The attorney usually visits the jail only when paid a retainer. The initial interview often takes place in a small room in which lawyer and client are separated by a window and must communicate by phone.

The first interview is more a get-acquainted talk than an in-depth discussion of the charges. The attorney obtains bond information and explains that, with certain exceptions, information communicated by the client is treated as privileged and cannot be disclosed without consent. The **attorney-client privilege** is intended to foster a good working relationship between them, one based on trust and full disclosure. The attorney next asks for the names of co-defendants and witnesses to determine whether there is a potential conflict of interest. If there is, the attorney may decline employment or ask for an advisory opinion from the bar association. If, as is frequently the case, defendants want to know how long a sentence they will serve if convicted, the attorney explains the applicable sentencing guidelines or statutes.

If not already hired, the attorney establishes the requirements for being retained and openly discusses the topic of fees. One of the requirements is that the fee be paid before the disposition of the case. A tactic that some attorneys use to buy time so that their clients can raise money to pay the fees is to request a continuance because "Mr. Green hasn't arrived yet." A continuance is a postponement of judicial proceedings. The judge understands that "Mr. Green" is a code term for fees.[11] Such requests are granted by some judges but denied by others. Irreconcilable differences are sometimes the reason for an attorney's request to withdraw from a case; such differences often stem from the client's inability to pay the fee. Some judges grant this sort of request for withdrawal, particularly if it is made early in the court process.

At the start of a case, the client signs a retainer agreement with the lawyer, establishing what the attorney is expected to do for the fee the client pays. There are a variety of ways of setting the amount of the fee. One is to estimate how long the case is likely to take. For example, a week-long murder trial might take 300 hours—60 hours for the trial and 240 hours for the preparation. A $100-an-hour lawyer would charge a fee of $30,000. Of course, if it takes 400 hours instead of 300, the attorney may lose money because an attorney in a criminal case will usually charge a flat fee that the client pays up front.

The attorney's fee is based on a number of criteria. One thing that allows the lawyer to claim a higher fee is reputation. Recent law school graduates who need the business are likely to take whatever clients they can get. The experienced attorney whose clients include the celebrated charge over $200 an hour. The nature of the case is another criterion. All things being equal, a case involving an aggravated battery is likely to be less time-consuming than a murder case. So is a case in which the defendant cops a plea, as compared with a case tried before a jury. A related consideration is the fact that a negotiated plea is likely to involve a reduction in charges. Aggravated battery, for example, may, through negotiation, become battery. Finally, most lawyers probably rank clients in terms of social or economic status. Undoubtedly, some adjust their fee according to that status.

If defendants cannot afford to hire an attorney, the court appoints one. There are several ways of providing indigents with an attorney. In Virginia, the court appoints them from a list of private attorneys who have volunteered to represent indigent defendants. An alternate approach, one that is used in New Jersey, is for the court to rotate appointments among all members of the practicing bar. While in most places they are paid a fee generally lower than that charged in private practice, in some jurisdictions where private attorneys are assigned, counsel are expected to represent indigent defendants free of charge (**pro bono**). It is considered a professional responsibility. A third way to enlist the aid of counsel is for the court to appoint a public defender, a salaried government employee who works full-time representing indigent defendants. Although the public defender system began in Los Angeles in 1914, it was not until the 1960s that this approach became popular. The newest way to appoint defense is through the contract system. In Pensacola, Florida, for example, the government enters into a contract with law firms to provide services in conflict-of-interest cases. If the public defender is representing one of two indigent co-defendants, but cannot represent both because of a conflict of interest, the court assigns a law firm to represent one of the co-defendants. The public defender represents the other.

Pretrial Preparation

One of the attorney's early concerns is securing the release of clients on bail. If they are out on bail, the second interview between attorney and client occurs in the attorney's office. Otherwise, it usually takes place in a room at the jail where they may talk face to face. The attorney may be accompanied by a private investigator. Questioning during the second interview can take up to three or four hours. The questions concern the victim, co-defendant, alibi, and the crime itself. In addition, the attorney warns clients not to talk about the case with a cellmate, law enforcement officer, co-defendant, or victim. Statements made to a co-defendant may be admissible later at trial, and contacts made with a victim can lead to possible tampering charges.

The attorney and investigator attempt to verify the facts in the case and determine the extent to which they may rely on the observations of their clients. While clients may not have lied, the information they provide may be incomplete and is almost certainly biased. The attorney or investigator also visits the scene of the crime and goes to the property room of the arresting agency to inspect the physical evidence that the prosecution is likely to introduce at trial. In addition, the attorney issues subpoenas and deposes witnesses.

The prosecutor is a powerful official who exercises wide-ranging discretion. It is important that the defense attorney find out early who has been assigned to prosecute the case. Defense attorneys who are familiar with those who work in the prosecutor's office will know whether they can work out a deal with the prosecutor or whether the case is likely to go to trial. By talking to lawyers with whom they are not familiar, defense attorneys can find out about these lawyers' experience with similar cases. By talking to friends in the criminal bar, defense attorneys can obtain additional information about their adversaries, such as their reputation for winning cases and their courtroom style.

The defense often formulates the strategy it will pursue long before the trial has begun. One approach is to create a reasonable doubt in the minds of jurors by undermining the prosecution's case through skillful **cross-examination.** Another strategy is for defendants to take the stand and deny their guilt. In the alibi defense, defendants produce the name of a witness who is willing to testify that the defendants were elsewhere at the time the crime was committed. In the affirmative defense, it is argued that, although what the defendants did might ordinarily be considered criminal, under the circumstances the actions were justified. Self-defense is an example. A variation of this approach is one in which defendants admit their wrongdoing but argue that they should be excused from liability. To plead insanity is an example.

Defendants may be found not guilty by reason of insanity if it is determined, usually by a jury at the end of a trial, that they were insane at the time of the offense. The jury makes its determination on the basis of the testimony of expert witnesses. Insanity excuses criminal liability because the defendants suffered from a mental disease when they allegedly caused the harm for which they were prosecuted.

According to the insanity test used in twenty-four states, the District of Columbia, and the federal courts, defendants are not criminally liable if, at the time of the crime, they lacked substantial capacity either to appreciate the criminality of their conduct or to conform it to the requirements of the law. This test is referred to as the American Law Institute test, Model Penal Code test, or **substantial capacity test.** The **M'Naghten rule** is in force in twenty states. According to this test, defendants are not criminally liable if, as a result of their mental illness, they did not know the nature and quality of what they were doing or did not know that what they were doing was wrong.

Motions

In addition to investigating the physical evidence, deposing witnesses, scoping out the opposition, and deciding on a defense strategy, pretrial preparation also involves the filing of motions. A motion is a request that the judge make a ruling or take some action. Some of the more familiar motions are those involving continuance, change of venue, suppression of evidence, severance of trials, severance of defendants, and incompetency.

Continuance, Speedy Trial, and Statute of Limitations

The Sixth Amendment guarantees the right to a speedy trial in federal courts. Under the due process clause of the Fourteenth Amendment, the Supreme Court held that this right also applies in state courts.[12] The right to a speedy trial takes effect once the arrest is made. A delay in arresting suspects does not violate the defendants' right to a speedy trial. While that right still commences when they are arrested, too long of a delay may result in their case being dismissed for causing substantial prejudice to a fair trial.[13]

Although seldom guides to actual practice, speedy trial statutes exist in all states and at the federal level. They vary widely. In one state, for example, every person charged with a felony must be brought to trial within 175 days of arrest. If the accused demand a speedy trial, the trial must be held within sixty days of the filing of the demand. If the prosecutor exceeds the deadline, the accused may file a motion for discharge. At a hearing on that motion, held no later than five days after the filing, the judge will order that the accused be brought to trial within ten days. If, through no fault of the accused, they are not tried within that time, they must be discharged from the crime forever.[14]

Defendants may waive their right to a speedy trial and file a motion for continuance (see Exhibit 3-2 and Exhibit 3-3). If they do, it may be part of a defense strategy to win the case or simply an indication that the defense needs more time to prepare. Judges may grant a continuance at their discretion or on motion of the defendant or prosecutor (see Exhibit 3-4).

The **statute of limitations** prevents the state from holding indefinitely the threat of arrest and prosecution over a suspect. It requires that the government make an arrest and start prosecution of the person identified as the perpetrator of a reported crime within a specified period of time. In noncapital felony cases, a federal statute sets the time limit of five years on the federal government.[15] The limits on felonies in state statutes vary from state to state, with the exception of murder. A few states specify offenses other than murder, such as embezzlement of public funds, for which there are no statutory limits.

Change of Venue

In court language, venue refers to the place where a case is to be tried. Proof of venue usually is established by a law enforcement officer

```
                              IN THE CIRCUIT COURT OF THE
                              SECOND JUDICIAL CIRCUIT, IN
                              AND FOR LEON COUNTY, FLORIDA.

                              CASE NO. 85-4810

      STATE OF FLORIDA,

              Plaintiff,                      1236 C        3/14/86

      -vs-

      JOHN WESLEY PEAVY,

              Defendant.

      _____/
```

WAIVER OF SPEEDY TRIAL

I, JOHN WESLEY PEAVY, by execution of this instrument
do hereby waive all of my rights to a speedy trial as guaranteed
to me by the law and Constitution of the State of Florida and
Constitution of the United States.

DATED this _____ day of March, 1986.

_____
JOHN WESLEY PEAVY

Exhibit 3-2 Waiver of the right to speedy trial, filed by John Wesley Peavy.

testifying about the specific location of a crime scene. Typically, a case
is tried in the county where the crime was committed. Defendants
may motion for a change of venue before the trial by filing a written
request with the court. The court will then hold a hearing at which
defendants present evidence in support of their request. Basically, defendants will argue that adverse publicity or community hostility
makes it impossible for them to obtain an impartial jury from the
county in which the crime was committed. They might contend that a
town's citizens already believe that the defendants are guilty because
of widespread publicity, or they might argue that people are prejudiced against them because they are strangers to the community,
whereas the victim may have been a popular lifelong resident.

Usually, the prosecution will oppose a change of venue because it
believes that it has a better chance of getting a conviction locally. The
state will argue that it is expensive to move witnesses and staff to a
distant city for a lengthy trial. It will maintain that, despite widespread publicity, there is no reason why jurors who could set aside
their opinions and try the case impartially cannot be found locally.
Where the case has received statewide coverage in the media, the
prosecution will contend that it would be just as difficult to find an
impartial jury elsewhere.

```
                        IN THE CIRCUIT COURT OF THE
                        SECOND JUDICIAL CIRCUIT, IN
                        AND FOR LEON COUNTY, FLORIDA.

                        CASE NO. 85-4810

    STATE OF FLORIDA,

            Plaintiff,

    -vs-

    JOHN WESLEY PEAVY,

            Defendant.
    _____/
```

                                                    3/14/86

MOTION FOR CONTINUANCE

COMES NOW the Defendant, JOHN WESLEY PEAVY, by and through
his undersigned lawyer, Anthony L. Bajoczky, and pursuant to
Rule 3.190(g), Florida Rules of Criminal Procedure, requests this
Honorable Court to continue the trial of this cause presently
scheduled for Tuesday, April 1, 1986, to some other date mutually
agreeable between counsel, and as a basis for this Motion would
allege as follows:

    1. The trial of this above-referenced case is tentatively
scheduled for Tuesday, April 1, 1986.

    2. The undersigned lawyer has been retained to represent
the Defendant and has commenced said representation.

    3. The undersigned lawyer has received and is reviewing
a massive amount of discovery materials provided by the prosecutor.
Much of this material consists of scientific evidence and the
results of laboratory analysis that must be further studied by
scientific experts retained by the defense.

    The State is in possession of additional discovery
materials that have not yet been completed or submitted to the
Defendant for his review and study.

    4. The State has listed approximately 200 persons as
potential witnesses for the prosecution. The Defendant and his
undersigned lawyer are in need of additional time to fully investigate the facts of this case; interview and depose witnesses; and,
to otherwise properly prepare their defense for presentation at
trial.

Exhibit 3-3 Motion for continuance, filed by Peavy and Anthony Bajoczky, his defense
attorney.

A change of venue is uncommon. Only on rare occasions when the
court is convinced that it is impossible for the defendant to find an
impartial local jury is a change of venue granted and the trial shifted

5. The Defendant has waived his right to speedy trial. (See Exhibit "A" attached hereto.)

6. Mr. Anthony S. Guarisco, Deputy State Attorney, has reviewed this Motion and has no objections to same.

WHEREFORE, the Defendant, JOHN WESLEY PEAVY, respectfully requests this Honorable Court to continue the trial presently scheduled in this case from Tuesday, April 1, 1986, to some other date mutually agreeable between counsel.

_____
ANTHONY L. BAJOCZKY

BARRETT AND BAJOCZKY
131 North Gadsden Street
Post Office Box 1501
Tallahassee, Florida   32302
(904) 222-9000

Lawyer for Defendant

CERTIFICATE OF GOOD FAITH

I, ANTHONY L. BAJOCZKY, do hereby certify that this Motion is filed in good faith and not for the purpose of unnecessary delay.

_____
ANTHONY L. BAJOCZKY

STATE OF FLORIDA
COUNTY OF LEON

Sworn to and subscribed before me this _13th_ day of March, 1986.

_____
NOTARY PUBLIC

My Commission Expires:
Notary Public, State of Florida
My Commission Expires Nov. 22, 1989
Bonce...

-2-

Exhibit 3-3 Continued.

IN THE CIRCUIT COURT OF THE
SECOND JUDICIAL CIRCUIT, IN
AND FOR LEON COUNTY, FLORIDA.

CASE NO. 85-4810

3/14/86

STATE OF FLORIDA,

      Plaintiff,

-vs-

JOHN WESLEY PEAVY,

      Defendant.

_____/

ORDER GRANTING CONTINUANCE

     THIS CAUSE came on before the Court for hearing upon the
Defendant's Motion for Continuance, and after reviewing the Court
file and being otherwise fully advised of the circumstances, it
is hereby

     ORDERED AND ADJUDGED that the Defendant's Motion for Con-
tinuance should be and it is hereby GRANTED.

     The trial of this above-styled cause presently scheduled
for April 1, 1986, is hereby continued to some other date mutually
agreeable between counsel.

     DONE AND ORDERED in Open Court at Tallahassee, Leon County,
Florida, this _____ day of March, 1986.

CHARLES D. McCLURE
Circuit Judge

Copies furnished to:

Anthony L. Bajoczky
Anthony S. Guarisco

Exhibit 3-4 Order granting the defense's motion for continuance, filed by Circuit Judge
Charles McClure.

to another locale. In most changes of venue, the trial will be moved to
an adjacent county, although the cost of the trial will still be paid by the
county in which the offense occurred.[16] A refusal to grant a change of
venue may be grounds for an appeal if the defendant is convicted.

Motion to Suppress Evidence

If the defense learns, as the result of pretrial discovery, that the prosecution intends to introduce at trial evidence that the defense thinks

was obtained illegally, the defense may file a motion to suppress that evidence. Grounds for such a motion might be that property used as evidence was seized without a warrant, that the warrant had incomplete or inaccurate facts, that the property seized was not the property described in the warrant, that no probable cause existed for believing the grounds on which the warrant was issued, or that the warrant was illegally executed.[17] A confession or admission may also be excluded if it was obtained illegally from the defendant.[18]

When the defense moves to suppress evidence or a confession, the court will usually hold an **evidentiary hearing.** Testimony is taken at the hearing to determine whether the search and seizure of evidence or the admission of a defendant is legal. If evidence was obtained through a warrantless search and seizure, the prosecutor has the burden of proving that the search and seizure was legal. If the search and seizure was conducted pursuant to a warrant, the defense attorney must prove that the search and seizure was invalid by attacking the legal sufficiency of the warrant.

The inadmissibility of unlawfully obtained evidence is referred to as the **exclusionary rule.** The rule was first formulated by the Supreme Court in *Weeks v. United States* in 1914, when the Court held that the Fourth Amendment bars the use of evidence obtained through illegal search and seizure.[19] The rule, however, applied only to federal law enforcement officers.

It was not until 1961, in *Mapp v. Ohio,* that the Supreme Court extended this right to the states. The police went to the residence of Dolree Mapp, believing that a suspect in a bombing was hiding there. They also had information indicating that materials for operating a numbers game were kept on the premises. When the police forcibly entered her house, Mapp demanded to see a search warrant. When a piece of paper alleged to be a warrant was produced, she grabbed it; but the police officers wrestled it away from her before she could examine it. When her attorney arrived, the police would not let him into the house. After the police thoroughly searched the house, Mapp was arrested for possession of obscene materials found in a trunk in the basement. No search warrant was produced as evidence at her trial. In *Mapp v. Ohio,* the Supreme Court held that it is wrong for a state prosecutor to use evidence illegally seized when, under *Weeks,* a U.S. attorney is barred from doing so. The state, by admitting such evidence, "serves to encourage disobedience to the Federal Constitution which it is bound to uphold."[20] Evidence obtained during an illegal search and seizure could no longer be admitted in state courts.

In recent years the Supreme Court has modified its stand on the exclusionary rule. The Supreme Court recognized the **good faith exception** in *United States v. Leon.* In *Leon,* the police obtained evidence from a search that was in violation of the exclusionary rule. A confidential informant of unproven reliability told a Burbank, California, police officer that he knew two people who were selling drugs at their residence and that he had witnessed a sale there five months earlier. On the basis of this tip, the police conducted an investigation that culminated in the indictment of three people on the charge of conspiracy to possess and distribute cocaine. A federal district court granted a motion to suppress the evidence seized during the search of several residences. The court held that the affidavit the police used in applying for the search warrant was insufficient to establish probable cause because it relied on information supplied by an informant whose credibility was unproven. It also did not help that the information about the sale he witnessed was considered "fatally stale." Neither the district court nor the court of appeals was willing to recognize a good faith exception. The Supreme Court was willing, though, holding that evidence obtained by law enforcement officers acting in reasonable reliance on a search warrant issued by a detached and neutral magistrate should be admissible.[21]

In *Nix v. Williams,* the Supreme Court established the **inevitable discovery exception.** Robert Williams was suspected of abducting a ten-year-old girl in Des Moines, Iowa, on December 23, 1968. He was seen carrying a bundle wrapped in a blanket. When he put it in his car, a fourteen-year-old boy who witnessed the incident said, two legs were sticking out of the blanket. When Williams's car was found abandoned in Davenport, Iowa, on December 25, the court issued a warrant for his arrest on the charge of abduction. On December 26, a lawyer went to the Des Moines police station and told officers that Williams had called him, saying that he wanted to turn himself in to the police in Davenport. When Williams did, the Davenport police phoned to notify the police in Des Moines. During that call and in the presence of the Des Moines chief of police and a veteran detective, the lawyer told Williams that he was not to discuss the case with the detectives who were coming to bring him back to Des Moines. Williams was given his Miranda warnings. On the 160-mile drive from Davenport to Des Moines, he told the detectives that he would tell them the whole story once he could confer with his lawyer. One of the detectives knew that Williams was a former mental patient. Knowing also that Williams was deeply religious, the detective delivered what has come to be known as the "Christian burial speech":

> I want to give you something to think about while we're traveling down the road. . . . Number one, I want you to observe the weather conditions, it's raining, it's sleeting, it's freezing, driving is very treacherous, visibility is poor, it's going to be dark early this evening. They are predicting several inches of snow for tonight, and I feel that you yourself are the only person that knows where this little girl's body is, that you yourself have only been there once, and if you get a snow on top of it you yourself may be unable to find it. And, since we will be going right past the area on the way into Des Moines, I feel that we could stop and locate the body, that the parents of this little girl should be entitled to a Christian burial for the little girl who was snatched away from them on Christmas [E]ve and murdered.

And I feel we should stop and locate it on the way in rather than waiting until morning and trying to come back out after a snow storm and possibly not being able to find it at all. . . . I don't want to discuss it further. Just think about it as we're riding down the road.[22]

Williams told the detective where he had buried the girl. In *Brewer v. Williams,* the Supreme Court held that the police had violated Williams's constitutional right to the assistance of counsel. At the second trial, the prosecution did not offer Williams's statement as evidence; nor did the prosecution try to show that he had led the police to the girl's body. However, it did present the results of postmortem tests as well as other forensic evidence. In *Nix v. Williams,* Williams argued that the second trial court erred in admitting that evidence because the state may not use evidence obtained directly or indirectly from police misconduct. The trial court replied that the state had proved that the little girl's body would have been found shortly if the search had not been stopped and that Williams had not led the police to the victim. The Supreme Court agreed, saying that "if the government can prove that the evidence would have been obtained inevitably and, therefore, would have been admitted regardless of any overreaching by the police, there is no rational reason to keep that evidence from the jury in order to ensure the fairness of the trial proceedings."[23]

Motion for Severance

For reasons of economy and efficiency, two or more defendants who are jointly charged with the same offense are usually tried together. On the motion of a defendant, the court can order a severance of defendants and separate trials. The petitioner, however, might have to show that such an action is necessary to promote a fair determination of the verdict or to protect the defendant's right to a speedy trial.[24] For example, it could be argued that, although the evidence against a co-defendant does not apply to the defendant, the jury would have difficulty keeping the non-applicable evidence separate from the evidence that applies. Likewise, perhaps the confession of a co-defendant should not be admissible unless all references to the defendant were deleted. In this situation, separate trials may be the only way to salvage intact the confession of the co-defendant and avoid prejudicing the case against the defendant.

The defendant who commits more than one crime and is caught can be tried for all of the offenses at one time if the crimes occurred in the same jurisdiction over a relatively short period of time. For the crimes to be joined in one information or indictment, however, they must be of the same general nature; or, if they are different, they must be part of the same transaction. A rash of burglaries, for example, would be of the same general nature. Burglary, larceny, and possession of burglary tools, although different crimes, could then be parts of a single transaction. Such consolidation saves expense by eliminating separate trials for each crime. The disadvantage is that it may be prejudicial to the defendant. For example, the jury may cumulate the evidence of various crimes charged and find guilt when, if the crimes had been considered separately, it would not. If two or more offenses are improperly charged in a single information or indictment, the court will grant a severance of charges on motion of the defendant. It will also grant a severance of charges to promote a fair determination of the verdict when two or more charges of related offenses are joined in a single information or indictment.[25]

Incompetency

Although defendants can be found not guilty by reason of insanity, they cannot be tried while they are insane. Defendants are not competent to stand trial if they are mentally incapable of consulting with their lawyer or of understanding the nature of the proceedings.[26] Their competency is determined by a judge at a pretrial hearing, based on the testimony of expert witnesses. If it is determined that the defendants are incompetent, the proceedings must be stopped until they are able to participate rationally.

Although procedures for determining incompetency vary from one jurisdiction to another, it may help to understand the general process by examining the specific procedure of a particular state. In Florida, for example, if the defense observes that a client may not be mentally competent, it files a motion to that effect, giving specific reasons for such an observation. The court then sets a time for a competency hearing, usually no later than twenty days from the time the motion was filed. Defendants who are thought to be incompetent are examined by two or three mental health experts.[27] The experts make their examination and report their findings to the court. Among other things, their findings indicate whether defendants are fully conscious of the charges against them and of the range of penalties should they be convicted, whether they understand the adversary nature of the judicial process and are able to assist their attorney in preparing the case, and whether they are motivated to help themselves and are able to manifest appropriate courtroom behavior.[28] Although the court is not bound by the findings of the experts, such findings are usually given considerable weight.

If the court finds defendants incompetent, it may commit them to the forensic ward of a mental hospital or order their release for treatment on an outpatient basis. Mental health experts evaluate the status of the defendants' competency every few months. If the incompetency lasts for five years, the court must conduct a hearing to determine whether there is any substantial likelihood that the defendants will ever be competent to stand trial. If no likelihood exists, the court must dismiss criminal charges. This does not necessarily mean that the status of the defendants is as it was before they were accused. If they meet the criteria for involuntary hospitalization, set forth by law, the court may commit them to a mental hospital, but not as patients of a forensic ward.

Gag Order

The Supreme Court ruled in 1975 that a trial court cannot forbid the press from publishing information about a case.[29] In a 1979 decision, it held that a trial court may close pretrial hearings to the press and public.[30] Later, it decided that the media have a right to be present at a criminal trial.[31] The apparent inconsistency in these findings indicates a fundamental conflict in principles in the Bill of Rights. While the First Amendment protects the freedom of the press, the Sixth Amendment guarantees a defendant a fair and impartial trial.

Trial courts usually do not close pretrial hearings. Instead, they order participating lawyers not to talk with reporters. Such orders, referred to as gag orders, are given on those infrequent occasions when the court believes that pretrial publicity would deny a defendant a fair trial because such publicity would make the selection of an impartial jury impossible. In *Sheppard v. Maxwell*, for example, the Supreme Court criticized the trial judge for making no effort to restrain pretrial publicity in a case in which a prominent Cleveland doctor was accused of killing his wife. The press published the names and addresses of the prospective jurors. As a result, "anonymous letters and telephone calls, as well as calls from friends, regarding the impending prosecution were received by all of the prospective jurors."[32] The press also published accounts of the police interrogation of the defendant and stories about his personal life and love affairs.

In a later decision, the Supreme Court tended to discourage the use of gag orders, maintaining that such restraint should be used only when publicity represents a clear threat to a fair trial.[33]

Study Questions

1. Why would defense attorneys not insist upon bringing Peavy to trial under the right to a speedy trial? Six months in jail awaiting trial seems much better than fifteen months.

2. Theorize an insanity defense for Peavy. What would be the defense's argument? What flaws would the prosecution see in such a defense?

3. If the Peavys had not given investigators permission to search their property, what evidence could have become the subject of a motion to suppress?

Endnotes

1. *Gideon v. Wainwright*, 372 U.S. 335, 344 (1963). For an excellent account of the Gideon case, see Anthony Lewis, *Gideon's Trumpet* (New York: Vintage Books, 1966).

2. *Argersinger v. Hamlin*, 407 U.S. 25 (1972).

3. *Kirby v. Illinois*, 406 U.S. 682, 689 (1972).

4. *United States v. Wade*, 388 U.S. 218 (1967).

5. *Kirby v. Illinois*, 406 U.S. 682 (1972).

6. Yale Kamisar, Wayne R. LaFave, and Jerold H. Israel, *Basic Criminal Procedure: Cases, Comments, and Questions*, 7th ed. (St. Paul, MN: West Publishing Co., 1990), 71–72.

7. *Miranda v. Arizona*, 384 U.S. 436 (1966).

8. *People v. Samuels*, 49 N.Y. 218 (1980).

9. *Blue v. State*, 558 P.2d 636 (1977); *Sobczak v. State*, 462 So.2d 1172 (Fla. 4th DCA 1984).

10. *Faretta v. California*, 422 U.S. 806, 834 (1975).

11. Paul Wice, *Criminal Lawyers: An Endangered Species* (Beverly Hills, CA: Sage Publications), 1978, 111.

12. *Klopfer v. North Carolina*, 386 U.S. 213 (1967).

13. *Barker v. Wingo*, 407 U.S. 514 (1972).

14. *Florida Rules of Criminal Procedure*, rule 3.191 (1987).

15. 18 U.S.C.A. §3282.

16. Gilbert B. Stuckey, *Procedure in the Justice System*, 3d ed. (Columbus, OH: Charles E. Merrill, 1986), 101.

17. For example, see *Florida Rules of Criminal Procedure*, rule 3.190 (1987).

18. For example, see *Florida Rules of Criminal Procedure*, rule 3.190 (1987).

19. *Weeks v. United States*, 232 U.S. 383 (1914).

20. *Mapp v. Ohio*, 367 U.S. 643, 657 (1961).

21. *United States v. Leon*, 468 U.S. 897 (1984).

22. *Brewer v. Williams*, 430 U.S. 387, 392–93 (1977).

23. *Nix v. Williams* (Williams II), 467 U.S. 431, 447 (1984).

24. For example, see *Florida Rules of Criminal Procedure*, rule 3.152 (1987).

25. For example, see *Florida Rules of Criminal Procedure*, rule 3.152 (1987).

26. *Dusky v. United States*, 362 U.S. 402 (1960).

27. *Florida Rules of Criminal Procedure*, rule 3.210 (1987).

28. *Florida Rules of Criminal Procedure*, rule 3.211 (1987).

29. *Times-Picayune v. Schulingkamp*, 419 U.S. 301 (1975).

30. *Gannett Co. v. DePasquale*, 443 U.S. 368 (1979).

31. *Richmond Newspapers, Inc. v. Virginia*, 448 U.S. 555 (1980).

32. *Sheppard v. Maxwell*, 384 U.S. 333, 342 (1966).

33. *Nebraska Press Association v. Stewart*, 427 U.S. 539 (1976).

4

Selecting the Jury

CASE STUDY

Finding a Dozen to Sit in Judgment

Another Christmas had come and gone since Peavy's arrest. For fifteen months, he had sat locked in jail, still innocent until proven guilty, waiting for his day in court.

Finally, that day came in March 1987.

Instead of flimsy blue cotton pants and a shirt with the words "Leon County Jail" stamped on back, Peavy wore a neat navy blue suit. He was already seated at the defendant's table before prospective jurors filed into the courtroom. That way, they wouldn't see the silver shackles hidden beneath the table above his shiny shoes.

Before long, the biggest courtroom at the Leon County Courthouse was packed and abuzz with everyday people called on to find justice in the murder case of the *State of Florida v. John Wesley Peavy.* Some came armed with paperbacks and needlepoint projects, prepared for the tedious process that would take most of the week.

Others looked bored or impatient during the long wait on hard wooden benches. From hundreds summoned to perform their civic duty, a dozen would be chosen to sit in judgment. Another three would be named as alternates, ready to step in if any of the twelve could not see the trial through to the verdict, for whatever reason.

Smiles dropped when Circuit Judge Charles McClure warned the group that this was a serious case, involving two counts of murder (see Figure 4-1). Some shifted uneasily in their seats when he told them that the trial was scheduled to last a month and that those selected as jurors would live out of a suitcase, sequestered in a motel room each night after courtroom testimony. Their personal lives would take a back seat to Peavy's trial for weeks.

Some prospective jurors were ready and willing for duty; others mentally plotted excuses that would let them off the hook.

McClure delivered a civics lesson pep talk by saying, "Our system of justice can function effectively only to the extent that each of you is willing

Figure 4-1 Circuit Judge Charles McClure, who presided over the trial of Peavy. Phil Coale.

to invest time and effort and thought in a commitment to serve conscientiously as a juror when called upon to do so."

Valid excuses for not performing jury duty included a man who said he was scheduled for an operation later in the week, a mother of two young children whose husband was in the service in Wisconsin, a full-time student in a college doctoral program, and a man who complained that this was the third time he had been called to jury duty in the past year. Also excused was a woman who had worked as a crime analyst on Peavy's case.

But Eric Davies's reason would not be good enough. Raising his hand, he said, "I'm a full-time professor . . . at Florida A&M University."

The judge asked, "Well, are you able to get someone to take over your classes?"

"I'm not certain of that," Davies said. "I can check into it."

"I can't excuse you on that basis," Judge McClure said. "The students, I can understand, because they might fail. But the professors . . . I hope you will be understanding."

Days later, as it turned out, Davies would be chosen as one of the twelve jurors to decide Peavy's case.

Later, it came time for the lawyers to use their peremptory challenges, the power to remove a person from the jury without giving a reason. The defense attorneys could keep secret why they did not want a particular person on the jury. For their own use, they jotted down their reasons:

- One removed woman was described as a "snaggletooth country woman with a mustache." More importantly, she knew Peavy.

- A man was excluded because he knew defense attorney Bajoczky, his father was a police officer, and he knew a witness in the trial.

- Another woman was not included because she had gone on a religious crusade with Herb Morgan, a local politician and brother of one of the victims, Mary Lee Driggers. She also remembered previously meeting prosecutor Guarisco.

- Also considered undesirable was a relative of State Attorney Willie Meggs. The relative also knew a witness.

The courtroom full of prospective jurors ranged from eighteen-year-old college students to seventy-year-old retirees. Some wore diamonds and gold, while others wore humble denim overalls or threadbare suits that no doubt had served a couple of decades as Sunday best.

Some had college degrees, while others were high school dropouts with calloused hands. Some had been to court before, as jurors, witnesses, or spectators in other cases. Others had never before ventured into this solemn room where crime victims choked on painful details and liberty was plucked from the convicted.

From this wide assortment of local humanity, the lawyers were to select good listeners and fair judges of the facts. Qualities desired in a juror depended on whether one asked the defense or the prosecution.

From the prosecutors' standpoint, it was partially a numbers game, rating people on a scale of zero to ten. A week or so before the trial, they obtained the lists of prospective jurors and ran criminal background checks. They sent a list around to lawyers in the state attorney's office and to well-connected and interested police officers, like Major Larry Campbell, to see if they recognized any names and spotted any problem-jurors.

They wanted to get rid of liberals, persons who had been arrested in the past but were not open about their history, or those enmeshed in lawsuits.

During voir dire, in which prospective jurors were examined for competence, one prosecutor asked questions while the other observed body language, looking for hints about personalities. Notes were taken, and each person was scored. An example of a zero might be the sloppily dressed male college student sporting a diamond stud in one ear. That was a loud and clear signal that he was too anti-establishment for the prosecution's liking, Deputy State Attorney Anthony Guarisco and Assistant State Attorney Ray Marky explained (see Figures 4-2 and 4-3).

Rating a nine might be a former prisoner of war who was now a member of a civic club and the Baptist church, the epitome of a conservative and stable citizen.

A college-educated black woman scored a perfect ten. She answered questions precisely and paid strict attention to the lawyers. She would take her job seriously, they figured; and she represented the strong, traditional family type.

Another ten was a man with a pleasant demeanor who had served on a county grand jury before.

Figure 4-2 Assistant State Attorney Jack Poitinger (left), and Deputy State Attorney Anthony Guarisco. Hal Yeager.

Figure 4-3 Assistant State Attorney Ray Marky, who worked for the prosecution against Peavy. Phil Coale.

The average person scored a seven. Prospective jurors might gain an extra point or two for owning his or her own business, showing independence.

But all of this was an inexact science, a mix of objective criteria and gut feeling. Lawyers from both sides knew that the jury selection process was a critical legal strategy session that could make or break their case.

"I don't think you can overstate the importance of the jury selection process," Robert Augustus Harper, one of Peavy's lawyers, said later. "And it is very important that you choose people who are capable of making decisions. In my opinion, it's important to choose people you can communicate with. I think a lot of the lawyers put it in the perspective of saying you want to find a jury who will convict, if you are a prosecuting attorney, and a jury who will acquit, if you are a defense attorney. But I really think what you're trying to do is to find a jury who will listen to your side of the case and who you feel will listen to your arguments and your presentation. So that's why I call it choosing a jury who you can communicate with."

Fancy formulas and preparations exist for picking the right jury for a particular case. Lawyers have hired psychologists to scrutinize jurors' answers on written questionnaires, or have enlisted investigators to dig up background information.

And even though he estimated that he had spent fifty hours preparing for jury selection in this case, Harper would depend mostly on his gut feelings when he looked each juror in the eye, sized them up face to face, and looked for visible clues as to their personality, integrity, and reliability.

"Probably ninety percent of it is done in the courtroom, when they are called in the box and you have a chance to see if they're comfortable," Harper said. "To see if they communicate with you, see if they seem to be responding to you one way or another. Sometimes you get very hostile looks and gestures, and during the course of the voir dire, you find that the jurors are very antagonistic, though they look good on paper. There's something in their life that makes them totally unsatisfactory as a juror."

But before the lawyers were allowed to question the potential jurors, it was the judge's turn to talk.

"Nobody is trying to be nosy," McClure told them. "We all have a job to do. Let me also advise you that if you are asked to step down for one reason or another, you may or may not know that reason. However, this does not mean that you are any less of a person; and we're not saying that you are not qualified to act as a juror in any other trial. It's just that, for one reason or another, you may be asked to step down. So, please don't be offended. If we ask questions that pinch a little, it's just a job that we have to do."

The most probing questions would examine the jurors' feelings about the death penalty. But McClure couldn't assume they knew anything about Florida's death penalty laws. So, to row after row of somber faces, the black-robed man sitting high on the mahogany bench delivered a legal lesson. He told them when it was legal to take a convicted murderer's life,

and he told them reasons why people may not be suited to make that
tough decision.

After delivering a wordy monologue approved by the Florida Supreme
Court as standard jury instructions, McClure asked the prospective jurors
to search their souls and prepare to answer questions on their death penalty views.

It was then prospective juror Harold Bryant's turn to speak his mind.
His mini-autobiography revealed that he was a retired state worker, married, and a member of Tallahassee Heights Methodist Church, the Masons, and the Shriners. And he was a disabled American veteran.

"Are you opposed to the death penalty?" McClure asked him.

"Yes," Bryant answered.

"Would you automatically vote against the imposition of the death penalty without regard to the evidence shown or the instructions of the court?"
McClure asked.

"Yes, sir," Bryant said.

"You would," the judge said, with a nod. "Would your views on the
death penalty interfere with or substantially impair your ability to return a
verdict of guilty or not guilty under the facts of the case and the law that
I instruct you on?"

"No, sir," Bryant answered.

But Paul Atkinson, another prospective juror, faced a greater moral dil-
emma concerning the death penalty.

"Mr. Atkinson, are you opposed to the death penalty?" McClure asked.

"Yes, I am." Atkinson was quick to respond, saying that he would automatically vote against the death penalty no matter what the judge instructed
about the law.

After a bench conference, the lawyers returned to their seats (see Figure 4-4). Judge McClure said, "Mr. Bryant and Mr. Atkinson, I need to ask
each of you this question. Would your view, Mr. Bryant, prevent you from
finding the defendent guilty if the evidence so warranted, because you
might be concerned the death penalty would be imposed?"

"No, sir," Bryant answered.

But Atkinson answered, "I think it would, because I participated in de-
monstrating against the death penalty at the Capitol. I'm definitely against
the death penalty."

"So you feel like your views on the death penalty would prevent you
from finding the defendant guilty if the evidence so showed?" McClure
asked.

"I think so," Atkinson said.

And so Atkinson was excused for cause. Later, Bryant changed his
mind. The more he thought about it, the more he realized that his views
on the death penalty would affect his judgment in deciding guilt or innocence. And that was all it took for the judge to excuse him, too.

That strong opponents of the death penalty are never allowed to sit on
a jury is a complaint of many defense attorneys and has been the subject

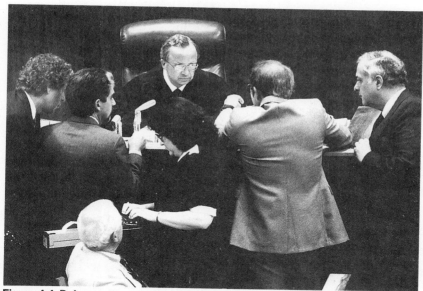

Figure 4-4 Defense attorneys Anthony Bajoczky and Robert Augustus Harper huddle with prosecutors Jack Poitinger and Anthony Guarisco (from left to right) with the judge at a bench conference to discuss the striking of potential jurors. The court reporter takes down every word, but the lawyers and judge speak in hushed tones so the prospective jurors cannot hear their comments. Hal Yeager.

of legal appeals. As Harper said, "I would like to have every juror up there strongly opposed to the death penalty. But, by law, I'm not going to have those people; so that takes out a large class of jurors who would be favorable to the defense to begin with."

Those left, he said, were "law-and-order" types who believed in the death penalty. The defense's goal was to keep those who did not approve of the death penalty, but who agreed they could follow the judge's instructions without being blinded by fear of sentencing an individual to the death penalty.

"We would like as many people as possible who have a strong feeling about the death penalty being unfair," Harper said.

During jury selection, so many questions about the death penalty created an undercurrent of guilt in the room. Peavy's defense attorneys had to make sure that jurors kept open minds not only about the possible penalty, but about Peavy's continued presumption of innocence.

Tony Bajoczky paced before a group of prospective jurors sitting in the box and asked, "Anybody up here think just because we've talked about the death penalty that it must be a foregone conclusion that he's going to get convicted? And this is all some kind of a circus until we get around to deciding whether he's going to get 'the chair' or he's going to get life in prison?"

Bajoczky's mission, the mission of the defense, was to continually reinforce the constitutional right that Peavy sat before these people as innocent as they were. Prospective jurors locked glances with the tense-jawed man in the navy suit, but they were not to burrow their eyes into Peavy's nervous face and secretly brand him guilty, just because investigators and prosecutors said he was.

Make them prove Peavy's guilt, said the defense attorneys, as they pounded away to pluck out anyone already leaning toward a guilty opinion of their client.

"Anybody here feel that because we have all these charging papers and documents, that because we've gone through this paperwork, he must be guilty?" Bajoczky asked.

Not willing to take any chances, Bajoczky told the prospective jurors that one of the victims, Mary Lee Driggers, was the sister of a well-known politician, Herb Morgan.

"Does anybody here feel that because one of the victims came from an important family, that somebody has to pay for this crime? [W]e just can't let a murder go unsolved of somebody important?" Bajoczky asked.

Over and over, the defense reminded the prospective jurors that the state was weighed down with the burden of proof. But, because the prosecutors wanted to make sure jurors would not hold the prosecuting attorney to an unfair burden, Guarisco openly presented the big weakness in the state's case: that the murder weapon was never found.

"If all the evidence indicates to your satisfaction that this defendant committed the crimes with which he stands charged," Guarisco asked, "do any of you have a state of mind that would preclude you from finding him guilty simply because the state did not produce the murder weapon for you?"

In their search for impartial judges of the facts, the lawyers had to discover whether people were leaning one way or another before they had heard the first word of testimony. And a fertile area of questioning focused on what effect television news or newspaper stories appearing at the time of the killings may have had on the prospective jurors' abilities to be fair and impartial.

To get the most honest answers to these questions, the judge brought each prospective juror into a little hearing room, where he or she could answer beyond earshot of the others waiting back in the courtroom.

Sarah Goodwin was one woman who had already made up her mind.

"When it first happened," she said, "I read that Mr. Peavy went to the— I believe they were living in a trailer home. He shot them through the window. They were sitting at the table. You know, in conference. I do remember that."

"Have you read or listened to any broadcast of this type since that time?" McClure asked.

"No," Goodwin said. "Other than Sunday night, you know, when they said the trial was coming up."

"What you read and saw on the TV, would it in any way affect your decision in the case?" the judged asked.

"No," she answered.

But when defense attorney Harper probed deeper, he discovered her bias.

"How did you understand or come to understand that it was Mr. Peavy that was involved in this instead of some other person?" he asked.

"Well," Gaines answered, "by keeping up with the articles. I would read the newspaper."

"When did you have it in your mind that he went to the trailer and fired the shots?" Harper insisted. "When did you get it in your mind that [the killer] was John Peavy?"

"When they said it in the papers, the investigators," Goodwin said. "You know, when they said that they had him or he was held for that.

"So, do you think now that Mr. Peavy probably did that?" Harper asked.

"Well, as the judge said, he's innocent until proven guilty," Goodwin said with a shrug.

"I understand that," Harper continued. "But what I was asking you is, from what you've heard and from what you've seen going on, do you think he probably did it?"

"I do," Goodwin said, nodding. "I really do."

"And you have that opinion already, ma'am?" Harper asked.

"Well, to be frank and honest, I do," Goodwin admitted.

"We would ask that Ms. Goodwin be excused for cause, Your Honor," Harper said to McClure. The judge granted his request.

Another woman was removed from the pool of potential jurors because she had forgotten the judge's order, given the day before, to avoid all media accounts of the case.

"We've noticed some newspapers that you've brought with you," Judge McClure said to the full courtroom awaiting another day of the selection process. "Has anyone read or seen or watched any news accounts of this trial? I instructed you yesterday."

A pause. A hand sent up. The judge studied the list before him, then asked, "Mrs. Smith?"

"Yes," Mrs. Smith replied.

"You read the article in the paper today?" McClure probed.

"I'm so used to going through everything in the paper," Smith offered apologetically. Then she stammered, "Did—did I read it?"

"You sat down and read the entire article?" the judge sternly asked.

"Yes," Smith confessed.

The judge summoned the lawyers to the bench. Bajoczky muttered, "Quite frankly, if she's not going to follow your instructions, I want her bounced for cause. I think that's atrocious, to be honest with you."

The judged leaned over and said, "I agree, but I'm not going to chastise her."

"I don't want you to chastise her," Bajoczky said. "I want her bounced."

And so the judge removed Smith for cause, and she was sent home where she could read as much of the newspaper as she wanted.

The questioning and scrutinizing and whispering at the bench dragged on for a week. Finally, the judges of Peavy's fate came down to these twelve:

- Bob Clay, an accountant for the Florida Department of Health and Rehabilitative Services' Medicaid program. His wife was an elementary school teacher, and they attended St. John's Episcopal Church in Tallahassee.

- Cathy Simon, a single woman holding down two jobs, one in an office at Florida State University and one at a luggage shop in a mall. She graduated from FSU with a degree in visual arts, and she liked to jog and lift weights.

- Eric Davies, an assistant professor of economics at Florida A&M University, and the father of three children ranging in age from two to sixteen. He liked to fish, belonged to Elva Missionary Baptist Church, and was a member of Phi Beta Sigma fraternity.

- Cliff White, a maintenance worker for the Florida Department of Agriculture for fourteen years and an Air Force veteran. He was married to a nurse working for Grandpeople, a program for the elderly. He had two daughters, ages twenty-five and twenty-six. He liked baseball and basketball and was Catholic.

- James Perry, a maintenance man for Investors Realty for three years, who had lived in Tallahassee for six years. He was not active in church or civic clubs, but liked to ride bicycles. He served in the Air Force for four years, and his father was a judge in the United States Army. He had studied anthropology and history at Florida State University.

- John Masters, retired from the Coast Guard, had become a physical education teacher at Rickards High School in Tallahassee. He and his wife, a homemaker, had five grown children ranging in age from twenty-six to thirty-five. He was a Catholic who did not attend church.

- Charles Johnson, a bachelor who was a computer troubleshooter at the Florida Department of Law Enforcement. He knew juror Davies because he was once his student at Florida A&M. He was once the victim of a crime when he was robbed while driving a cab. He liked to fish and cook.

- Patricia Dickson, a secretary for a judge at the First District Court of Appeal. Her husband was the director of personnel at the Florida Department of Agriculture. They had two children, ages seventeen and twenty-two. She was not active in civic groups or church, but she liked to read, walk, and cross-stitch.

- Joy Weaver, a program audit supervisor in the Office of the Auditor General for the State of Florida. She was single, did not attend church, and was a member of the Sierra Club, the Audubon Society, and the North Florida Masters.

- Mabel Brown, a cooperative education teacher at Rickards High School and a member of First Baptist Church.

- Christine Marshall, worked in buildings services at Florida A&M for thirty years and who had seen juror Davies, the professor, on campus. She had eight children, all grown. One was a Florida Highway Patrol trooper, but her oldest son had served two years in prison. She sang in the choir at Bethel Missionary Baptist Church and liked to jog and to watch wrestling and football.

- Dan Mathews owned a business selling custom software and business services, had been divorced and remarried. His second wife was an interior decorator. He had a little ranch outside of Tallahassee. He liked to read and do computer work.

And three alternates sat interspersed with the other jurors:

- Richard Beattie, a young bachelor and a traveling pharmaceutical salesperson.

- Max Durham, a supervisor at the Florida Department of Environmental Regulation's underground injection control section. His wife was an elementary school teacher on maternity leave with two young children. He liked outdoor sports, camping, and collecting rocks and minerals.

- Leah Spradley, a high school teacher. Her husband worked for the Florida Department of Community Affairs, and they had two children.

These fifteen chosen ones were given time to pack their suitcases, say goodbye to their families, inform their bosses, and make other arrangements for their absences from various routines.

For the next three weeks, they would resume their same seats in the jury box, scribbling notes on legal pads as they listened to testimony and viewed evidence all day long. Then, they would climb into vans and return to their motel, under the watchful eyes of bailiffs. They were a cluster of men and women, mostly strangers, who were now insulated from their real worlds. They were flung together to decide whether a man was a murderer, and, if so, whether he should die to pay for his crime.

Only after the jurors left the courthouse would the bailiffs come to get Peavy. Only when no jurors were around to watch the incriminating spectacle did Peavy stand up in his pressed suit and polished shoes, shuffle in chains to the elevator, which took him down to the courthouse basement, and climb into the van for the crosstown ride back to his cell.

═══════ PROCEDURAL DESCRIPTION ═══════

Although the procedures by which jurors are selected vary widely, trials usually begin with the assembly of a group of people presumed to represent a cross section of the community. The judge and attorneys examine them in order to determine who is qualified to serve. Those who are not are exempted from jury duty. The remainder of jury selection, sometimes elaborate and time-consuming, consists mostly of questions and challenges directed at the individual members who qualify. Body language as well as verbal responses provide clues as to the roles jurors are likely to play during deliberations.

Obtaining Jurors

Defendants have the right to a jury trial, but some choose a **bench trial** instead. The choice between jury and judge may be influenced by whether the judge is known to be prosecution-minded or defense-minded. The nature of the case may also be a factor in such a decision. For example, the defense may prefer a bench trial if its case is strong but the facts would be shocking to a jury because the crime is so heinous.[1]

In a jury trial, the selection of jurors is important because it allows the attorneys to choose the finders of fact, the people who evaluate the evidence and decide the verdict. Each party is looking for jurors who will return a verdict favorable to its side. The prosecutor wants jurors who will convict. The defense wants jurors who will acquit. Some say that, with both sides injecting into the selection process their idea of what constitutes a good jury, they inevitably will select a fair and impartial jury that will return a just verdict.[2]

The jury trial begins by assembling names for the **master jury list,** sometimes called the master wheel or jury wheel. Sources of names

JUROR QUESTIONNAIRE

PLEASE ANSWER THESE QUESTIONS AND RETURN IMMEDIATELY IN ATTACHED RETURN ENVELOPE.

GIVE THE FOLLOWING INFORMATION FROM
YOUR JURY SUMMONS:

COURT APPEARANCE DATE: _____

NAME OF JUDGE YOU REPORT TO: _____

YOUR JUROR NUMBER (SHOWN BESIDE YOUR NAME ON THE SUMMONS) _____

1. NAME _____
     FIRST   SECOND OR INITIAL   LAST

2. HOME ADDRESS _____

3. YEARS OF RESIDENCE: IN FLORIDA _____ IN THIS COUNTY _____

4. FORMER RESIDENCE _____

5. MARITAL STATUS (MARRIED, SINGLE, DIVORCED, WIDOW OR WIDOWER) _____

6. YOUR OCCUPATION AND EMPLOYER _____

7. IF YOU ARE NOT NOW EMPLOYED, GIVE YOUR LAST OCCUPATION AND EMPLOYER _____

8. IF MARRIED, NAME AND OCCUPATION OF HUSBAND OR WIFE _____

9. HAVE YOU EVER SERVED AS A JUROR BEFORE? _____

10. HAVE YOU OR ANY MEMBER OF YOUR IMMEDIATE FAMILY BEEN A PARTY TO ANY LAWSUIT? _____ IF SO, WHEN AND IN WHAT COURT _____

11. ARE YOU EITHER A CLOSE FRIEND OF OR RELATED TO ANY LAW ENFORCEMENT OFFICER? _____

12. HAS A CLAIM FOR PERSONAL INJURIES EVER BEEN MADE AGAINST YOU OR ANY MEMBER OF YOUR FAMILY? _____

13. HAVE YOU OR ANY MEMBER OF YOUR FAMILY EVER MADE ANY CLAIM FOR PERSONAL INJURIES? _____

NOTIFICATION PURPOSES:
JUROR'S PHONE NUMBER:

DAY _____

NIGHT _____

_____
JUROR'S SIGNATURE

Exhibit 4-1 Questionnaire completed by prospective jurors.

include voter registration lists, utility customer lists, driver's license lists, city directories, and telephone directories. In one jurisdiction that uses voter registration lists, the chief judge of the major trial court randomly picks a number that commences the process by which jurors are selected. For example, if the number five is picked and it is decided that 20,000 prospective jurors are needed for the year and there are 80,000 registered voters in the county, names are selected at intervals of four, starting with the fifth name of the list. These names are kept in a locked box until needed.

The **venire,** sometimes called the array or panel, is the group of people from whom the jury is selected. It is chosen from the master jury list whenever it is needed. The court clerk issues summons for those whose names have been picked for jury duty. Each prospective juror is asked to complete a questionnaire (see Exhibit 4-1).

Present on the first day of trial are the judge, attorneys, defendant, deputy court clerk, court reporter, bailiffs, and members of the venire. Everybody stands up when the bailiff or deputy court clerk announces the judge: "Oyez, oyez, the Court of [name of jurisdiction] is now in session, the Honorable [name of judge], presiding; draw near and give attention and you will be heard; God save this honorable court." The judge greets the members of the venire, informs them of the charges against the defendant, and tells them how long the trial is likely to last and whether the jury will be **sequestered.** When a jury is sequestered, it is confined to a hotel or motel when the court is not in session in order to prevent exposure to outside influences such as trial publicity, jury tampering, and personal threats. This isolation, the judge explains, lasts the duration of the trial. If it is a case in which the death penalty may be imposed, the judge then instructs prospective jurors that their attitudes toward capital punishment are a proper subject of inquiry during the selection process. After these introductory remarks, the venire is sworn en masse. The oath requires that prospective jurors swear to answer truthfully questions concerning their qualifications.

The judge usually begins **voir dire,** the examination of members of the venire, by inquiring whether there is anyone legally disqualified from serving as a juror. Often, public officials, such as sheriffs, police officers, court clerks, and judges, are excluded by law. So are those who are not at least eighteen years old, those who are not citizens of the state, or those who are not registered electors of the county (see Excerpt 1).[3] Excluded also are those presently under prosecution or who have been convicted but have not had their civil rights restored.

EXCERPT 1

THE COURT: Let me ask if each of you is at least eighteen years of age, a citizen of this state, and a registered elector of Leon County. Would you say yes or no? Anyone whose answer is different, please raise your hand.

MR. TAYLOR: I ain't never been registered.

THE COURT: Tell me what your name is.

MR. TAYLOR: Alvin Taylor. I have never been registered.

THE COURT: You don't vote in elections?

MR. TAYLOR: No.

THE COURT: What is your juror number?

MR. TAYLOR: Sixty-three.

THE COURT: I think we're going to have to excuse you. You may be excused.

The judge may also ask if anyone present, who does not want to serve, is seventy or older, has served on a jury in the last two years, or is suffering from an illness. Those volunteering such an excuse are often excluded. If the trial promises to be long, the judge asks if anyone present, who does not want to serve, is an expectant mother, a single parent with custody of young children, a person responsible for the care of someone who is ill, or a person for whom a long absence would be an economic hardship. Usually, those responding affirmatively are excused. Some judges will also excuse college students, those who have long-standing appointments that cannot be broken easily, and those who have made advance reservations that cannot be cancelled without substantial penalty. Those who are excused because of the length of the trial are frequently asked to be on call should they be needed for shorter jury duty in another courtroom. The judge has the bailiff call a specified number of prospective jurors. Juries vary in size from one jurisdiction to another. Although the majority of states authorize juries of fewer than twelve, most allow such small juries only in civil or misdemeanor cases.[4] Those who are called are instructed to take seats in the jury box.

The judge may call or have the bailiff call additional names to be impaneled as jury alternates. These alternates are selected in the same way as principal jurors.[5] If principal jurors become unable to perform their duties, they are replaced by alternate jurors. Except in a complicated case where deliberations are expected to be long, alternate jurors who do not replace principal jurors may be discharged when the jury retires to consider its verdict. Alternate jurors in a capital case may be required to replace principal jurors in the penalty phase of a trial even though they did not participate in the deliberations that led to the defendant's conviction.[6] A capital case is different from other criminal cases in that the penalty, whether it be life imprisonment or death, is determined separately from the issue of guilt or innocence. When no alternates are impaneled, the judge may declare a mistrial if a juror becomes unable to serve and the defendant has not waived the right to be tried by less than twelve jurors or by whatever the number of jurors is legally required.

The judge continues asking questions of prospective jurors once they have taken seats in the jury box:

- Have you ever served on a jury before? Was it a criminal case or civil case? Were you able to reach a verdict?

- Have you or any members of your family ever been the victim of a crime? What kind of crime?

- Have you or any member of your family ever been arrested? For what? When?

- Have your ever filed a suit or been sued?

- Have you ever been a witness in a trial or given a deposition in a case?

- Do you know anyone else in the jury box?

- Do you work in law enforcement or know anyone who does?

Affirmative responses always evoke the follow-up question: Would it affect your ability in this case to sit as a fair and impartial juror?

The judge introduces the attorneys and defendant and asks if any prospective juror knows them personally. Then the judge asks the attorneys to read out loud the names of witnesses who are likely to be called to give testimony during the trial. The judge asks prospective jurors if they know any of the persons whose names have been called (see Excerpt 2).

EXCERPT 2

THE COURT: Does anyone on the panel know any of the witnesses whose names were called off by Mr. Guarisco [a prosecutor] or Mr. Harper [a defense attorney]?

MR. PETERS: Probably Major Campbell [from the sheriff's office], yes.

THE COURT: Probably Major Campbell? Do you feel that you would give his testimony more weight or less than you would any other witness?

MR. PETERS: Probably more.

THE COURT: [Speaking to the attorneys] You want to approach the bench?
    (Whereupon a bench conference was held.)

MR. BAJOCZKY [a defense attorney]: Obviously, Your Honor, Mr. Peters has mentioned Major Campbell and has for the record indicated that he would probably give his testimony greater weight than any other testimony: he's prejudiced. And we would ask that he be struck.
    (End of bench conference.)

THE COURT: Mr. Peters, I'm going to ask you to step down, if you will. Call the next juror.

The court may excuse prospective jurors it does not think are qualified to serve. If it does not, the prosecutor or defense attorney may challenge the jurors. Those who are excused are replaced by other prospective jurors who are asked the same questions. Replacements are called in sequence from a list of members of the venire. If the attorneys have copies of this list and questionnaires for every member, they know who will be called next each time a prospective juror is struck.

If a case has received pretrial publicity, the judge is likely to require that members of the venire be interviewed individually in a nearby hearing room. In attendance are the judge, attorneys, defendant, deputy court clerk, court reporter, and bailiffs. The judge initially conducts questioning. Then each attorney is given a chance to ask questions. The following are typical of the questions asked:

• What have you read or seen in the media concerning this case?

• Have you discussed this case with anyone?

- Do you know anything about the facts of this case?

- Have you formed an opinion?

- Could you set aside your opinion and listen to the facts?

Prospective jurors may be excused if they have formed an unalterable opinion, based on what they have seen or heard in the media, that the defendant is guilty (see Excerpt 3).

EXCERPT 3

THE COURT: Do any of you know anything about the facts of this case?

MS. DOUGLAS: What I've read in the paper.

THE COURT: Do you recall any specifics or have you formed any opinion about this case?

MS. DOUGLAS: To be perfectly honest, yes.

THE COURT: Do you feel that opinion would affect your ability to sit and listen to the facts in this case and apply the law that I would instruct you on?

MS. DOUGLAS: I would hope not.

THE COURT: [speaking to a defense attorney]: You want to approach the bench?

MR. HARPER: Your Honor, the problem I am beginning to have with this juror is she's indicated she's formed an opinion, as opposed to merely having knowledge; and the fact that she is having to set aside a preconception or preconceived opinion as opposed to setting aside some knowledge gives me grounds to renew our motion to remove her for cause.
[Ms. Douglas was then excused.]

In a capital case, the judge asks prospective jurors their opinion of the death penalty. Just because some members of the venire may have objections to capital punishment does not disqualify them automatically. In *Witherspoon v. Illinois,* the prosecutor challenged nearly half of the venire for having qualms about the death penalty after the trial judge said, "Let's get these conscientious objectors out of the way, without wasting time on them."[7] The Supreme Court held that potential jurors cannot be excluded merely because they have conscientious scruples about the death penalty. In *Adams v. Texas,* it ruled that "to exclude all jurors who would be in the slightest way affected by the prospect of the death penalty or by their views about such a penalty would be to deprive the defendant of the impartial jury to which he or she is entitled under the law."[8]

Once the judge has finished examining prospective jurors, the attorneys begin their questioning. Voir dire serves three purposes for the attorneys. One of them is to establish rapport. In light of the suspicion and controversy surrounding a criminal case, it is important for attorneys to create an atmosphere in which prospective jurors can feel free to be candid. During voir dire, attorneys should substitute their role as cross-examiner with that of interviewer, making prospective jurors feel that the attorneys are genuinely interested in them and what they have to say.[9] Another purpose of voir dire is to elicit information from prospective jurors about their backgrounds and attitudes to determine if they are qualified to serve. The attorneys need this information if they are to exercise their challenges intelligently. The juror questionnaire, where it is used, may also provide background information. Finally, voir dire gives attorneys an opportunity to try to influence jurors. If they can get jurors to think about the case in a favorable way before the trial has actually begun, they have a decided advantage.

Challenges

There are three kinds of challenges: **challenge to the panel, challenge for cause,** and **peremptory challenge.** A challenge to the panel, which must be made before individual members are examined, is a challenge to the whole venire. It alleges systematic exclusion of potential jurors on the basis of such criteria as gender, race, or religion. The attorney who makes this challenge must produce substantial evidence of discrimination. For example, just showing that the percentage of blacks on the venire is not the same as the percentage of black electors from which the venire was chosen is not sufficient. It would be sufficient, though, to prove that a quota system had been used to systematically exclude a certain percentage of blacks.[10]

If it appears during voir dire that a prospective juror cannot fairly judge a case, an attorney may challenge that person for cause. Usually out of hearing of the venire, the attorney moves to strike that person. If the judge sustains the motion, the prospective juror is excused. Each attorney may make an unlimited number of challenges for cause.

The grounds for challenging for cause are several. An attorney may want to exclude a prospective juror who has a preconceived idea of the defendant's guilt. The person interviewed in Excerpt 3 is a good example. An attorney may also move to strike a prospective juror who appears to be prejudiced toward a particular class of people. The person interviewed in Excerpt 2 seems to have a bias toward law enforcement officers that would work against the defense. A prospective juror's being related to the defendant could also be grounds for a challenge for cause. Such a relationship could be one of landlord and tenant or of employer and employee. Being related by blood or marriage would certainly qualify.

With one exception, attorneys can exercise peremptory challenges without having to explain their reasons for doing so (see Excerpt 4).

No grounds need be stated, but the number of challenges is limited by law. The judge, however, may grant additional challenges in certain situations. For example, the judge might increase the number of peremptory challenges when an indictment or information are consolidated in a trial.[11]

EXCERPT 4

MR. BAJOCZKY [a defense attorney]: Anyone that wants to go home and has other things to do, I do not want to be sitting up here worrying that you are in a hurry to do this case, to give justice to my client, because you have to get home and do something. I want us to take the time to do it right. Any questions? You want off, Mr. Knight?

MR. KNIGHT: I would rather be somewhere else.

MR. BAJOCZKY: Your Honor, I would ask to use my peremptory for him.

THE COURT: Mr. Knight, I'll ask you to go ahead and step down. Thank you very much.

Peremptory challenges usually are not subject to judicial discretion. Racial discrimination is an exception. In *Batson v. Kentucky*, a case involving a black man accused of second-degree burglary and receiving stolen goods, the prosecutor used his peremptory challenges to eliminate four black members of the venire. The counsel for the defense objected, but the trial judge observed that "the parties were entitled to use their peremptory challenges to 'strike anybody they want to.'"[12] The Supreme Court reversed the conviction, holding that when a defendant makes a prima facie case of discrimination, the state has the burden of proving that its challenges were not made solely on the basis of race.

The attorneys begin usually questioning by explaining the purpose of voir dire and apologizing for questions potentially embarrassing to prospective jurors. Defense attorneys often ask prospective jurors whether they would vote to acquit the defendant before any evidence has been presented. This tactic enables them to instruct members of the venire that a person accused of a crime is presumed innocent until proven guilty and that the state has the burden of proving that guilt.

Both sides ask prospective jurors sitting in the jury box about their backgrounds:

- Where do you live?

- What is your occupation? What kind of work does being a [title of occupation] involve?

- Are you married? What is your spouse's occupation? Do you have any children? What are their ages?

- Did you serve in the military? What branch? What was your rank? Were you a military police officer or an officer in a court-martial?

- What school did you last attend? Did you receive a degree from [name of college or university]? What was your major field of study?

- Do you belong to any civic organization? Do you hold a position in any of these organizations?

- Are you a member of a church?

- What do you do in your spare time?

There are no hard-and-fast rules about which questions attorneys should ask prospective jurors. They are free to be spontaneous. For example, an attorney might ask potential jurors if they have any bumper stickers on their cars. Answers to this and to other questions could reveal something about a person's attitudes or abilities that might make an attorney want to challenge that person. The defense attorney whose client is black or Jewish would probably challenge someone who admitted having a bumper sticker promoting the white supremacist Aryan Nations. A study of jurors indicated that certain background characteristics, taken singly or in combination, were predictive of how jurors voted.[13] For example, it was found that secretaries and managers tended to convict. So did females who had at least an associate of arts degree.

In addition to background questions, attorneys ask prospective jurors about their attitudes toward different topics, depending on the type of case. If the trial involves a defendant whose penchant for firearms is central to the state's case, the prosecutor is not likely to want an avid gun enthusiast on the jury because the juror might identify with the defendant. If the case involves the violent death of a victim, the defense attorney would be concerned with how potential jurors are likely to respond to gruesome photographs of the body or graphic descriptions of the wounds. Those for whom such evidence is especially upsetting might feel compelled to convict (see Excerpt 5). If the state's key witness is black and the prospective jurors are white, the prosecutor might try to uncover the extent of their racial prejudice. A blatant admission of racism would likely be grounds for a challenge for cause. Such challenges are rare, however, because people tend to give answers that are socially acceptable, thus forcing attorneys to use instead their peremptory challenges.

EXCERPT 5

MR. BAJOCZKY [a defense attorney]: Parts of this case are going to be quite gruesome. We've got guns. We're going to have sex and adultery most likely testified about, drugs definitely, murder definitely. Anybody here feel that because of the nature or the sensitivity of any of these issues that you'd rather not sit on the jury?

Both sides must make wise use of their peremptory challenges because such challenges are limited in number. A rule of thumb for most attorneys is to never use all of their peremptory challenges and to always save at least one. This is important where **back-striking** is permitted, in which an attorney exercises a peremptory challenge after having earlier passed over a prospective juror.[14] It is also a good idea for an attorney to know at any given time exactly how many peremptory challenges an opponent has used. Good attorneys are resourceful in their use of challenges for cause. Instead of resorting early to peremptory challenges, they will word questions in such a manner as to educe causes for successful challenges.

For this purpose, open-ended questions often are better than closed-ended questions. Closed-ended questions are worded so as to evoke a straightforward *yes* or *no* response. They are useful when an attorney is trying to get prospective jurors to commit themselves to a particular position (see Excerpt 6).

EXCERPT 6

MR. BAJOCZKY [a defense attorney]: Anyone got a feeling that if the defendant has money or the family has money, that must mean he's guilty? To go out and hire him a fancy-pants lawyer to come in here, he has a lot of money; he can just get off with everything, here? Anybody feel like that?

Open-ended questions typically begin with words such as *what* or *why*. Used skillfully, they can lead potential jurors to make statements revealing biases that open them to challenges for cause (see Excerpt 7).

EXCERPT 7

MR. GUARISCO [a deputy state attorney interviewing prospective jurors during individual voir dire]: What bothers me, Mr. Kavetti—and I don't want you to get the wrong idea that I'm picking on you—but I'm a little concerned here about what you said while you were in the [jury] box there that, in essence, you are pro-defense. I don't want to be representing the state of Florida and start off with two strikes against me. Maybe you can explain what you meant by that comment.

Because prospective jurors tend to give answers that are socially acceptable, attorneys often look to body language for an expression of true feelings.[15] Potential jurors who fold their arms across their chests, lean back in their chairs, or turn sideways when questioned may convey a closed or rejecting orientation toward the inquiring lawyer. Increased eye contact may reveal hostility. Body rigidity may indicate anxiety. And auditory cues, such as tense laughter, rapid speech, or a condescending tone, may signal the presence of anxiety or deception.

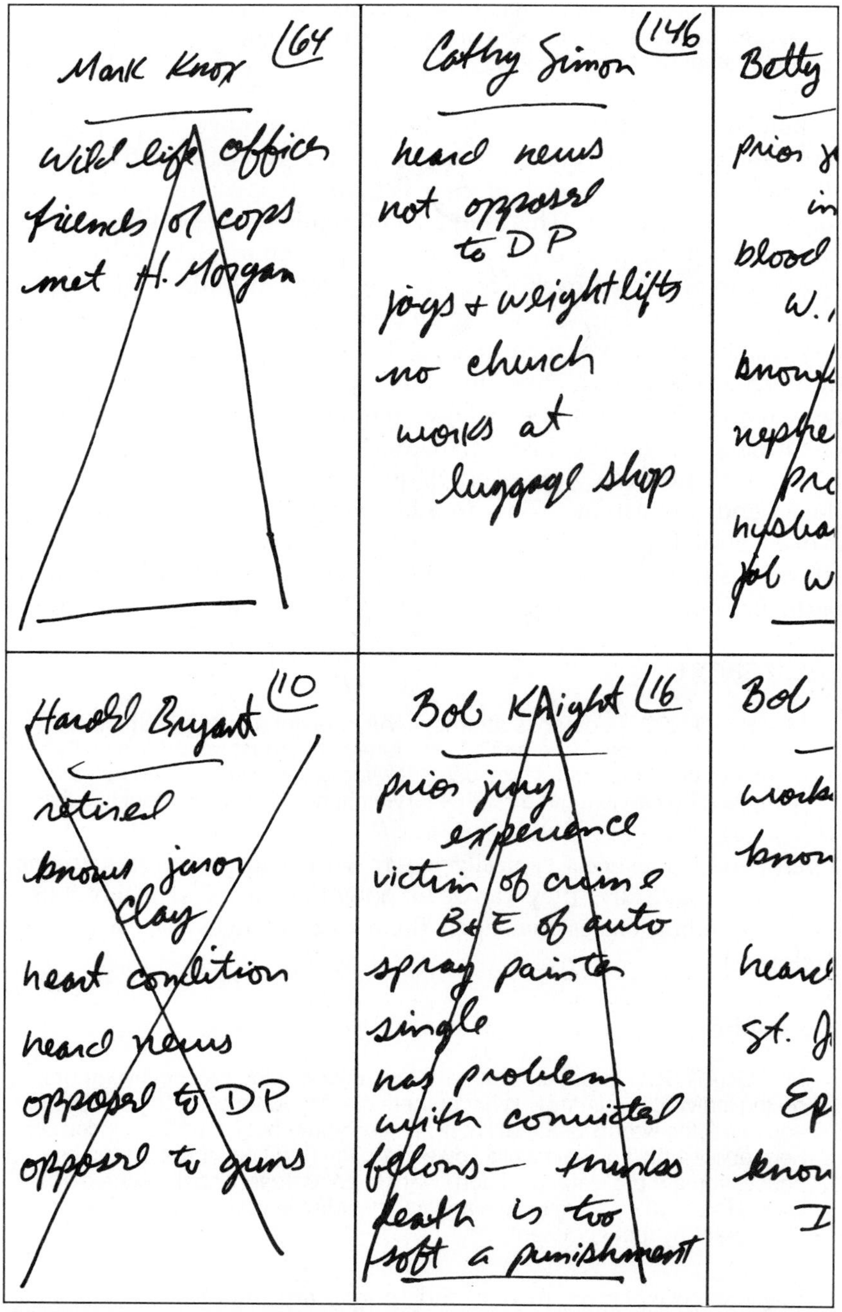

Exhibit 4-2 Jury seating board, including actual observations recorded by a defense attorney in the Peavy case. The large deltas refer to peremptory challenges made by the defense. The large X refers to a challenge for cause.

It can also be very telling when a prospective juror, confused by an attorney's question, looks to the opposition for clarification.

Attorneys do much of their observing of body language during voir dire. Recess, however, can also be a rich source of cues. For example, if a prospective juror moves away abruptly when approached by the defense attorneys in the hallway during a break, the attorneys might infer that they are being rejected.[16] During voir dire, where often teams of two lawyers work together, one typically observes while the other asks questions. The one observing usually records facts that might be useful later in deciding whom to challenge (see Exhibit 4-2). It is not uncommon for attorneys to bring in persons expressly to observe prospective jurors' body language. Sometimes they are experts. Often, though, they are not. Defense attorneys frequently ask their clients for observations, too.

Juror Roles

Attorneys' perceptions of the roles people might eventually play in the deliberations of the jury affect their choices of jurors.[17] Basically, a jury is a task-oriented group. Its goal is to reach a verdict. Except for the requirement that there be a foreperson, little structure exists initially in a jury. Likewise, there are few rules on how to reach a verdict. That means that the juror emerging as the leader can play a pivotal part in bringing order to the jury and influencing the process by which it reaches the verdict. Signs of leadership include occupational status, strong will, articulate speech, and leadership experience.

Whenever any doubt exists about a prospective juror who shows signs of leadership, there is a propensity to strike that person, often leaving the jury leaderless. This can be especially perilous for the defense. Jurors tend to be biased against the defendant. Unless a leader emerges to take a stand in favor of acquittal and to try to persuade others, the jury is likely to reach a guilty verdict without much deliberation.

In addition to leaders, juries also have followers, fillers, and holdouts. Followers are individuals who actively support the leader. They may have reached a verdict independently of the leader, but they lack the skills or self-confidence to present their positions. Fillers find it difficult to reach any verdict on their own. They are passive individuals who tend to be intimidated by the whole process of the trial and who are likely to go along with whatever the majority decides. Holdouts are individuals who resist the buildup of pressure during deliberations as others around them surrender to the growing majority. Whether they are isolates from the very beginning or leaders who later become isolates, they are stubborn. It is rare, though, that a lone juror is able to produce a **hung jury.**[18]

Once the jurors and alternates have been selected, the trial continues with the swearing in of the jurors. The judge briefly instructs the jurors before the attorneys present their opening statements (see Excerpt 8).

EXCERPT 8

THE COURT: Is the State ready to proceed?

MR. POITINGER: The State is ready, Your Honor.

THE COURT: Is the Defense ready to proceed?

MR. BAJOCZKY: We are, Your Honor.

THE COURT: Bring the jury in.
   (Thereupon, a jury of twelve persons, plus [three] alternate jurors, having previously been selected, returned to the courtroom.)

THE COURT: Ladies and gentlemen, I hope you had a comfortable weekend. Let me ask you to stand, please; and I am going to ask the Clerk to administer the oath.
   (Thereupon, the twelve jurors, plus three alternates, were duly sworn.)
[Afterward, the judge continued his opening comments:]

THE COURT: Let me admonish you not to form any definite or fixed opinion about the merits of this case until you have heard all the evidence, the final arguments of the attorneys, and the instructions of the law given to you by myself. And until that time you should not discuss the case among yourselves.
   [The judge instructed the jurors as to the defendant's rights:]
   In every criminal proceeding the defendant has the absolute right to remain silent, and at no time is it a duty of a defendant to prove his or her innocence.
   From the exercise of a defendant's right to remain silent, a jury is not permitted to draw any inference of guilt; and the fact that a defendant did not take the witness stand must not influence your verdict in any manner whatsoever.
   [The judge then instructed the jurors as to how they should interpret motions made by the State, the Defense, and the Court:]
   When an objection is made, you should not speculate on the reason why it is made. Likewise, when an objection is sustained or upheld, you must not speculate on what might have occurred had the objection not been sustained, or what a witness might have said had he or she been permitted to answer.
   [The judge then addressed the prosecution:]

THE COURT: Are you ready with your opening statement?

MR. GUARISCO [deputy state attorney]: Yes, sir.

THE COURT: You may proceed.

Study Questions

1. How might jury selection have been different had the murders been committed on the other side of the Ochlockonee River, in rural Gadsden County where Peavy resided?

2. Why would defense attorneys not want prospective jurors to see Peavy's shackles? Jurors would surely expect that a man charged with two counts of first-degree murder would be held in secure custody.

3. Why do you suppose the prosecutor revealed to prospective jurors the biggest weakness in the state's case?

4. The defense used a peremptory challenge to get rid of Bob Knight. Can you tell from looking at the jury seating board what it was that he said or did that prompted the challenge? Why do you think Harold Bryant was struck?

Endnotes

1. See Thomas A. Mauet, *Fundamentals of Trial Technique* (Boston: Little, Brown, and Co., 1980), 24–25.

2. Thomas A. Mauet, *Fundamentals of Trial Technique* (Boston: Little, Brown, and Co., 1980), 31.

3. This excerpt and subsequent ones are adapted from the transcript of the trial of John Wesley Peavy in the Second Judicial Circuit Court in Tallahassee, Florida, in March 1987. The presiding judge was Charles McClure.

4. *Florida v. Williams*, 399 U.S. 78 (1970).

5. For criticism of alternate jury systems, see Gilbert B. Stuckey, *Procedures in the Justice System*, 3d ed. (Columbus, OH: Charles E. Merrill, 1986) 210–21.

6. *Florida Rules of Criminal Procedure*, rule 3.280 (1987).

7. *Witherspoon v. Illinois*, 391 U.S. 510, 514 (1968).

8. *Adams v. Texas*, 448 U.S. 38, 50 (1980); see also *Wainwright v. Witt*, 469 U.S. 412 (1985).

9. See Marjorie Fargo and Beth Bonora, "Conducting the Voir Dire," in *Jurywork: Systematic Techniques*, eds. Beth Bonora and Elissa Krauss (Oakland, CA: National Jury Project, 1979), 156–58.

10. See Richard G. Lubin, "Jury Selection," in *Criminal Trial Practice in Florida*, ed. Gerald T. Bennett (Tallahassee, FL: Florida Bar, 1984), 23–24.

11. *Florida Rules of Criminal Procedure*, rule 3.350 (1987).

12. *Batson v. Kentucky*, 476 U.S. 79, 83 (1986).

13. Thomas Sannito and Edward Burke Arnolds, "Jury Study Results: The Factors at Work," *Trial Diplomacy Journal* 5 (1982), 6–10.

14. For a discussion of strategies of sequential and struck systems of selecting jurors, see Beth Bonora, Rosalyn Linder, Richard Christie, and Jay Schulman, "Jury Selection," in *Jurywork: Systematic Techniques*, eds. Beth Bonora and Elissa Krauss (Oakland, CA: National Jury Project, 1979), 214–16.

15. "Body Language: What You Should Look for in Jury Selection," *Bar Bulletin* (Tallahassee Bar Association), November 1989, 1, 3; see also Beth Bonora, Rosalyn Linder, Richard Christie, and Jay Schulman, "Jury Selection," in *Jurywork: Systematic Techniques*, eds. Beth Bonora and Elissa Krauss (Oakland, CA: National Jury Project, 1979), 209–11.

16. Robert Harper, criminal defense attorney, Tallahassee, FL, personal communication, 1 August 1989.

17. See Beth Bonora, Rosalyn Linder, Richard Christie, and Jay Schulman, "Jury Selection," in *Jurywork: Systematic Techniques*, eds. Beth Bonora and Elissa Krauss (Oakland, CA: National Jury Project, 1979), 206–7.

18. D. W. Broeder, "The University of Chicago Jury Project," *Nebraska Law Review* 38 (1959), 744–60.

5

The Trial

Cold-Blooded Killer or Innocent Man Wrongly Accused?

DAY ONE: POLAR POSITIONS IN THE COURTROOM

It would take three weeks of trial testimony and legal arguments to find out if John Wesley Peavy would win or lose.

On March 9, 1987, it was finally time for the jury to begin listening attentively, ready to jot notes on the pads resting in their laps. First to speak was Deputy State Attorney Tony Guarisco, who gave an outline of the crime, spiced with dramatic effect.

"This Halloween evening proved to be a night of tragedy, resulting in the deaths of Mary Lee Driggers and Bobby Harrison," he said, pacing before the jury. "They met their deaths in a hail of gunfire," he said, slowing his words for emphasis.

Guarisco started the Halloween night scene at the Shady Rest, painting a mental picture of the beer-drinking, pool-shooting hangout on a country road between Havana and Quincy. It was there, he said, where Harrison played cards and gambled in a back room while Driggers watched. Peavy, he said, showed up in the evening and got angry because Harrison and the other guys snubbed him and wouldn't let him join in the game.

Then Guarisco previewed the words the jury would hear again and again: "Peavy goes to the bar and says to the owner, 'What has Bobby got on them that they won't let me play?'"

Driggers and Harrison left the Shady Rest, Guarisco said; and Peavy soon followed the couple to Bobby's trailer on Fairbanks Ferry Court (see Figure 5-1). Guarisco argued that bad blood between Peavy and Harrison, his former brother-in-law, fueled by the defendant's alcohol problem, was sufficient motive for Peavy to kill both Harrison and Driggers. And Guarisco confidently told the jury the state had enough evidence to directly link

103

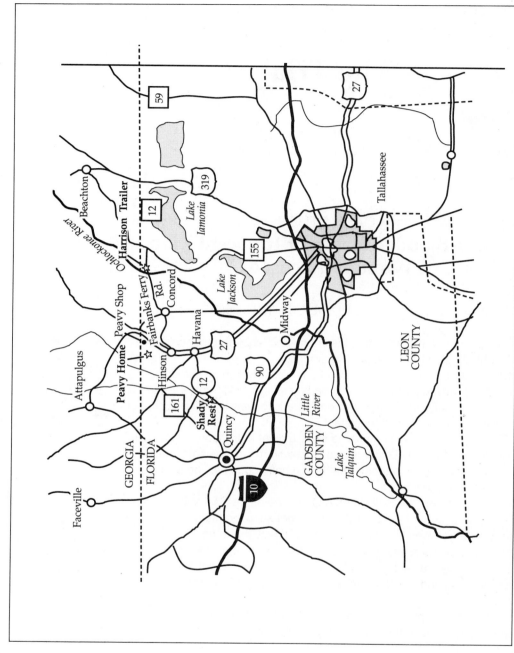

Figure 5-1 Map of Leon and Gadsden counties, showing the murder scene, Peavy's home, and the Shady Rest tavern. Harrison lived just over the county line, the Ochlockonee River, in Leon County.

Figure 5-2 Anthony Bajoczky, defense attorney for John Peavy. Mark Wallheiser.

Peavy to the killings. Among the state's key evidence was the fact that Peavy owned a 9mm semiautomatic pistol, known as a Tec 9, and that spent cartridges and live rounds fitting that gun were gathered from outside Harrison's home, as well as from several other locations Peavy frequented. Guarisco told the jury that an expert witness would tell them how those cartridges matched, linking Peavy to the murders.

"This will be a long and complicated trial," Guarisco warned the jurors. But after they had heard testimony from the state's potential list of 174 witnesses and viewed a possible 133 pieces of physical evidence, he promised, "Everything will point to the guilt of John Wesley Peavy."

Defense attorney Tony Bajoczky then gave his opening statement (see Figure 5-2). He began his counterattack by telling the jury that, at five-foot-eight in his shoes, John Peavy was too short to be guilty of murder. And he promised to bring on his own gun expert to prove his point. The expert, Bajoczky said, would testify that it would have been "absolutely impossible for anyone under six-foot-two" to have fired a gun through a high window, such as the window on Harrison's trailer, at the proper angle.

Rather than focusing on Peavy's character, Bajoczky directed the jury's attention to Bobby Harrison, describing him as "a rough-and-tumble guy who'd get into a fistfight at the drop of a hat."

More significant, Bajoczky told the jury, was the company that Harrison kept. The defense attorney said Harrison was "into dope and cocaine with Martha Munroe," the flamboyant owner of a cheesecake bakery in North Florida who had grabbed headlines the year before when she was convicted of conspiracy to traffic more than 400 grams of cocaine.

Harrison had had many enemies, Bajoczky told the jury—but Peavy wasn't one of them.

"Harrison knew weeks before he died that he was a marked man. He knew he was in over his head," Bajoczky said. He said Harrison had kept the drapes on his trailer windows drawn, even in the afternoon, acted paranoid, and told his daughter to keep a loaded gun with her at all times, even to go to the bathroom.

Before the trial was over, Bajoczky said, there would be several good suspects to the killings, enough to create the reasonable doubt necessary to set Peavy free.

"[Harrison] told people, 'I'm a walking time bomb. And anybody who hangs around with me will be wasted,'" Bajoczky said.

And, apparently, the one with Harrison at the wrong place at the wrong time was Driggers. Lead vapors and gunpowder on the bodies, Bajoczky told the jury, showed they were shot at close range through Harrison's kitchen window, from less than six feet of the bodies. And, the defense attorney continued, a gun expert would say the gun was most likely shot at a level angle through the high window. That meant the killer had to be tall, Bajoczky told the jury.

Responding to Guarisco's jab that Peavy had a drinking problem, Bajoczky said that he agreed Peavy was an alcoholic who was in and out of treatment centers. On the day of Harrison's funeral, Bajoczky said, an argument with his brother led Peavy to get drunk on whiskey. Peavy's father was about to admit him into another thirty-day stint at an alcohol treatment facility when he first suggested they clean out Peavy's truck.

That was where Peavy usually kept his 9mm gun, Bajoczky said; but it wasn't in the truck. That, along with appearing at the Shady Rest tavern on the night of the killings, was what got Peavy arrested, Bajoczky said, his voice revealing his disgust.

"When the police come and don't find the gun, they figure, 'This is it, Johnny. If you don't have your gun, you must be guilty.'"

A lot of people in Havana, Bajoczky said, owned 9mm guns; and he argued that the prosecutors couldn't positively link Peavy and his missing gun to the dead bodies.

Once Peavy was locked in jail, Bajoczky said, several convicts anxious to make deals with the state attorney's office came forward with lies that Peavy had confessed behind bars.

"All they have," Bajoczky told the jury, "is some shells, dead bodies, and confessions from jailbirds."

And so, on the first day of the trial, the jurors were left to ponder polar positions: the defense attorney saying he would prove Peavy was too short to be the killer and the prosecutor saying first-degree murder would fit Peavy just right.

DAY TWO: PRESENTING THE EVIDENCE

On the trial's second day, the jury was presented with a load of evidence, ranging from boxes that once held Bobby and Mary Lee's take-out chicken dinners to a window screen riddled with bullet holes.

Leon County Sheriff's Lieutenant Bill Gunter, the crime scene expert, was the prosecutor's vehicle for introducing a slew of evidence, focusing mostly on his theory about the bullets' paths of fire.

The end of the day brought a feisty cross-examination by Bajoczky, which at one point left Gunter stalled on the witness stand by a lack of conviction about what could actually be proven.

As things got heated, one courtroom spectator whispered to another a wish that Gunter would hit the defense lawyer with his pointer stick. And the judge had to urge lawyers for both sides to calm down.

The crux of Bajoczky's cross-examination of Gunter dealt with a dozen spent 9mm shell casings that Gunter had collected from the ground near the shattered kitchen window. That was the spot in which the prosecutors said Peavy had stood when he fired the gun.

For hours in court, Gunter tracked the direction and angle of bullets and lead fragments, holding up photos, pointing to a diagram, and matching it all up to the casings. But, by the time Bajoczky was through, Gunter wound up agreeing that:

- Some of the bullets were "chunks of lead" too fragmented for him to really say where they came from.

- He could not pinpoint how long the casings had been on the ground because no such test for time exists.

- He could not prove the casings came from the killer's gun. Nor could he positively link the spent casings to the dead victims.

Bajoczky focused jurors' attention on a target practice tree not far from Harrison's front porch. Pacing before Gunter, his arms folded and his voice rising, Bajoczky asked, "The bottom line is that the shell casings could have come from target practice; isn't that right?"

Reluctantly, Gunter testified, "That's a possibility."

In attacking Bajoczky's opening statement promise that the killer had to be at least six-foot-two, Assistant State Attorney Jack Poitinger asked Gunter for measurements from the bottom of the kitchen window to the ground.

"Five feet, seven inches," Gunter answered, adding that the farther away from the trailer he walked, the higher the ground sloped.

Poitinger hoped the jury grasped his point: that, at five-foot-eight, Peavy was tall enough to be the killer. Supporting that idea, Gunter testified that one exit hole showed a bullet had traveled at an upward angle, suggesting that the killer could have pointed the gun upward to blast through the high window.

On cross-examination, Bajoczky pounced on the fact that Gunter had never made sure the trailer was sitting level, thus casting doubt on the deputy's figures.

After hours of examination, cross-examination, and redirect examination, Gunter's voice and manner began to reveal his irritation with the grueling questions from the defense attorney who wouldn't give up.

Gunter gripped his pointer stick and said, "Whether it's level, upside down, or inside out would not affect my measurements!"

Bajoczky wound down his questioning, looking satisfied. He let the jury know that there were dozens of items taken from Harrison's trailer to be tested for fingerprints: everything from salt shakers to Marlboro cigarette packs. Peavy's fingerprints showed up on none of the items, Gunter acknowledged; and some of the prints did not match anyone known to frequent the trailer.

Tapping his hand on the diagram of Harrison's place, Bajoczky asked, "Is there anything at all that ties John Peavy to this scene?'"

Gunter answered dejectedly, "No, I guess not."

DAY THREE: THEORIZING A MOTIVE

Though it was not required that the prosecutors prove a motive, on the trial's third day, they shared their theory with the jury. For the motive, the prosecutors returned to the Shady Rest tavern.

The state's lineup of witnesses included Herman Mills, a construction crew supervisor from Bainbridge, Georgia, and one of the back room gamblers. The way Mills described it, Peavy walked into the room after it was already dark that Halloween night, and exchanged howdies. While still rolling the dice, Mills testified, Bobby "just looked up at him [Peavy] and dropped his head."

Peavy wanted to place side bets, Mills testified, but, he said, "Bobby told him he didn't have enough to cover him. Bobby crapped out, and I took the dice and I told him [Peavy] I didn't have enough right then."

Peavy went to the bar, Mills said; and the game broke up somewhere between eight and nine P.M. On cross-examination, Bajoczky focused on the way Harrison looked up from rolling the dice without saying a word.

"Did you take that to mean Bobby was mad at Johnny?" the defense lawyer asked. And Mills ended up agreeing with Bajoczky that no, that was just the way Bobby was. He also agreed that it seemed like a regular, friendly game, but that most of the gamblers were tired and had run out of money.

Bobby had been the big winner, another witness testified, pocketing hundreds of dollars that night.

Midway through the day, a break came for the prosecution. Poitinger successfully persuaded the judge to allow the jury to see thirteen color photos of Harrison's and Driggers' naked and decomposing bodies in the hospital morgue at the autopsy.

Defense attorney Robert Harper argued that any professed relevance the photos might have was "a red herring just to get some dirty pictures in front of the jury," and that the prejudice the inflammatory photos would cause Peavy outweighed any probative value.

But, Poitinger successfully argued, by paraphrasing a Florida Supreme Court opinion, someone accused of murder could expect to be confronted with pictures of it later, no matter how disturbing those pictures might be.

And so Dr. Woodward Burgert, Jr., the medical examiner who conducted the autopsies, was allowed to stand before the jury, hold up gruesome eight-by-ten-inch photos, and point to bullet holes. He testified that three bullets had ripped through Driggers and that all of them were fatal. Harrison, the doctor said, had been hit with five bullets, one fatal and one potentially fatal. For both, the doctor estimated, death had come within minutes.

Though the prosecutors had left the tavern for the sterile chill of the morgue, the Shady Rest held still more evidence against Peavy.

DAY FOUR: WITNESSES AND TESTIMONY

On the trial's fourth day, the prosecutors brought on Sam Castle, the owner of the Shady Rest, who lived in a trailer behind the tavern. Castle's right hand shook when he raised it to take the oath to tell the truth. On that fateful date, October 31, 1985, Castle remembered, he had opened the bar at ten A.M. for Mills and his work crew, who had been rained out of their construction job and were in the mood to drink beer and gamble.

It wasn't until around nine P.M., Castle testified, that Peavy walked in, went to the back gambling room, and came to the bar a few minutes later.

Castle was tending bar. He remembered serving Peavy a Miller draft and Peavy asking, "What's Bobby got on them that they won't play with me?"

Next, Castle testified, Peavy told him that Bobby Harrison was his ex-brother-in-law and he had lost Peavy's sister's house.

That quick exchange between a tavern owner and a beer-drinking customer took up hours of courtroom time. Castle answered a barrage of questions on the witness stand, while opposing lawyers tried to pinpoint the degree to which Peavy seemed bothered by not being allowed to gamble.

When Guarisco, the prosecutor, asked the questions, Castle said, "He was upset because they wouldn't let him play."

But when Bajoczky cross-examined him, Castle agreed with the defense attorney that Peavy was "concerned," not "huffing-and-puffing mad."

"When Peavy talked about his sister losing her house," Bajoczky asked, "was Peavy acting mad or just informing you?"

"I guess, informing," Castle answered with a shrug.

Guarisco was allowed another question: "Was he disturbed?"

"Disturbed? Yes," Castle concluded, adding that he really didn't know that much about Peavy's temperament, other than that Peavy was a pretty nice fellow who would come in for occasional beers and who had donated a cap to the collection Castle kept on the wall behind the bar.

Bajoczky persisted with this crucial semantics game: "Just because he's not happy doesn't mean he was in a rage, does it?"

"No, sir," Castle agreed.

On his way out of the courtroom, Castle cast a smile and a friendly nod in Peavy's direction.

Later in the day, Peavy's nephew, "Little Delacy," found himself testifying against Uncle Johnny. He had helped investigators gather up spent 9mm casings from Peavy & Son Construction property and from land the Peavys owned on the Ochlockonee River.

Little Delacy testified that his Uncle Johnny owned a Tec 9 semi-automatic pistol that fired 9mm cartridges like the casings found near the bullet-shattered window of Harrison's trailer.

By the time Bajoczky was through, Peavy's nephew agreed that a long list of gun-loving guys the Peavy family knew also had shot 9mm guns at those same target practice locations.

The fourth day of testimony ended with Leon County Sheriff's Detective Bill Moody, who told of December 6, 1985, the day Gloria Peavy stood by while he searched a closet at the Peavy's Havana home.

Gloria, Moody testified, had supplied him with an inventory of thirteen weapons her husband owned. But, Moody said, the closet only contained eleven. One missing gun, he said, Gloria could explain: for protection, she had taken a .38-caliber gun to her sister-in-law's house where she was staying.

But the other missing gun, Moody testified, was Peavy's Tec 9 semi-automatic pistol. Neither Gloria nor Johnny could explain why it was nowhere to be found.

DAY FIVE: WEAPONS TALK

Guns, bullets, spent shell casings, and more guns: on the trial's fifth day, the jury was pelted with round after round of firearms talk. Testimony came from a long line of investigators, sheriff's scuba divers with underwater metal detectors, and the gun dealer who had sold Peavy a semi-automatic 9mm pistol on December 20, 1984.

So far, the testimony showed clearly that Peavy owned a small arsenal of guns, including a missing Tec 9 that fired 9mm bullets. Not so clear was whether prosecutors could link Peavy to the gun that left fatal bullet holes in Driggers and Harrison. The testimony set the stage for the prosecutor's key witness, who would testify the following week: Don Champagne, the Florida Department of Law Enforcement ballistics expert. Prosecutors hoped that Champagne's testimony, along with testimony that Peavy's Tec 9 had mysteriously disappeared, would tie Peavy to the crime scene.

But Bajoczky drummed on the fact that the Peavys' river property and road construction business and Johnny Peavy's home, where investigators had seized spent 9mm cartridges, were used for target practice by many people.

Kevin Kelly, a gun dealer, produced records verifying that he had sold

Peavy a Tec 9 semiautomatic weapon. In the courtroom, he used one just like it for demonstration purposes. As he lifted the black paramilitary-style weapon from its box and held it up, several jurors flinched. Even unloaded, the gun was scary.

Testimony focused on a certain kind of ammunition found at the various locations: CCI Blazer 9mm Luger bullets. Kelly testified that he had probably sold more than a thousand boxes of that common ammunition and that it could be fired from hundreds of models of handguns. "Everybody who owns a 9mm handgun has tried it," Kelly testified, "because it's so cheap."

Furthermore, Kelly testified, ninety-eight percent of all 9mm handguns made hold twelve or more shots.

That was what the defense wanted in response to earlier testimony from Lieutenant Gunter of the sheriff's department, who said he had gathered twelve spent 9mm casings from the crime scene.

Bajoczky had already told the jury that they would learn that the gunman had used a gun with no rifling, steel grooves in the barrel that cause bullets to spiral out when fired. Someone would remove rifling, Bajoczky explained, so that the bullets could not be traced to the gun.

On cross-examination, Bajoczky asked Kelly whether Tec 9 guns are manufactured with rifling. And the gun shop owner answered, "To my knowledge, Tec 9s always come with rifling."

But Poitinger asked Kelly, "If someone bought a Tec 9, and there was something wrong with the barrel and there was no rifling, would you know about that?"

Kelly had to admit: "No sir, we would not."

DAY SIX: PEAVY'S "CONFESSORS"

After a weekend of rest, the trial resumed on Monday. Two jailbirds were cooped up on the witness stand, and Bajoczky, armed with razor-sharp questions, did his best to fricassee them.

One was Tommy Lee Johnson, a self-described cocaine addict and a five-time convicted felon currently serving a ten-year sentence. The other was Ricky Steven Osborn, doing time for stabbing a man to death.

Both had lived with Peavy in a twenty-man cell block at the Leon County Jail. Both gave riveting testimony about confessions from Peavy, all about killing Harrison and Driggers.

Peavy opened up to him, Johnson testified, when they were sharing woes about their addictions. For Johnson, it was cocaine. Peavy's downfall was alcohol.

"[Peavy] stated to me that if he hadn't been drinking, he wouldn't have did what he done," Johnson testified. He then supplied a version of the killing, supposedly told him by Peavy, that pretty much matched the prosecutors'.

Osborn's rendition had a spark of drug-dealing intrigue involving Martha

Munroe, the cheesecake baker and convicted cocaine dealer whom Bajoczky had mentioned in his opening statements.

Near dawn in the jail cell, Osborn testified, Peavy had muttered something in his sleep. Even though he really couldn't make out the words, Osborn admitted, he woke up Peavy and said, "You're telling on yourself."

"I told him he didn't have to worry about us; we wouldn't tell on him." And then Osborn proceeded to tell the jury the information with which he said Peavy had entrusted him: that Peavy's brother hired him to kill Harrison because a band of cocaine dealers didn't want Harrison testifying in Munroe's upcoming trial.

During Osborn's testimony, Peavy held a single finger over his lips, which were tilted into a smile, and turned to wink at a reporter.

Were the two convicts telling the truth or weaving lies to save themselves? That was a question for the jurors to ponder, and Bajoczky's cross-examination gave them plenty to consider.

For example, Bajoczky pointed out, in January 1986, when Johnson went to Leon County sheriff's investigators with his information, he was facing charges of attempted first-degree murder, aggravated battery, carrying a concealed weapon, and possession of a firearm by a convicted felon. During a plea negotiation, the state reduced the attempted-murder charge, which carried a term of life in prison, to aggravated assault. Johnson was sentenced to ten years and was excused from Florida's usual three-year minimum mandatory sentence for crimes involving firearms.

Johnson insisted that no deal was cut for his testimony. At the end of Bajoczky's grilling, Johnson flung one arm toward the judge and said, "I'm sitting up in a one-man cell looking out a window. I'm not to blame for the sentence I got. You're going to have to talk to the judge about that."

Despite Bajoczky's insinuation that Johnson had received a sweetheart deal for lying, Johnson insisted that he had come forward with his information because "I felt like it was the right thing to do."

But Bajoczky produced a transcript of Johnson telling a detective that his motives to help were "for protection for myself. You know, for what I'm facing."

Focusing next on Osborn, Bajoczky unveiled a plea negotiation, dated December 1, 1986, in which the capital offense of sexual battery of a seven-year-old girl was reduced to simple battery, a misdemeanor. For Osborn, life in prison with no chance of release for twenty-five years had been shaved down to a year in the county jail.

At that time, Osborn was still awaiting sentencing on his plea for the time he and five inmates had escaped from the jail and beaten a guard. The original charges included attempted first-degree murder, but the charges were reduced to aggravated battery.

A walking reminder of that jail escape fracas, Osborn limped to the witness stand, leaning on a cane. His testimony about Peavy's confession, he insisted, was the truth.

But Bajoczky clutched one of Osborn's court files, which held a letter to a judge adamantly denying he, Osborn, knew anything about the crime in which a man was stabbed to death. It also held his later guilty plea to third-degree murder in that case.

"What's the first thing you think of when charged with a crime?" Bajoczky asked, his voice sarcastic as he paced before Osborn. "How to get out of it?"

Eventually, Osborn answered, "Yeah."

"And the second thing you think of is how to lie? Right?"

"Sounds pretty good," Osborn said.

The jury was left to wonder whether Osborn was lying to them.

The jury was already en route to its motel when the judge granted Peavy a quick courtroom visit with his wife. It was Gloria and Johnny's wedding anniversary, and they seized the chance for hugs and kisses.

The lawyers were busy packing their briefcases when Bajoczky turned to Poitinger and said with a grin, "Truth, justice, honesty, and integrity: that's what we heard from the stand today."

The prosecutor bounced back, "You'll get your turn."

DAY SEVEN: TESTIMONY FROM THE EXPERTS

The seventh day was math and science day, as jurors jotted notes about intersecting lines and microscopic findings. First at the chalkboard was Broward Wilkes. Never before in his years as a veteran county land surveyor, he said, had he been asked to go to a crime scene and line up bullet holes.

He had hauled his tripod to Harrison's trailer to help the state disprove Bajoczky's assertion that Peavy, at five-foot-eight, was too short to be the killer.

Wilkes's finger had traced the intersecting horizontal lines projecting out from bullet holes in the walls at Harrison's trailer. According to Wilkes's figures, the gunman would have been standing three feet from the side of the trailer; and the entry bullet hole was five feet, seven inches from the ground. If the gunman stood four feet away, that bullet was fired five feet, five inches above the ground.

Defense attorneys would not allow the words "gun" or "bullet" to fall from a land surveyor's lips, because he wasn't a ballistics expert. Prosecutor Poitinger had to fashion his questions carefully. "Was what made the holes *above* the banister on the front porch?"

Wilkes answered, "Yes, about ten inches above the banister."

But the next expert witness was allowed to provide plenty of opinions involving ballistics. Don Champagne, the firearms examiner for the Florida Department of Law Enforcement, gave a lesson on his various microscopic tests. His job, Champagne said, was to figure out if the dozen CCI Luger 9mm cartridge casings found at the crime scene matched those found at places prosecutors said Peavy was known to practice shooting: the river acreage, the Peavy company, and Johnny's nearby home.

"I was able to determine that all [of the cartridge casings] were fired in the same weapon," Champagne testified, "even though I did not have the weapon."

Shaking a box to rattle the casings inside, Bajoczky asked, "There's a complete absence of evidence to show what gun was used, isn't there?"

Champagne agreed. Without a weapon to work with, Champagne said, there was no way to positively link the bullets to the casings or to any particular gun make.

Under his microscope, Champagne said, he had scrutinized the little scratches on the fired bullets. Using chalkboard drawings, Champagne explained that his efforts were in vain because the gun used did not have rifling, or grooves in the barrel that cause bullets to spiral out and leave characteristics markings when fired.

Champagne testified that someone could remove rifling by drilling out a barrel or by substituting a piece of pipe for the barrel. On cross-examination, Bajoczky drew from him the fact that specific makes of guns, like the H&K handgun, don't have the usual rifling.

After Bajoczky's series of questions with Champagne, the defense turned from the microscopic to the macroscopic. With a flair for the dramatic, and over prosecutors' objections, the defense lawyers erected a full-scale pine-and-Styrofoam mock-up of the front porch and exterior wall of Harrison's trailer (see Figure 5-3).

On the courtroom's green carpet, the lawyers laid down a wooden ramp to show how the land sloped higher farther from the trailer. Drawn on the Styrofoam in black was a window the size of the one shattered when bullets rained into Harrison's kitchen. Peavy sat in a chair near the banister, close to the spot in which the killer had stood on that Halloween night.

A few inches could make a mile of difference in sizing up the evidence against Peavy, the defense attorneys hoped, in trying to prove their theory that the killer had to be six inches taller than five-foot-eight Peavy in order to fire the gun through a high kitchen window at the proper angle.

Their man with the tape measure was Dale Nute, a forensic science consultant. Poitinger vigorously and unsuccessfully tried to keep Nute off the witness stand, arguing that he was not qualified to give an expert opinion.

After a twenty-five-minute bench conference, during which whispers unintelligible to onlookers and the jury swished through the courtroom, Judge McClure deemed Nute enough of an expert to share his opinions in the areas of crime scene analysis and trajectory, the path of bullets in flight.

From calculations made on his half-dozen visits to the crime scene, Nute estimated the distance from the entry bullet hole to the ground, to be six feet, one inch when one stood right at the trailer's exterior wall. That was two inches higher than the measurement made by Broward Wilkes, who had taken measurements at a crime scene for the first time in his surveying career.

Figure 5-3 John Peavy sits at the defense table, next to the mock-up of the front porch and window of Harrison's trailer. Hal Yeager.

Prosecutors positioned Peavy far enough from the trailer to stand on the upwardly sloping land, making him tall enough to be the gunman. But the defense tried to place the killer closer to the window by pinpointing the position of Driggers's body on the kitchen floor. As Champagne had testified earlier, lead vapors were detected on the bodies of both victims, and he had said that that only happens when a gun's muzzle is six feet away, or less, from a target.

One of Nute's opinions sparked a legal skirmish. The defense wanted to suggest that the killer could have come from the river, eliminating Peavy, who was at the Shady Rest tavern not long before the killings.

Figure 5-4 Defense expert, Dale Nute testifies that in his opinion, Peavy was too short to be the killer. Hal Yeager.

Earlier, the jury had heard from Harrison's neighbor, Jamie Fuller, who testified that he thought he heard a boat on the river that night, which was rather unusual, considering that the river was swollen with rain dumped by Tropical Storm Juan.

At first, in what seemed a damning blow to the defense paying for his testimony as a forensic science consultant, Nute said, "That's a very unlikely probability that someone came up from the river." (See Figure 5-4.)

Surprised, Bajoczky launched into a follow-up question, trying to salvage matters; but Poitinger objected, saying, "He's got to take the answer he's given."

To Bajoczky's relief, Nute was allowed to add that yes, the killer could have come up from the river, as long as he had a flashlight and used a pathway through the woods.

DAY EIGHT: WHERE THE KILLER STOOD

The next day brought a day-long tug-of-war with a yardstick. Bajoczky kept pushing the killer closer to the trailer, where the ground sloped lower; and, he argued, the gunman had to be taller than Peavy. Poitinger kept pulling the killer farther away.

The action took place up and down the porch rail of the mock-up of Harrison's mobile home that dominated the courtroom. With painstaking detail, Nute compared his charts and measurements to those of the state's witnesses. Projecting horizontal lines out from bullet holes marked on the mock-up's walls, the witnesses tried to pinpoint the spot in which the gunman had stood. All day, Nute traced a path from the mock-up's porch to a collection of charts, stretching and retracting his tape measure along the way.

A key factor in estimating where the gunman had stood was Champagne's testimony about lead vapors on Driggers's clothing, which meant the killer's gun muzzle had to have been within six feet of where she sat at the kitchen table.

Adding Champagne's lead vapors information to his trajectory computations, Nute placed the gun muzzle thirty-nine inches from the bullet hole in the trailer. He added another sixteen to eighteen inches for the gunman holding the gun. Rounding the distance to four feet from the trailer, Nute testified, the gun's muzzle would have been five feet, eight inches from the ground.

Considering that the killer would peer down the gun barrel to aim, Nute added, his eyes would also have been five feet, eight inches from the ground.

"In your opinion, could Mr. Peavy have fired the gun?" Bajoczky asked.

"Objection!" Poitinger jumped up. "That's an issue for the jury!"

Judge McClure ordered the lawyers to the bench. When Bajoczky resumed questioning, he rephrased his last question so that Nute was allowed to give his bottom-line opinion: According to his figures, Peavy's eyes were four inches too low to fit the gunman.

As soon as it was Poitinger's turn to ask the questions, he attacked Nute's credibility. Producing two thick editions of a book titled *Introduction to Criminalistics,* Poitinger asked Nute to find the chapters about trajectory.

The day before, during the battle over whether Nute could be certified as an expert witness, Nute had said that he was familiar with that book and that he had possibly gained some of his trajectory expertise through reading its chapters dealing with firearms or crime scenes.

With arms folded and a frown on his face, Poitinger paced the courtroom. The only sound was Nute flipping through the books' pages. Long minutes later, Nute said, "I don't find it."

Over at the mock-up porch, Poitinger tapped the Styrofoam wall with a pointer stick, indicating one of the key bullet holes, referred to as Hole One. Nute had depended on its location, along with the lead vapor and other information, in arriving at his conclusion.

"What evidence do you have there were lead vapors on Hole One?" Poitinger asked. Nute answered, "None."

"Aha!" Poitinger exclaimed, a smug aside revealing that Nute had made an assumption he couldn't prove: that Hole One, critical in Nute's calculations, had been made by a bullet fired at close range.

Defense attorney Harper shot up from his chair and said, "[I] object to the little noise the prosecutor made!"

Poitinger turned on his heels, looked at the defense attorneys, and said with irritation, "I guess I've picked up some bad habits."

Harper angrily replied, "You've got some bad habits and you didn't learn them from us!"

McClure again gathered the testy lawyers to the bench and sternly prohibited any more gratuitous remarks. The jurors grinned, relaxing during this break from the long, complicated, numbers-laden testimony.

DAY NINE: A PORTRAIT OF HARRISON

After another weekend break, Monday morning brought Bobby Harrison's two teenage children to the witness stand. "Dad" was one of the shooting victims, and "Uncle Johnny" was on trial for double murder. And Harrison's kids were witnesses for the defense.

Robert Lester Harrison, Jr., seventeen, and Kelly Harrison Phillips, nineteen, testified that their father and Peavy were good friends and drinking buddies—both before and after Harrison's divorce from Peavy's sister. Such testimony stabbed at the state's motive for the killings, which hinged on bad blood between the two men after the divorce.

And Harrison's children helped the defense plant seeds of reasonable doubt by testifying that their father had had enemies and had been acting paranoid the summer before his death. Several weeks before the killing, Harrison, Jr., told the jury, his father began crying, hugged him, and told him they would all be better off when he was dead. And the night before that fatal Halloween, he testified, his father broke their plans for spending a long weekend together. Never before, he testified, had his dad told him not to come over.

Phillips's testimony echoed her brother's. While she lived with her father during the summer of 1985, Phillips testified, he insisted that she keep a gun with her at all times. He told her to put a pistol on the seat of her car when she drove to work at Peavy & Son Construction and to carry a gun from room to room when she got home.

Names the children mentioned in their testimony suggested that their father was somehow entangled in drugs. Harrison, Jr., told the jury about a man named Bruce Evans who once lived with his father. Evans, a pipe fitter who lived fifty miles away in Perry, Florida, was the state's paid informant in Martha Munroe's cocaine trafficking trial. Evans had testified that he had run drugs cross-country for Munroe several times, in exchange for cocaine.

"I asked Dad about Bruce one day," Harrison, Jr., testified. "He snapped at me and said, 'I don't want to hear his name again. Bruce back-stabbed me.' And Dad said he was going to get him."

Phillips told about the time she arrived at her father's place to find Munroe talking to Harrison. It was about the beginning of August 1985, she said, while Munroe was awaiting her trial.

At her January 1986 trial, Munroe had testified that she had planned to call Bobby Harrison as a key witness and that he was killed the day her trial was originally set to begin. Serving an eighteen-year prison sentence, when Peavy came to trial, Munroe was listed as a possible witness in Peavy's case. She was transported from prison to a courthouse holding cell, but was never called to the stand.

On that August day, Phillips testified, her dad had tried to get her out of the house by telling her to feed the dogs and wash the clothes. She eavesdropped instead.

But the jury was not allowed to hear what Phillips overheard between Munroe and her father. Judge McClure agreed with the prosecutors that such testimony would amount to inadmissible hearsay.

So, instead of pursuing the exact words spoken, Bajoczky settled for attempting to establish Harrison and Munroe's state of mind. Phillips said that Munroe was "acting very nervous, talking real fast and messing with her hands."

"Was your father consoling her?" Bajoczky asked.

"Yes, sir," Phillips answered. "They were real sweet to each other. When she left, he told me that he'd do anything in the world—"

An objection from Guarisco halted her sentence. The jury was left wondering. After days of bullet holes and measurements, of a missing gun and supposed confessions, the testimony had come to an end.

DAY TEN: CLOSING ARGUMENTS

The defense rested without calling Peavy to the witness stand or offering an alibi for his whereabouts at the time of the killings. It was time for the lawyers to sum up their cases in closing arguments.

Bajoczky made an impassioned plea to free Peavy, whom he described as an innocent man wrongly accused.

"We can do wonders with science. But we cannot replace the spark of life or replace the freedom of a man who sat in jail for fifteen months for a crime he did not do," Bajoczky told the jury. "Please, free him to go home to his family."

In contrast, Poitinger urged the jury to "release Mr. Peavy to face the consequences of his actions." The prosecutor depicted Peavy as a cold-blooded killer who crept up to his ex-brother-in-law's window and blasted him with a semiautomatic pistol. Driggers, the sister of the well-known politician, the prosecutor said, "just happened to be in the wrong place at the wrong time."

"While this has not been the greatest case in the world, and it's certainly not a textbook case, the evidence points unerringly to John Peavy's guilt," Poitinger told the jury, reiterating what Peavy had told the bartender at the Shady Rest tavern.

But Bajoczky argued that, as a motive for a killing, bad blood between Peavy and Harrison was so shaky as to be an absence of motive. And Bajoczky wove into his defense the names of a number of his own suspects.

"I'm trying to tell you that Bobby Harrison had enemies aplenty and [that] John Peavy [was] not one of them," Bajoczky argued.

But Poitinger reminded the jury that the state did not have to prove a motive. He concentrated once again on the ballistics testimony and offered his bottom-line conclusion: that, out of forty-seven casings recovered from the Peavy family property on the Ochlockonee River, at Peavy & Son Construction, and at Peavy's home, all identified positively to Little Delacy's Tec 9 or John Peavy's Tec 9.

The nephew's gun, Poitinger reminded the jury, was eliminated as the murder weapon because it was locked in a police property room in South Florida at the time of the killings. Peavy's Tec 9 was still missing.

"There's no question what gun was used in the killing," Poitinger told the jury. "The gun in this case was John Peavy's Tec 9."

But Bajoczky argued that the prosecutors were "forcing the evidence to fit the crime." He dismissed the shell casings as inconclusive because no one could link the common casings to the bullets in the victims or say positively what gun shot them. Furthermore, Bajoczky said, the Tec 9 gun prosecutors said was the murder weapon would have been altered to remove the manufactured rifling.

It was time to end the talk from the lawyers and to find out what the jury thought.

Dozens of Peavy's family members and friends, who kept a daily vigil at the thirteen-day trial, camped in the courthouse hallways awaiting the jury's decision. Winnie Harrison, the mother of Bobby Harrison, kept her vigil, too, traveling to the trial each day from Whigham, Georgia. But she sat alone on the other side of the courtroom, directly behind the prosecutors' table.

She may have been outnumbered by the Peavys across the aisle, but she smiled and said, "Me and the good Lord make a majority. That's who I've had with me every day."

At 9:45 P.M. on March 27, 1987, after four-and-a-half hours of deliberations, came the knock on the door separating the courtroom from the room in which the jury was deliberating. That meant the jury had made up its collective mind. The bailiff ran to signal the judge and lawyers. Everyone assembled in the courtroom, thick with tension.

Eyes and mouths drooping, the jurors filed wearily into the courtroom. Row after row, the Peavy clan assembled, clenching their hands, hoping to bring Johnny home. Gloria, in the front row, tossed these words over the oak banister to Johnny, in custody on the other side: "I love you."

The jury foreman handed the verdict forms to the court clerk, who handed them to the judge. Across the aisle, State Attorney Willie Meggs was already smiling, even before an official word was spoken.

"Good news," he whispered. The veteran chief prosecutor had followed Judge Charles McClure's gaze to where he knew the guilty choice was printed on the verdict forms.

But the Peavys, confident in winning what they considered a flimsy case based on circumstantial evidence, weren't braced for what they were about to hear. The judge handed the verdicts back to the clerk. Before the court clerk could finish reading the list of verdicts against Johnny, gasps and sobs erupted from row after row of the assembled Peavy clan.

For two counts of first-degree murder for the killings of Bobby Harrison and Mary Lee Driggers, Peavy was found guilty. For shooting into a dwelling, he was found guilty. And, for use of a firearm in the commission of a felony, the jury found him guilty.

By the first guilty verdict, wails were rising from the Peavys. Johnny clenched his jaw, while Gloria screamed from the front row, "Oh, no!" and lowered her head to her hands in tears.

McClure banged his gavel for order as emotion-charged chaos erupted. Just as the judge was preparing to poll each juror for the record, someone cried, "Somebody, get an ambulance!"

Gloria's father had slumped in his seat, and relatives clustered around him to prop up his head, take off his glasses, and give him pills. Johnny, who knew CPR, tried to convince the bailiffs to let him help; but they made him remain seated at the defense table, their hands ready on their nightsticks. Peavy looked caged and scared. While waiting for a hospital stretcher to arrive, the judge ordered the grim-faced jurors to leave the courtroom. Retreating to the deliberation room, they waited in silence.

Still sobbing, Peavy's family and friends hugged one another and exchanged shocked, disbelieving reactions. Just an arm's length away at the defense table, Johnny turned to Gloria and said, "I'm all right. I'm all right."

PROCEDURAL DESCRIPTION

The trial usually begins with both the prosecution and the defense making opening statements. The prosecution then starts by questioning witnesses testifying on its behalf. This questioning is referred to as **direct examination.** If either side requests it, witnesses are sequestered. That means they are not allowed in the courtroom during proceedings, except when they are giving **testimony.** The deputy court clerk administers an oath or affirmation to each witness who takes the stand. The defense is allowed to cross-examine each witness after the prosecution has completed its direct examination of that witness. If the prosecution wants, it can resume questioning its own witness once the defense has finished. This questioning, called **redirect examination,** is usually limited to clarifying facts brought out in cross-examination. The defense is permitted to **recross-examine** the same witness on facts brought out in redirect examination. When the prosecution is through questioning witnesses and presenting evidence, it rests.

This is when the defense usually moves for a **judgment of acquittal,** arguing that the prosecution has failed to prove its case. If the motion is denied, the defense presents its case; and the roles of examiner and cross-examiner are now reversed.

Once the defense rests, the prosecution may present additional evidence to rebut the evidence presented by the defense. Rebuttal evidence is not usually new evidence establishing the defendant's guilt. Should new evidence come to light and the judge permit its use, the defense is entitled to conduct a rebuttal or rejoinder, presenting its own evidence in an attempt to overcome the new evidence. After rebuttal, the defense usually moves again for a judgment of acquittal. If the motion is denied, as is usually the case, both sides present closing arguments; and the judge instructs the jury on the law.

Opening Statements

Unlike closing arguments, opening statements are not argumentative. Their purpose is to preview the testimony of witnesses and the content of exhibits. Much like the pictures on the boxes of puzzles, they help organize what might appear to be jumbled bits and pieces of evidence.

Opening statements are important because jurors often make up their minds on the basis of such statements.[1] The law of primacy explains the consistency of first impressions and jury verdicts. Briefly stated, the law of primacy is the principle that ideas based on first impressions are often resistant to change, particularly if such ideas go unchallenged.

The opening statement begins with a declaration of the theory of the case. There are actually two theories of any case: experiential and legal.[2] An experiential theory is a narrative consisting of interconnected concrete events that occur in chronological order. Here is an example: Bob, a crafty good-for-nothing, decided to make some fast money by peddling as valuable antiques pieces of furniture recently built but made to look old; although John didn't know much about antiques, he thought they might be a good investment; John paid Bob $5,000 for what he thought was an antique.

In contrast, a legal theory is an abstraction consisting of a set of legal elements. For example, the crime of false pretenses is obtaining ownership of another's property by means of false representation with intent to defraud. The elements of this theory include (1) obtaining ownership, (2) property of another, (3) false representation, and (4) intent.

At trial, it is necessary to establish a legal theory by proving the elements of that theory. The problem is that witnesses cannot testify to a legal theory because its elements lack factual content. The narrative of Bob and John, for example, is one of countless experiential theories to which the elements of false pretenses might apply. What bridges the gap between experiential and legal theories are factual propositions. A factual proposition is an element of a legal theory restated in language to which witnesses can testify. For example, no one could testify to the abstraction of false representation in the case of Bob and John; but John could testify to the factual proposition that Bob told him that the furniture he bought was antique; and an expert could testify to the fact that the furniture John bought was not antique. The jurors, it is hoped, would conclude that the testimony presented by John and the expert establishes that Bob made a false representation.

While prosecutors try to prove legal theories, defense attorneys try to disprove them. For example, if Bob were charged with false pretenses, his attorney might try to prove that Bob had no intent to defraud John. While the prosecution must try to prove all of the elements of its legal theory, the defense may have to prove only that element of its theory that disputes an element in the prosecution's theory. During opening statements and closing arguments, attorneys explicitly tell jurors the conclusions they should draw from the factual propositions.

Delivery techniques are important, particularly during opening statements. Attorneys strive to make good first impressions. To do so, they must appear to be in control. That is why they usually position themselves directly in front of the jury, where they can maintain eye contact with each juror and where are close enough to be heard and seen, but not so close as to make the jurors uncomfortable. It is better for attorneys not to use notes when making opening statements, but charts and diagrams can be effective visual aids if the judge permits their use. During opening statements, attorneys usually try to personalize their clients by referring to them by name. Opponents are referred to in depersonalized terms such as "the defendant" or "the state." It is important to avoid overly technical legal terms during opening statements. Terms such as "prima facie" and "**case in chief**" tend to undermine effective communication with the jury.

Certain comments are improper during opening statements. For example, prosecutors cannot comment on the failure of a defendant to take the stand.[3] They also cannot attack a defendant's character.[4] Furthermore, it is unethical for either side to talk about evidence during opening statements unless such evidence is relevant and likely to be admitted later during direct examination.[5]

The defense usually opens immediately after the state makes its opening statement at the outset of the trial. The principal advantage to opening then is the benefit of primacy. There are tactical advantages, however, for the defense to reserve its opening statement until after the state rests. Instead of having to anticipate what the state might say, the defense can fashion its opening statement to fit the evidence actually presented. Also, if the prosecution does not know the defense's case because of limited discovery, and the defense has a strong case, it may be to the defense's advantage to reserve its opening statement.

If the defense does open immediately after the state, it may commit itself to a particular theory or specific evidence (see Excerpt 9). It may also opt to make a noncommittal opening statement. In such an opening, the defense usually reminds jurors that the state has the burden of proof, that there are two sides to every case, and that jurors should keep an open mind until all the evidence is presented. The defense might pursue this tactic if it is not presenting any evidence or if it wants to keep its case a secret until after the state rests.

EXCERPT 9

THE COURT: Mr. Bajoczky [a defense attorney].

MR. BAJOCZKY: Your Honor, if it please the Court.
Ladies and gentlemen of the jury, again this is going to be an opportunity for me to speak with you like Mr. Guarisco [a prosecuting attorney] did, and give you a brief outline of what I believe the evidence that Mr. Guarisco has in this case is going to show and what it is not going to show, and what I think our evidence is going to show when we present our case. . . .
[Continuing, Mr. Bajoczky affirmed that a crime had been committed:]
Yes, there was a crime there because two people got murdered; and there is no doubt about that.
One element of the crime that we deny wholeheartedly, absolutely, and vigorously is that John Peavy had anything to do with the death of Bobby Harrison or Mary Lee Driggers. . . .
[Mr. Bajoczky explained how evidence to be presented would prove Peavy's innocence:]
We reconstructed the scene [of the murder], and Dale Nute [a forensic expert] will tell you that it is absolutely impossible for anybody under six-foot-two to have shot those shots into the window. You had to be six-foot-two because the bullets [fired into the trailer] go level.
I'm big enough to stand up and aim in the window level, but anyone under six-foot-two is going to either have to have a crate or a box to stand on; and there was never any crate or box found. Or, if they shot and they were less than six feet [in height], they were going to have to shoot up; and the bullets would go up. . . .
[Mr. Bajoczky concluded by stating Peavy's innocence in simple, non-technical terms:]
John Peavy is about five-foot-seven with his shoes on. He's not just too short; he's way too short to have fired the bullets that killed Mary Lee Driggers and Bobby Harrison.

Attorneys must decide whether to volunteer weaknesses in their cases. It is probably a good idea to do so if the other side knows about the weakness; such candor will soften its impact on the jury.

Direct Examination

After opening statements, witnesses are called individually to give testimony. The deputy court clerk administers an oath or affirmation before each takes the stand: "Do you solemnly swear (or affirm) that the evidence you shall give in this issue between the State and this defendant shall be the truth, the whole truth, and nothing but the truth, so help you God?" If the witness opts to affirm, "so help you God" is omitted. Witnesses are then examined by the side on whose behalf they are called. The witnesses for the state begin first.
There are several types of witnesses. The most common are **occur-**

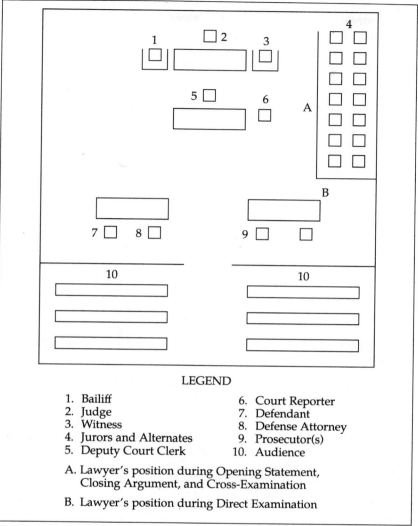

LEGEND

1. Bailiff
2. Judge
3. Witness
4. Jurors and Alternates
5. Deputy Court Clerk
6. Court Reporter
7. Defendant
8. Defense Attorney
9. Prosecutor(s)
10. Audience

A. Lawyer's position during Opening Statement, Closing Argument, and Cross-Examination

B. Lawyer's position during Direct Examination

Figure 5-5 Diagram showing the courtroom positions of participants in the trial of John Wesley Peavy.

rence witnesses, who saw, heard, or did something related to the case.[6] For identification purposes, direct examination usually begins with the attorney asking the witness's name and address. The questioner next asks the witness for a description of the scene and people he or she witnessed. The bulk of the direct examination focuses on the occurrence. In a series of questions, the attorney asks the witness to describe in detail what happened (see Excerpt 10). During questioning, the attorney usually occupies a position so as to minimize eye contact with the jury (see Figure 5-5). All eyes should be on the occurrence witnesses as they occupy center stage.

EXCERPT 10

BY MR. GUARISCO [a prosecutor]:

Q: Would you please state your name, sir?

A: Samuel L. Castle.

Q: And where do you reside?

A: Shady Rest.

Q: OK. Are you the owner of the Shady Rest?

A: Yes, sir.

Q: And what type of an establishment is the Shady Rest?

A: Beer, wine, pool tables, dancing.

Q: OK. Did you own the Shady Rest back on Thursday, October 31, 1985?

A: Yes, sir. . . .

[Mr. Guarisco asked Mr. Castle to describe what occurred on October 31, 1985:]

Q: And what time did you open for business that day?

A: About four-thirty or five.

Q: And when you opened up for business that day, do you recall basically who was there when you opened up?

A: Herman Mills and his group was mostly there.

Q: Now, did you also see anyone else besides the group that was there earlier?

A: Bobby, Mary Lee.

Q: Bobby Harrison?

A: Yes, sir.

Q: And do you know where they were when you saw them?

A: They came out front.

Q: And on that date did you have occasion to see John Wesley Peavy?

A: Yes, sir.

Q: In the morning or evening?

A: Evening.

Q: Do you see Mr. Peavy in the courtroom today, sir?

A: Yes, sir.

Q: And would you please point him out?

(The witness indicated Peavy.)

Q: And please describe what he's wearing.

A: That day?

Q: No, what he has on today.

A: He's got on a light suit.

MR. GUARISCO: OK, would the record reflect that [the] witness has pointed to the defendant?

THE COURT: The record will so reflect.

BY MR. GUARISCO:

Q: Now, after you saw the defendant, John Peavy, where did he go when he came in?

A: He went in the back room.

Q: OK. And did you go back there and see what he was doing?

A: No, sir.

Q: All right. About how long did he stay in the back room?

A: Somewhere between five and ten minutes.

Q: OK. And what happened after that? Did he come out, or . . .

A: He came out.

Q: And what did he do when he came out of the back?

A: I got him a beer.

Q: He ordered a beer?

A: Yes, sir.

Q: OK. Did Mr. Peavy say anything to you at that time?

A: Yes, sir, he did.

Q: What did he say?

A: He said, "What has Bobby got on me that they won't play with me?"

Q: OK. And what else did he say?

A: And then he said, "Bobby is my ex-brother-in-law and lost my sister's house."

Q: OK. Did he elaborate on that?

A: No, sir.

Q: Now, based on that statement he made to you and your observations of him, how did he appear?

A: Well, he was upset because they wouldn't play with him.

With certain exceptions, attorneys must be careful not to ask **leading questions** during direct examination. A leading question is one which suggests the desired answer. It is permissible for an attorney to lead when the witness has difficulty understanding the questions or is adverse or hostile.

An **adverse witness** is one presumed to favor the opposition and one whose testimony could be harmful. The only way an attorney can exert control over such a witness is to act as if he or she were cross-examining the witness and to ask leading questions.

A **hostile witness** is one who unexpectedly exhibits hostility toward the questioning attorney. Such a sudden turnabout also justifies the attorney examining this witness as if on cross-examination. First, though, it is necessary to have the court declare the witness hostile before the attorney is permitted to ask leading questions.

Witnesses ordinarily cannot express their opinions or draw conclusions. The rules of evidence prohibit them from doing this. An exception is the **expert witness.** Experts such as a medical examiner or a forensic specialist are allowed to give opinions and draw conclusions because they have extensive knowledge of subjects that might assist jurors in reaching their verdict (see Excerpt 11).

EXCERPT 11

BY MR. GUARISCO [a prosecutor]:

Q: Based on the autopsy you performed on Mary Lee Driggers, within the bounds of reasonable medical certainty, have you formed an expert opinion on the cause of death of Mary Lee Driggers?

A: [Dr. Woodward Burgert, Jr., medical examiner] Yes. Three fatal gunshot wounds.

Experts who do not have firsthand experience with the facts in a particular case may be asked to testify to hypotheticals. In this case, the attorney will supply the pertinent facts during direct examination. Asking the expert to assume these facts are true, the attorney then will invite him or her to express an opinion.[7]

Although attorneys may stipulate to expert witnesses' qualifications, it is customary to qualify such witnesses. Qualification entails asking the witnesses about such matters as their education, licenses, professional experience, membership in professional organizations, and nature of expertise (see Excerpt 12).

129
Procedural
Description

EXCERPT 12

BY MR. GUARISCO [a prosecutor]:

Q: Sir, would you please state your name for the record?

A: Yes, sir. My name is Woodward Burgert, Jr., M.D., associate medical examiner.

Q: Are you licensed to practice in the state of Florida?

A: Yes, I am, since 1971.

Q: Would you please, Doctor, outline your educational background and medical training.

A: Yes. After graduating from college, I spent four years at Cornell Medical School in New York City, followed by a year of internship in medicine and pathology at Bellevue Hospital, also in New York City.
    I was drafted, and spent a couple of years in the paratroopers in Okinawa and Vietnam.
    I returned to New York City to New York Hospital as a resident in anatomic pathology, which is the type of pathology that allows you to examine whole bodies and pieces of bodies, and biopsies, for the diagnoses of medical disease.
    From 1968 until 1970 I spent two years in laboratory medicine, which is that branch of pathology which deals with diagnosis by the use of chemicals and toxicology studies, and that sort of thing.
    From 1970 until 1971 I was back in New York City, and spent a year as a fellow in chemistry pathology.
    From 1971 until this time I have been in the practice of pathology here.
    I was given my specialty boards in anatomic and chemical pathology. . . .

[Mr. Guarisco then asked the witness about additional expert qualifications:]

Q: Do you belong to any type of professional organization, sir?

A: Yes, I do. I belong to the local medical society, the Capital Medical Society, and the Florida Medical Society, and the Florida Pathology Society, and the International Academy of Pathology, and the American Medical Association, and the American Association of Blood Banks, and the College of American Pathology, and the American Society of Clinical Pathology, and the American Society of Psychology.

Q: And your specialty, again, is . . . ?

A: Pathology.

Q: And are you certified in pathology?

A: Yes, since 1970.

Q: Are you presently associated with the medical examiner's staff?

A: Yes, I am; I'm an associate medical examiner. . . .

[Mr. Bajoczky acknowledged Dr. Burgert's qualifications:]

MR. BAJOCZKY [a defense attorney]: Your Honor, we would stipulate to Dr. Burgert being an expert.

If defendants choose, they may be sworn as witnesses in their own behalf. The prosecution cannot comment on their silence should they decide not to testify.

Attorneys make a distinction between direct and indirect evidence. **Direct evidence** is testimonial evidence from a witness who actually saw or heard something. It is based on personal observation and directly proves a fact. Indirect or **circumstantial evidence** is testimonial evidence based on facts from which jurors can make inferences about other facts. In this situation, the proof is indirect. For example, jurors might infer that the defendant, Jane Doe, had been outside in the rain if witnesses testified that they saw her indoors wearing wet shoes. The witnesses did not actually see the defendant outside in the rain, but they might infer that she had been outside in the rain.

Testimony is an important type of evidence. So are **exhibits.** Broadly speaking, exhibits include any type of tangible evidence that can be offered to the court for inspection.

The procedure for getting an exhibit admitted as evidence includes a number of specific steps:

- Have the deputy court clerk mark the exhibit;

- Show the exhibit to the opposing counsel;

- Ask the court leave to approach the witness;

- Ask the witness to examine the exhibit;

- Lay the foundation for the exhibit;

- Move for admission of the exhibit into evidence;

- Ask for permission to show the jurors the exhibit;

- Show the jurors the exhibit.

Attorneys frequently ask to publish the exhibit. To publish is to show the exhibit publicly.

Laying the foundation is authenticating the exhibit. Counsel must show that the exhibit is what it purports to be. This is accomplished through the recitation of certain formulaic phrases (see Excerpt 13).

BY MR. POITINGER [a prosecutor]:

Q: I am going to show you what has previously been marked as State's Exhibits Forty-two through Fifty-three [bullet casings], and I ask if you recognize those?

A: [Deputy Sheriff William Gunter] Yes, sir.

Q: And when they were collected, what happened to them, sir?

A: They were collected and placed in a paper bag and sealed and transported to the Department of Law Enforcement Crime Laboratory.

Q: And you indicated that you either collected them or they were collected under your supervision?

A: That's correct.

Q: You were present when they were collected?

A: Yes, sir.

Q: And you have looked at the casings?

A: Yes, sir.

Q: And is there any indication from your examination that those casings . . . have been in any manner substantially altered?

A: No, sir.

Q: Modified?

A: No, sir.

Q: You indicated that they were nine millimeter casings. How were you able to determine that?

A: It says on the face of the casing: "nine millimeter."

Q: Does it give any other information, other than nine millimeter?

A: It says, "nine millimeter Luger" and "CCI."

Q: So . . . the writings on them would indicate that they are nine millimeter Luger CCI; is that correct?

A: Yes, sir.

Q: Are you familiar with ammunition and handguns?

A: Yes, sir.

Q: Are you a hunter?

A: Yes, sir.

Q: What does "CCI" stand for?

A: It is a name brand of ammunition.

Q: And "nine millimeter" designates what?

A: The caliber.

Q: And what does "Luger" mean?

A: It's a type of round determined by Luger.

Q: Nine millimeter?

A: Yes, sir.

MR. POITINGER: Your Honor, at this time, the State would move Exhibits Forty-two to Fifty-three into evidence.

Attorneys are confronted with three problems in direct examination.[8] First, they must follow certain rules, such as those governing the admission of evidence. If they do not, they may not be able to present the evidence they need to win. Second, they must be effective in their presentation. If they are not, it does not matter what evidence they present. Third, they must preserve an effective record by making timely and appropriate objections. If they do not, errors in rulings on evidence and other matters go uncorrected.

In presenting a case, attorneys must follow certain rules of evidence. When they jump up and object to testimony as irrelevant, immaterial, or incompetent, they are questioning the admissibility of the evidence their opponent is trying to introduce. The court, applying the rules of evidence, decides whether or not to sustain the objection. It is the jury's duty to weigh the admissible evidence once the trial is completed.

Cross-Examination

While witnesses command the jury's attention during direct examination, attorneys occupy center stage during cross-examination. There, they usually ask short questions or make statements to which they invite witnesses to respond. Attorneys are permitted to ask leading questions during cross-examination. Although their questions should not go beyond the subject matter of the direct examination, judges often allow inquiry into additional matters.[9] The proverbial slip of the tongue by a witness during direct examination also can open the door for the cross-examiner to explore otherwise inadmissible topics.

Attorneys do more than merely ask questions during cross-examination. They perform before the jury. They project self-confidence. They feign ignorance or incredulity. When their witness unexpectedly says something bad, they assume a poker face, giving the jury the impression that their case has suffered no damage.

Cross-examination has two purposes: to elicit favorable testimony from witnesses and to discredit witnesses and their testimony. Obviously, it is to the cross-examiner's advantage to get witnesses to admit facts that are consistent with the cross-examiner's theory of the case (see Excerpt 14). This is not always as difficult as it appears because seldom is the direct examination entirely damaging. A resourceful cross-examiner can get witnesses to repeat favorable testimony.

EXCERPT 14

BY MR. BAJOCZKY [a defense attorney]:

Q: All right. Now the next thing, Johnny [Peavy] comes out of the back room. How long was he back there?

A: [Samuel Castle, witness for the prosecution] Somewhere between five and ten minutes.

Q: All right. Now these people who are back there, they've been playing cards or shooting [craps] or drinking beer—it's nine o'clock at night. They've been in there since ten, ten-thirty in the morning, haven't they?

A: Yes, sir.

Q: They've been shooting, [playing] cards, and drinking for almost twelve hours, haven't they?

A: Close.

Q: OK. Now, during this time when Johnny [came] back out, what did he do when he came out?

A: I got him a beer.

Q: OK. Did he come out kind of storming and weaving back and forth like he was mad?

A: No, sir.

Q: Did he come out huffing and puffing or [showing] any facial expressions that would indicate that he was mad or angry?

A: No, sir.

Q: Did Johnny act . . . anything other than normal?

A: Normal, all except he said they wouldn't play with him.

Q: All right. Now let's go into that. He came out and he told you—what did he say? What's his verbatim quote?

A: "What's Bobby got on me that they won't play with me?"

Q: All right. Now, did he say it real nasty?

A: No.

Q: Just kind of, you know, "[I] wonder what I did to him"; or "I wonder what he's got that they don't want to play with me"?

A: Something like that.

Q: All right. Did you think that Johnny was ready to fist-fight anybody?

A: No.

Q: Did he scream when he said it?

A: No, sir.

Q: At any time you talked to Johnny, did he ever cuss Bobby or say anything nasty about Bobby?

A: No, sir. . . .

[Mr. Bajoczky asked Mr. Castle to recall any other comments Peavy might have made:]

Q: Did he ever make any kind of comment like, "I'm going to fix him," or "I'm going to get them," or "I'm going to show them"? Did he ever make any comment like that?

A: No, sir. . . .

[Mr. Bajoczky questioned Mr. Castle further about Peavy's attitude and actions:]

Q: Is there anything that he did on Halloween night that would make you think he left there [the Shady Rest] with a grudge or vendetta against Bobby?

A: No, sir.

Q: Or vendetta or grudge against Mary Lee Driggers?

A: No, sir.

Q: Did it seem like Johnny was pretty normal in every way that night?

A: Yes, sir.

There are a variety of ways to discredit testimony. One is to question the competence of the witness:

- A hearing-impaired witness claims to have overheard a conversation, but experiences difficulty hearing the cross-examiner's questions;

- A witness says he had ample opportunity to observe an event, but he finds it hard to remember details when asked about the event months later;

- A victim of a violent crime identifies the defendant, but admits under cross-examination that it was not easy to see on the night of the crime because of poor lighting.

Lay witnesses are not the only ones to have their competence questioned. Attorneys may also attempt to undermine the testimony of experts by challenging their competence (see Excerpt 15).

EXCERPT 15

BY MR. POITINGER [a prosecutor]:

Q: Did I not ask you yesterday, after I read the list of books, which book you referred to in doing your trajectory work, and [according to] my recollection, . . . your answer was O'Hara and Ostenberg's *Introduction to Criminalistics?*

A: [Dale Nute, forensic expert for the defense] I said I thought that book would have it [the trajectory information] in it. I did not say any specific book [had] it [the information] in it because I don't remember any specific book.

Q: Did you not tell the jury that book contained at least one chapter on firearms and that, if it did, it [the chapter] probably contained information on trajectory?

A: That was what I thought, yes, sir.

Q: But it doesn't contain any chapter on firearms, does it, sir?

A: It's got some chapters on. . . .

Q: Does it contain any chapters on firearms, sir?

MR. HARPER: Your Honor, I object to counsel badgering the witness. The witness was in the middle of answering.

MR. POITINGER: Your Honor, I think it's. . . .

THE COURT: Objection overruled.

MR. POITINGER: If anyone can recognize badgering. . . .

THE COURT: Objection overruled.

BY MR. POITINGER:

Q: Answer my question, Mr. Nute.

A: There is no specific complete chapter on firearms.

Q: Thank you, sir.

Another way to discredit testimony is to attack the credibility of witnesses by showing that they previously said something inconsistent with their testimony. The earlier statement could have been made for a deposition. Impeachment procedure requires that the cross-examiner read the prior statement and allow the witness to admit making it. The cross-examiner should present the witness's different statements to the jury so that the contrast is readily apparent.

The cross-examiner may attack the credibility of witnesses by asking about their previous criminal convictions (see Excerpt 16). The procedure is to ask the witness if he or she has ever been convicted of a felony and, if so, how many times. The cross-examiner may not inquire about arrests or accusations that did not result in felony convictions.[10]

EXCERPT 16

BY MR. BAJOCZKY [a defense attorney]:

Q: Excuse me, sir. You still cheat at cards anytime you play, don't you?

A: [Tommy Johnson, cellmate of Peavy] Well, I haven't played since—in quite a while.

Q: You are still cheating when you do play, don't you, sir?

A: If I get the chance.

Q: All right. That is a bit more of an indication of the kind of person you really are, isn't it?

A: No, it's not what I am. That is what I'm adapted to. When you are living with wolves, you have to live like a wolf.

Q: You have been convicted of stealing and dishonesty offenses before?

A: No, no more than just stealing.

Q: No more than just stealing. Stealing is a crime that involves honesty or integrity, doesn't it?

A: No. I was under the influence of drugs when I stole.

Q: OK. So, not only are you a thief and a card cheat and a five-time convicted felon, but then you are also a drug addict?

A: Yes, sir, I am a drug addict.

Q: What kind of drugs were you addicted to?

A: Cocaine.

Finally, the cross-examiner may attack a witness's credibility by showing that he or she had a stake in the outcome of the trial or was biased toward one side or the other. An appellate court held that a romantic interest between a prosecution witness and an investigating officer was a proper area of cross-examination.[11] So, in another trial, was the fact that a defendant owed a witness money.[12]

Objections and Motions

If the prosecution leads a witness during direct examination, the defense may object, arguing that the state is leading the witness. The judge responds by either sustaining or overruling the objection. The objection is to the form of the question, which can usually be rectified if the attorney rephrases the question (see Excerpt 17). Other objections to form are that the question is argumentative, that it assumes facts not in evidence, or that it calls for a conclusion. A question is argumentative when it states a conclusion and invites the witness to argue about it. Assuming facts not in evidence occurs frequently in connection with hypothetical questions. A fact not in evidence (or even in dispute) is simply assumed in the question. And a question calls for a conclusion when it asks the witness to deduce a conclusion from the facts. As a rule, witnesses testify to facts. With the exception of expert witnesses, only jurors are permitted to draw conclusions.

EXCERPT 17

BY MR. POITINGER [a prosecutor]:

Q: Mr. Johnson, I'm going to show you what has been marked as State's Exhibit Number Eighteen [a complaint/arrest affidavit]. This is a charge that was not prosecuted against you.

THE COURT: Is that Defense or State?

BY MR. POITINGER:

Q: Defense Exhibit, I believe. Do you remember that incident?

A: [Tommy Johnson, Peavy's cellmate] Yes, I do.

Q: What did that offense involve, sir?

A: I got my arm stuck in a commode.

Q: Excuse me. I don't think we all heard you.

A: I got my arm stuck in a commode.

Q: How did you happen to get your arm stuck in a commode?

A: Oh, well, I was trying to unclog the commode that night. It had a big wad of paper in it and I stuck my hand down in it . . . I had recently had pins took out of my hand, and I tried to come [out] with it, and my arm wouldn't come out. So they had to take the commode off, take it to the fire station, solder it, torch it off, and get my arm out.

Q: So, what it was is you got your hand stuck in a toilet, and they had to get the fire department to cut it off of you, and then they charged you with it for having to cut it off your hand. Is that right?

A: Right.

Q: And what is the reason indicated as to why that crime was not prosecuted? What does it say by the signature of Jack Poitinger?

A: It says, "No information will be filed in the above-styled cause; no evidence of criminal intent."

Q: "No evidence of criminal intent." Did you intend to destroy that toilet, sir?

A: No, I did not.

Q: You just got your hand stuck, and the fire department—

MR. BAJOCZKY [a defense attorney]: Object, Your Honor, to leading question.

THE COURT: Sustained.

An objection can also involve the substance of a question. If the judge sustains the objection, the testimony will be excluded unless the questioner can persuade the court to change its ruling by making an offer of proof. An **offer of proof** is a statement of what the witness would say if allowed to testify. Some of the most common objections are that the question calls for an immaterial answer, that the question calls for an irrelevant answer, that the question calls for a hearsay answer, or that the question is speculative. If evidence does not relate directly and significantly to the matter at issue, it is immaterial. If the evidence is not **probative,** it is irrelevant. Hearsay is the statement of a witness testifying to an out-of-court statement made by another person. Generally, such secondhand testimony is not admissible. A question that requires a witness to speculate about what would have happened in a given situation is considered improper (see Excerpt 18).

EXCERPT 18

BY MR. POITINGER [a prosecutor]:

Q: OK. And was anyone else present at the time, sir, when he made these statements [alleged confession made by Peavy while in jail]?

A: [Tommy Johnson, cellmate of Peavy] No, not when he made those statements; no, there was no one else present.

Q: And do you remember about what month, year, these statements would have been made to you in, approximately?

A: They were made in December because they moved me out of the cell in December, from 2-E to 2-F, of '85.

Q: Were you specifically asking Mr. Peavy to tell you about this, sir?

A: No, sir, I wasn't.

Q: From your conversation with him, did you get the impression that he wanted to tell you about this?

MR. BAJOCZKY [a defense attorney]: Object, Your Honor. Speculation.

THE COURT: Sustained.

The procedure for objecting is to say "objection" and then state the grounds on which the objection is based. Objections should be timely. If the judge sustains an objection to testimony already given, the questioner should move to strike that testimony. If it is not stricken, the jurors may consider it in their deliberations. If the judge overrules the objection, the questioner may appeal later if it is thought that the judge's ruling was improper. If the adversary is asking a series of questions, it is appropriate to request a "continuing objection" rather than to object to every question. A continuing objection preserves the objection for appeal. If an objection to a question is sustained, the attorney trying to pose the question may ask for clarification. Some objections can be met by simply rephrasing questions.

Objections occur mostly during direct examinations and cross-examinations. Although it is permissible to raise them during opening statements and closing arguments, attorneys rarely do, because interrupting an opponent's speech is always risky. Objecting attorneys, particularly if their objections are not sustained, are likely to appear discourteous.

Attorneys use motions at trial to achieve substantive goals and to preserve the record for appeal. Three of the most common motions are for judgment of acquittal, the **motion to strike,** and the motion for **mistrial.** If the defense claims insufficiency of evidence, it may move for a judgment of acquittal after the state has presented its evidence or after all the evidence in the case has been presented (see Excerpt 19). The defense must set forth the specific grounds for its claim. Failure to make a motion in a timely fashion may cause the motion to be denied when later appealed. If the judge opines that the evidence is legally insufficient to warrant a conviction by the jury, he may enter a judgment of acquittal.

EXCERPT 19

THE COURT: What says the Defense?

MR. HARPER: Your Honor, we are prepared to announce rest. And we would, at this point, ask the Court to reconsider the motion for judgment of acquittal made at the conclusion of the case in chief by the State, renewed at this time on the grounds previously stated, as well as the additional grounds of the evidence, as a whole at this point and this stage of the proceedings, fairly viewed even in the light most favorable to the State, does not establish a prima facie case of guilt, and justifies the Court entering a judgment of acquittal at this time.

THE COURT: What says the State?

MR. GUARISCO: Judge, in response to that, I think there is sufficient evidence to go to the jury; and it's up to the jury to decide as to the credibility of the witnesses that have been put on. We have put on a prima facie case to go to the jury; and it's up to them to decide on the credibility of [the] witnesses.

THE COURT: Anything further, Mr. Harper?

MR. HARPER: No, sir, not on that point.

THE COURT: It appears from hearing the evidence and having previously ruled on sufficiency or prima facie sufficiency, I still feel that it's a case for the jury to decide, as the finders of facts. So I will deny your motion for judgment of acquittal.

Once inadmissible testimony has been given, it can only be eliminated if the attorney moves to strike it and the judge instructs the jury not to consider the offensive testimony. Usually, the objection is made *after* the question has been asked but *before* the inadmissible testimony is given. If the witness answers before the objection is made, the attorney may move to strike.

If inadmissible evidence is so prejudicial that its impact cannot be lessened by the judge's instruction, the defense may move for mistrial (see Excerpt 20). Inadmissible evidence is prejudicial if its introduction denies the defendant a fair trial because the jury is unable to reach a verdict on the merits of the case. It is also improper for the prosecutor to comment on the defendant's bad character. Witnesses are permitted to testify to the truthfulness of the defendant, but only if the defendant has testified. Other grounds for mistrial include, warning the jury of future misconduct should the defendant be acquitted, playing on the jury's sympathy for the victim, commenting on the defendant's silence, and finding that the jury is unable to reach a verdict.

EXCERPT 20

BY MR. POITINGER [a prosecutor]:

Q: In your experience, sir, in jail, is it unusual for people to talk about their crimes to fellow inmates?

MR. BAJOCZKY [a defense attorney]: Objection, Your Honor.

THE WITNESS [Tommy Johnson, cellmate of Peavy]: No, it's not unusual.

MR. HARPER [a defense attorney]: Objection. I would ask the Court to please instruct the witness when counsel makes an objection to quit answering and trying to bolster the State's case.

MR. POITINGER: Your Honor, if we can—

THE COURT: Wait just a minute.

MR. POITINGER: May we approach the bench for just a minute, sir?

THE COURT: All right. Approach the bench.

(Whereupon, the following discussion was held at the bench:)

THE COURT: What I want you to do, if you object, [is] just one of you stand up and object.

MR. BAJOCZKY: We will try, Judge. But when we hear him keep talking, I don't know if Mr. Harper is going to make it.

MR. POITINGER: One of the things I would like this Court to do—as I understand it, both the State and Defense have a right to a fair and impartial trial and all of these gratuitous remarks like "bolstering the State's case"—I'm inclined to move for a mistrial on the basis of all these—

MR. BAJOCZKY: Let him move.

THE COURT: Motion denied.

Closing Arguments

In closing arguments, the side that goes first often goes last, too, as the first side to speak is allowed to rebut the other side. In Florida, for example, the speaking order of the closing arguments depends on whom the defense calls to testify during direct examination.[13] If the defense presents evidence or questions witnesses other than defendant, the prosecution speaks first and last. Otherwise, the defense speaks first and last.

Closing argument begins with an introduction. Attorneys thank the jurors for their attention and set the mood for the remainder of the argument (see Excerpt 21).

EXCERPT 21

MR. GUARISCO [a prosecutor]: If it please the Court.
Ladies and gentlemen, Mr. Poitinger and I, of course, would like to take this opportunity to thank you for serving on this jury, for your patience, and for listening closely and taking notes.
This has been a very long trial. It's been a very complex trial. And you have made sacrifices to serve on this jury. And we realize that, and we really appreciate it. You have performed the greatest duty that a citizen can perform here in these weeks we've been in trial.

As the judge has mentioned, arguments are not evidence. We are going to explain; we are going to summarize the facts and our theories of the case.

You have listened to the testimony; you have listened to the witnesses; you have made your observations. And whenever in doubt, please trust your recollection.

We have been busy trying this case. Sometimes, things slip up on us. I want to remind you, please, don't go outside the testimony and evidence that has been presented here. Don't speculate.

The body of the closing argument consists of a summation in which the attorney marshals evidence and draws conclusions. Here, attorneys use analogies, rhetorical questions, and exhibits to argue their theories of the case. Although in many states the judge does not instruct the jury on the law until after the lawyers have completed their closing arguments, in states in which this practice is observed, the judge and lawyers customarily discuss the contents of the instructions before closing arguments. The attorney who weaves elements of the judge's instructions into a closing argument increases the argument's impact (see Excerpt 22).

EXCERPT 22

MR. BAJOCZKY [a defense attorney]: Now, the judge will tell you, ladies and gentlemen, that the defendant is not required to prove anything. So the fact that we bring Dale Nute up here, and we bring Kelly Harrison Phillips, and we bring Bob Harrison [Jr.], yeah, we are trying to show to you and to prove to you, scientifically [that John Peavy is innocent]. Lieutenant Gunter couldn't prove anything scientifically to tie John Peavy in this case.

Don Champagne could prove nothing, scientifically, to tie John Peavy in this case.

I am trying to prove scientifically to you that John Peavy could not have committed these killings, period. It is impossible.

Now, if I fall short in proving it is impossible, that's nothing to upset you. I don't have to prove anything.

But, ladies and gentlemen, we didn't fall short. There is no proof beyond a reasonable doubt in this case.

Although, during closing arguments, it might seem folly to tell the jury about a case's shortcomings, volunteering weaknesses can minimize their negative effect by deflating the opposition's argument and gaining the speaking attorney the respect of the jury. Because the verdict depends on the credibility of witnesses, attorneys support the credibility of their witnesses while attacking the credibility of their opponent's witnesses during their closing arguments (see Excerpt 23).

EXCERPT 23

MR. BAJOCZKY [a defense attorney]: Dale Nute [forensic expert for the defense] stood up here for half a day, under intense cross-examination by Jack Poitinger to impeach his credibility.

And I ask, when you get in the back—we've got the original chart by

Dale Nute—look on Dale Nute's chart and show us one correction, one correction to that chart, that was put on there by Mr. Guarisco or Mr. Poitinger or their witnesses. Show me one correction. He [Poitinger] spends all day haggling Dale Nute about a book: "Well, did you have *Criminalistics, Introduction to Criminalistics* Number [edition] One or Number [edition] Two?

"And what was the copyright date on that book?"

"And what are the chapters in it?"

And Dale Nute tried to answer truthfully: "I think there is a chapter in *Criminalistics* about firearms, and trajectory would be in there. I've got fifteen years' worth of magazines. I've got a lot of other books."

They didn't ask him about the other books. We did. We had Dale Nute bring in his other books on trajectory, and his magazines and his articles.

All day long, they haggled Dale Nute about his book, about why he left the Florida Department of Law Enforcement, trying to embarrass that man or humiliate that man or put that man down in front of you, over things that have nothing to do with his profession or expertise.

They didn't attack his drawings for holes being wrong and offset. They didn't attack his window for being one foot when it was a three-foot window; they didn't attack the rail for being two inches off, when it was not in the right place. They never, ever attacked Dale Nute's chart.

The conclusion affords attorneys a chance to tell the jury forcefully what verdict it should return. When the opposition has the last word, the other side may tell the jurors that this is its last opportunity to speak to them. It may invite them to anticipate points the opposition is likely to raise in its rebuttal.

As in opening statements, delivery can play an important part in closing arguments. Attorneys position themselves in front of the jury so as to maximize eye contact with each juror. Summation is given at a comfortable distance. A rule of thumb is that closing argument should be no longer than ten minutes a side for every day that evidence was presented at trial.[14]

Jury Instructions and the Verdict

The judge usually instructs the jury after both sides have given their closing arguments. The purpose of jury instructions is to inform jurors of the law applicable to the case at hand. Instructing jurors often is referred to as charging the jury.

In many jurisdictions, judges use standardized instructions in charging the jury. It is not required that they recite them word-for-word, but if they depart from the instructions substantially, they must state why on the record or in a separate order. Attorneys may recommend changes in the instructions by submitting their requests in writing, usually before closing arguments are made. If the judge fails to give the recommended instructions, the attorneys may object, out of the presence of the jury.

Grounds for objecting to instructions might state that the instructions:

- Are vague, ambiguous, and confusing;

- Are incorrect statement of the law;

- Are argumentative;

- Are not supported by evidence;

- Invade the province of the jury.[15]

The failure of the judge to give certain instructions, for example, can be grounds for later reversal of the conviction on appeal.

Before closing arguments, the judge and lawyers convene informally in the judge's chambers or formally in open court, without the jury, to determine the instructions to be given and the forms to be used. The court reporter's presence is required in order to preserve for appeal the record of all requests, objections, and rulings. While it is customary for defendants to attend court proceedings, they need not be present at this conference. If a defendant chooses not to attend, as a cautionary measure, the attorney may request that the defendant's waiver become a matter of record.

The judge's instructions to the jury include a recitation of the elements of the offense charged and the **lesser included offenses** (see Excerpt 24). A lesser included offense consists of some of the elements of the greater offense, but it does not have any element not already included in the greater offense.

EXCERPT 24

THE COURT: Before you find the defendant guilty of murder in the first degree; premeditated [murder]; or first-degree, premeditated murder, the State must prove the following three elements as to each charge of first-degree murder, beyond a reasonable doubt.

One: Mary Lee Driggers and Robert Lester Harrison are dead.

Two: The death of each was caused by the criminal act or agency of John Wesley Peavy.

Three: There was a premeditated killing of Mary Lee Driggers and Robert Lester Harrison.

Killing with premeditation is killing after consciously deciding to do so. The decision must be present in the [killer's] mind at the time of the killing.

The law does not fix the exact period of time that must pass between the formulation of the premeditated intent to kill and the killing by the defendant.

The premeditated intent to kill must be formed before the killing.

The question of premeditation is a question of fact to be determined by you from the evidence.

It will be sufficient proof of premeditation if the circumstances of the killing and the conduct of the accused convince you beyond a reasonable doubt of the existence of premeditation at the time of the killing.

In addition, the judge may also inform jurors that:

- If you have a reasonable doubt, you should find the defendant not guilty;

- You should use your common sense in deciding which is the best evidence and on which evidence you should not rely in considering your verdict;

- You should consider how the witnesses acted, as well as what they said;

- You may not speculate on what an answer might have been when an objection to a question was sustained;

- If you find an absence of evidence suggesting a motive for the defendant to commit the crime charged, you should consider the absence of such a motive; but proof of motive is never necessary for a conviction;

- The opinion of experts is only reliable when given on a subject about which you believe them to be expert;

- The defendant exercised a fundamental right by choosing not to be a witness in this case; you must not view this choice as an admission of guilt or be influenced in any way by this decision;

- The case must be decided only upon the evidence that you have heard from the answers of the witnesses and that you have seen in the form of exhibits in evidence, and these instructions;

- The case must not be decided for or against anyone because you feel sorry for anyone or because you are angry at anyone.

After the judge has charged the jury, the jurors retire to the jury room, where they select a foreperson from their ranks. The foreperson is responsible for signing the verdict forms once the jury has completed its deliberations.

The bailiff is usually charged with keeping close guard on the jurors. Unless the judge orders it, no one is permitted to enter the jury room or speak to the jurors. The judge may permit jurors to take into the jury room the approved verdict forms, evidence presented during the trial, and jury instructions. Out of concern that jurors might become preoccupied with legal issues, judges rarely used to permit jurors to take the jury instructions. Such permission is more common today.

In some jurisdictions, jurors are permitted to take notes. They may be instructed, though, that their notes are for their own use and not to be shared with others during deliberations. A recent American Bar Association study found that notetaking aids juror recall and comprehension.[16]

If the jurors want testimony read to them or need additional instruction, the bailiff brings them back into the courtroom. There, the judge orders the court reporter to read the testimony or provides the jurors with the needed instruction. Both attorneys are notified of

IN THE CIRCUIT COURT OF THE
SECOND JUDICIAL CIRCUIT, IN
AND FOR LEON COUNTY, FLORIDA.

CASE NO. 85-4810CF

STATE OF FLORIDA,

-vs-   VERDICTS

JOHN WESLEY PEAVY,
_____/

COUNT I

WE, the Jury, find the defendant, JOHN WESLEY PEAVY, guilty as charged of Murder in the First Degree With a Firearm of Mary Lee Driggers.

SO SAY WE ALL this 25 day of March, 1987.

Bob Clay
FOREMAN

WE, the Jury, find the defendant, JOHN WESLEY PEAVY, guilty of the lesser included offense of Murder in the Second Degree With a Firearm of Mary Lee Driggers.

SO SAY WE ALL this _____ day of March, 1987.

_____
FOREMAN

WE, the Jury, find the defendant, JOHN WESLEY PEAVY, guilty of the lesser included offense of Murder in the Third Degree With a Firearm of Mary Lee Driggers.

SO SAY WE ALL this _____ day of March, 1987.

_____
FOREMAN

Exhibit 5-1 Verdict form on which the jury found Peavy guilty of killing Mary Lee Driggers.

these activities. However, the judge cannot recall the jurors to hear additional evidence once they have retired to consider their verdict.

When a jury is deadlocked, the court may have the jurors return to the courtroom to inquire about their progress. It may not ask them how they voted. Nor may it give them the impression that they must return a verdict or that the court is setting a time limit on the deliberations. Some states permit the judge to give what is called the **Allen charge,** or "dynamite charge," to jurors that seem hopelessly deadlocked.[17] Among other things, the judge instructs the jury that:

> We ask each of you on one side to carefully consider the discussion points of view of those on the other side. And we point out to you that this case ought to be decided. If it is tried again in all likelihood the jury will be no better equipped than yourself; the jury will be similarly selected as you were in all likelihood, the evidence will be the same. And therefore, it is incumbent upon you to reach a verdict. Bearing in mind, however, that we do not expect any of you to vote one way or the other except according to your own conscience based upon the evidence and upon these instructions. I will now ask you to retire to deliberate further.[18]

The purpose of this instruction is to encourage jurors to reach a verdict. Courts in several jurisdictions have stopped using the Allen charge because these courts feel that such encouragement threatens jury impartiality.

When the jurors have reached a verdict, they return to the courtroom; and the judge asks the foreperson whether an agreement has been reached as to the verdict. If the answer is affirmative, the judge instructs the foreperson to give the verdict forms to the deputy court clerk, who reads the verdict out loud (see Exhibit 5-1 and Excerpt 25).

```
        WE, the Jury, find the defendant, JOHN WESLEY PEAVY, guilty

of the lesser included offense of Manslaughter With a Firearm of

Mary Lee Driggers.

        SO SAY WE ALL this _____ day of March, 1987.




                              FOREMAN _____
--------------------------------------------------------------------
        WE, the Jury, find the defendant, JOHN WESLEY PEAVY, not

guilty.

        SO SAY WE ALL this _____ day of March, 1987.




                              FOREMAN _____
```

Exhibit 5-1 Continued.

The court can poll the jury if it wishes or if asked by the prosecution or defense. Should one of the jurors dissent, the jury must return to the jury room for further deliberations. The judge discharges the jury when its members are in agreement, except in capital cases, where their presence is required for sentencing.

EXCERPT 25
Proceedings at 9:45 P.M., March 25, 1987:

THE COURT: Mr. Bailiff, bring the jury in.

(Whereupon, the jury was returned to the jury box.)

THE COURT: Let the record reflect the jury has returned to the jury box, and all members are present.
    Ladies and gentlemen, have you reached your verdict as to each count?

JURY FOREMAN: Yes.

THE COURT: Is it a unanimous verdict as to each count?

JURY FOREMAN: Yes.

THE COURT: All right. I will at this time excuse the alternate jurors. You can have a seat in the audience. You are welcome to stay.
    Mr. Clerk, would you receive the verdicts.

(The verdicts are received by the clerk and viewed by the court.)

THE COURT: I'm going to hand you the original instructions.
    Mr. Clerk, will you publish the verdicts, please, naming them by counts?

THE CLERK: As to Count Number One: We, the jury, find the defendant, John Wesley Peavy, guilty as charged of murder in the first degree, with a firearm, of Mary Lee Driggers. So say we all this twenty-fifth day of March, 1987.

(Noise in the audience.)

THE COURT: Order in the Court.

THE CLERK: (Continuing) As to Count Two: We, the jury, find the defendant, John Wesley Peavy, guilty as charged of murder in the first degree, with a firearm, of Robert Lester Harrison. So say we all this twenty-fifth day of March, 1987.
    As to Count Three: We, the jury, find the defendant, John Wesley Peavy, guilty as charged of shooting into a building. So say we all this twenty-fifth day of March, 1987.
    As to Count Four: We, the jury, find the defendant, John Wesley Peavy, guilty as charged of using a firearm in the commission of a felony. So say we all this twenty-fifth day of March, 1987.
    Each count signed by the foreman of the jury.

THE COURT: Does either side wish to have the jury polled?

MR. HARPER: [a defense attorney]: Yes, Your Honor.

THE COURT: OK. Ladies and gentlemen, polling the jury means that I am going to ask each of you if this was your verdict as to each count.
We will start with you, Mr. Johnson.
Mr. Johnson, was that your verdict as to the four counts?

JUROR JOHNSON: It was.

A few states permit nonunanimous verdicts in non-capital cases to avoid hung juries caused by the dissent of one or more jurors. The Supreme Court upheld this practice in a Louisiana case in which the verdict was 9-3 and in an Oregon case in which the verdict was 10-2.[19] The verdict of a jury composed of only six members, however, must be unanimous for non-petty offenses.[20]

Study Questions

1. Though it is not required that the defendant prove anything, what were two big weaknesses in the defense's case?

2. If the state does not have to prove the defendant's motive, why did the prosecution offer the jury one for Peavy?

3. Were there any particularly noteworthy "performances" by either the defense or the prosecution during cross-examination?

4. Find where the prosecution impeached a witness who then had to be bolstered back by the defense, and vice versa.

5. What details did the defense seize upon in arguing that there was reasonable doubt that Peavy was guilty of murder?

Endnotes

1. Craig Spangenberg, "Basic Values and Techniques of Persuasion," *Litigation* 3 (1977), 13–14.

2. Paul Bergman, *Trial Advocacy in a Nutshell*, 2d ed. (St. Paul, MN: West Publishing Co., 1989), 9–30.

3. For example, see *Florida Rules of Criminal Procedure*, rule 3.250 (1987).

4. *Post v. State*, 315 So.2d 230 (Fla. 2d DCA 1975).

5. For example, see *Florida Rules of Professional Conduct*, 4-3.1 (1989).

6. See Thomas A. Mauet, *Fundamentals of Trial Techniques* (Boston: Little, Brown and Co.), 1980, 98–171.

7. Rules of evidence in some jurisdictions have done away with the need for hypotheticals by allowing non-percipient witnesses to become acquainted with the facts from other sources. For example, see *Federal Rules of Evidence*, rule 703 (1989).

8. Thomas A. Bratten, "Direct Examination," in *Criminal Trial Practice in Florida*, ed. Gerald T. Bennett (Tallahassee, FL: Florida Bar, 1984), 113.

9. For example, see Florida Statutes 90.612 (2) (1989).

10. See Robert Link, "Objection to Evidence," in *Criminal Trial Practice in Florida*, ed. Gerald T. Bennett (Tallahassee, FL: Florida Bar, 1984), 209.

11. *Sweet v. State*, 235 So.2d 40 (Fla. 2d DCA 1970).

12. *McDuffie v. State*, 341 So.2d 840 (Fla. 2d DCA 1977).

13. For example, see *Florida Rules of Criminal Procedure*, rule 3.250 (1987).

14. Thomas A. Mauet, *Fundamentals of Trial Techniques* (Boston: Little, Brown and Co.), 1980, 302.

15. For example, see Rom W. Powell, "Jury Instructions," in *Criminal Trial Practice in Florida*, ed. Gerald T. Bennett (Tallahassee, FL: Florida Bar), 1984, 281.

16. *Jury Comprehension in Complex Cases*, Report of the Special Committee on Jury Comprehension of the American Bar Association Section on Litigation, Chicago, 1990, 34–37.

17. *Allen v. United States*, 164 U.S. 492 (1896).

18. *State v. Marsh*, 260 Or. 416, 422 (1971).

19. *Johnson v. Louisiana*, 406 U.S. 356 (1972); *Apodaca v. Oregon*, 406 U.S. 404 (1972).

20. *Burch v. Louisiana*, 441 U.S. 130 (1979).

6

Sentencing

Life-or-Death Decision

While the courtroom cleared, defense attorney Tony Bajoczky sat hunched in his seat, looking stunned by the verdict. And M. D. Peavy, Johnny's father, stood and shot a piercing look of bitterness and betrayal at the FDLE investigators who sat on the other side of the room.

It was far from over. Soon would come the penalty phase and the jury's life-or-death decision. As drained as they were, the jurors still faced deciding between the recommended sentence of life in prison with no chance of release for twenty-five years, or death in the electric chair.

Two days later, in the morning, the two vans driven by bailiffs returned to the courthouse. One brought the jury from the motel; the other carried Johnny from the jail. The jury was ready to proceed, but Johnny was not.

Saying that he had no faith in the jury that wrongfully convicted him, Johnny asked the judge to bypass its recommended sentence and allow him to make his own decision. He made it clear that he did not want the jury playing any more roles in deciding his fate.

But Judge McClure, who had approved a Valium prescription for Peavy, proceeded with the penalty phase. First, though, in a small hearing room, Peavy, the lawyers, and the judge gathered. Bajoczky put on the record what his client had told him in a holding cell minutes earlier: "He told me that he's not guilty and that this has been a miscarriage of justice," Bajoczky said. "He said he doesn't want to participate in any further miscarriages of justice."

McClure advised Peavy that he had the right to waive his presence in the penalty phase hearing. But, finally, Peavy said, "No, sir, no; I don't want to waive it; no." And he gave his word that there would be no emotional outbursts in the courtroom.

The jury assembled, and the hearing proceeded with a parade of Peavy family members taking the stand to testify their support: his wife, mother, sister, and the children of Bobby Harrison, Peavy's niece and nephew. When Peavy's thirteen-year-old son, John Peavy, Jr., took the stand and testified that he would visit his father in prison, the defendant wiped away his first public tears.

Soon thereafter, Peavy, the lawyers, and McClure returned to the little hearing room; and Bajoczky told the judge, "He's restated his innocence, and he doesn't want to dignify this jury by having his family testify for him."

McClure put Peavy under oath. The solemn-faced defendant told the judge: "The jury gave the wrong verdict, and, I'm sorry, but I don't have any faith in them. I've thought about it, and thought about it, and thought about it. I'd rather put it in your hands, Judge."

But Assistant State Attorney Jack Poitinger argued, "I can understand his frustration with the jury. But the purpose of a jury is for justice to both sides."

The prosecutor made it clear that the state wanted to continue the penalty phase. Noting that Peavy had been given tranquilizers and was under great stress, McClure decided to continue the hearing over Peavy's objections. Peavy returned to his chair in the courtroom, to suffer through the rest of the trial's penalty phase.

Besides Peavy family members, the defense brought on Dr. Peter Macaluso, a self-described alcoholic who was also addicted to Demerol, a narcotic pain reliever. Over the objections of the prosecutors, Macaluso was allowed to give his opinion about Peavy's alcoholism.

Macaluso testified that after interviewing Peavy the night before at the jail, and after reviewing his alcohol treatment record, he concluded that Peavy was in the advanced stages of alcoholism. He said that he had reviewed a lab report of a urine sample taken from Peavy on November 6, 1985, a week after the Halloween night killings. The sample showed a blood alcohol level of 0.49, Macaluso testified, which could be lethal, even for some alcoholics. (In Florida, 0.10 is the legal presumption of intoxication.) But, even with that high reading, the doctor testified, Peavy was talking and walking, which showed how chronic Peavy's alcohol problem was (see Figure 6-1).

Peavy had been hospitalized for alcoholism in 1982 and 1984. And, in 1985, Macaluso testified, Peavy's family asked that he be involuntarily committed to treatment, if necessary. The doctor said that Peavy took his first drink at the age of seven or eight, was first intoxicated at age fourteen, and was drinking daily by the time he was in high school.

Defense attorney Robert Harper used Peavy's drinking problem to argue to the jury that Peavy's mental condition was impaired by a long-standing bout with alcoholism. He further argued that Peavy had been shot in the head as a child and suffered severe headaches.

But Poitinger showed little belief in Macaluso's credibility and little sympathy for Peavy's alcohol problem.

"All of us have problems of some kind," Poitinger told the jury. "But society requires that we keep our problems in check and, certainly, not

Figure 6-1 Robert Augustus Harper (left), one of Peavy's defense attorneys, confers with defense expert Dr. Peter Macaluso, who testifies about Peavy's alcoholism during the trial's penalty phase. Hal Yeager.

kill. I'm not asking for vengeance. I'm asking for a penalty that speaks the truth. On that night, he ended two human lives. The only appropriate penalty, acting fairly and impartially, is the death penalty for John Wesley Peavy."

Urging the jurors' mercy, Harper told them, "You have played the role of judge, and today you play the role of God."

Out of nine possible aggravating factors that could incur capital punishment, the judge found that only one applied to this case: that Harrison and Driggers were killed in a "cold, calculated, premeditated manner without any pretense of moral or legal justification."

After receiving that instruction, the jury left to deliberate. And, after this twelve-hour day of testimony and legal arguments, the jury took only fifteen minutes to decide to spare Peavy's life.

When the jury promptly returned with its merciful recommendation, there were plenty of smiles of relief among the Peavy clan. The judge allowed a visit in the corner of the courtroom, where Gloria and Peavy's mother, Virginia, took turns hugging him. It was an upbeat contrast to the wails of anguish flooding the courtroom two nights earlier.

The marathon trial had kept the jurors sequestered in a motel for three weeks. And a gag order had sealed the lawyers' lips. Lugging his law books out of the courtroom, Poitinger was finally able to say, "It's been a long and difficult case for everyone. But I had faith in this case going in. And I feel the jury had faith in the case, too."

Faith also remained with the Peavy family, who insisted that Peavy was not a murderer and that their legal fight was not yet over. M. D. Peavy's blue eyes glistened with a hint of tears when he recalled the guilty verdict that sent a shock wave through his unprepared family.

"We thought we were going to bring him home," Peavy's father said. And Gloria said she told her children, ages thirteen and eight: "This is not the end for Daddy. We'll just start over, and it'll just take longer for Daddy to come home." She fought back tears when she added, "I have to believe that, or I couldn't go on."

Nearly a month passed before the judge sentenced Peavy on April 23, 1987. The jury's advisory sentence of life in prison was only a recommendation that the judge could override.

The prosecutors were ready to argue again that Peavy deserved to be strapped in the electric chair. But before sentencing began, clashing lawyers waged agitated arguments on the validity of the jury's verdict.

"I think the verdict in this case shocked everybody in the courtroom," Bajoczky told the judge. "To say it shocked me is to put it mildly. And I believe this court was as shocked as everybody else."

But Poitinger said, "The jury did a good job. The jury did an honorable job with a difficult case."

At one point in the three-hour-long, sometimes stormy hearing, Bajoczky held up a thick brown envelope and said, "I'm not the only one who's lost confidence in the jury system and is shaken by the verdict. . . . I've got 3,500-plus people on a petition asking for a new trial. Many are relatives of Bobby Harrison. Many watched the trial and heard about this trial in the eighteen months this case developed."

Once the petitions were introduced, prosecutor Guarisco nearly exploded. He jumped up from his seat, his voice rising with anger:

"This is absolutely unbelievable that he'd try to put something like this on!"

Thrusting his finger repeatedly in the direction of the envelope the defense attorney still held, Guarisco continued, "Those people [on the petition] didn't sit in the jury box and take notes. I'm absolutely shocked he'd do something like that in this courtroom, and I want it stricken from the record!"

It would be an abuse of the judge's discretion, Guarisco argued, to pit his judgment against that of the jury.

When the bickering was over, McClure said, "I'll not grant a new trial based on community petitions. That's not a valid point of law." He added, "I find the case was circumstantial and is best decided by the jury. I find the verdict was not contrary to the weight of the evidence or to law."

Much of the hearing was spent reviewing what Bajoczky called "missing links" in the chain of circumstantial evidence:

- That the Tec 9 gun prosecutors proved to the jury was the murder weapon came from the manufacturer with rifling (grooves in the barrel that cause fired projectiles to spiral out and that leave telltale markings on the bullets). Yet, Bajoczky argued, the deadly bullets in this case had no rifling; and there was no evidence that Peavy had altered the barrel of his gun.

But Poitinger reiterated trial testimony that four days after Peavy purchased his Tec 9 in December 1984, he fired it in the presence of his nephew, Little Delacy Peavy. That bullet, lodged in a radiator at the Peavy and Son Construction Company shop, along with others fired on at least two occasions at other locations, Poitinger stressed, had no rifling.

Bajoczky then produced another missing link:

- That the only witnesses who could link Peavy to the crime scene were two "jailbirds" who, Bajoczky said, had "an appalling lack of credibility." He reminded the judge that the two felons who testified that Peavy had confessed to them in jail each provided a different version of the supposed confession.

But, Poitinger argued, the jury had apparently believed everything Osborn and Johnson had said, in spite of extensive cross-examination. Other unsuccessful defense arguments for a new trial included:

- That the jurors, waiting one day to be taken to their motel after the trial had recessed, never should have seen Peavy being led to a transport van in shackles. Seeing Peavy in chains, with speculations that he was dangerous, the defense attorney argued, had affected jurors' abilities to be fair.

But Poitinger successfully argued that it would be up to the defense attorneys to prove there had been actual prejudice to Peavy.

Bajoczky also argued:

- That the jury was swayed by morbid autopsy photos that showed gruesomely extended limbs and wires running through bodies not found until several days after the killings. But McClure agreed with Poitinger that the photos were relevant in helping the medical examiner explain his testimony.

Once the motion for a new trial was denied, the prosecutors asked the judge to override the jury's recommendation for mercy. Guarisco called the crime "an ambush killing" and "execution murder."

Bajoczky countered that the prosecutors, who zealously defended the jury's wisdom in the guilt phase, should not "talk out of both sides of their mouth" by asking the judge to disregard the jurors' decision on the penalty.

After hearing all that was to be said—the prosecutors' arguments for the death penalty and the defense's plea that an innocent man deserved a new trial—it was time for the judge's decision.

McClure decided to abide by the jury's recommendation. For the counts of murder, the judge sentenced Peavy to two consecutive life sentences, for a total of fifty mandatory years in prison under Florida law. On the pair of less-serious felonies, McClure ordered thirty-month concurrent sentences (see Figure 6-2).

Figure 6-2 John Peavy at the penalty
phase of the trial. Hal Yeager.

Before he was led back to his jail cell, Peavy stood in shackles to
deliver his message to the judge: "In the eyes of the law, I stand before
this court a convicted man. But, your honor, in the eyes of God, I stand
before the court an innocent man."

Gloria sat in the front row, flanked by the couple's young son and
daughter. She wiped away tears while her husband told the judge, "I honestly believe if the verdict had been given by you and you alone, I'd have
walked out of this court a free man."

PROCEDURAL DESCRIPTION

Although the court sentences offenders when they are convicted, the
imposition of a sentence is usually preceded by a presentence investigation (PSI) and a sentencing hearing. The probation officer conducts the PSI, inquiring into the offender's prior record and current
situation, and makes recommendations. These recommendations often
become the basis of the court's sentencing decision. The sentencing
hearing provides witnesses a chance to testify about such matters as
the offender's character and the victim's loss. The type of case determines how the hearing is conducted. A hearing in a noncapital case is
often informal. It is always formal in a capital case because a jury must
consider the appropriateness of the death penalty. In a case involving
plea bargaining, a hearing tends to be formulaic because the judge is
required to recite a set of predetermined questions about the defendant's waiver of certain constitutional rights.

Although PSI procedures vary widely, it may help to understand the general process by examining the specifics of a particular jurisdiction. In plea negotiations, where the defendant pleads guilty or no contest, the judge may impose a sentence without a PSI if both the state and defense waive it. In this case, the probation officer routinely conducts a postsentence investigation, similar in most respects to the PSI, and sends its findings and recommendations to the agency where the defendant will serve time. The recommendations may be used in developing a plan for the treatment of the defendant. For example, the report might recommend that, as part of probation, the defendant should complete high school, enroll in a substance-abuse program, or learn a trade.

When a defendant is convicted of a felony, the judge customarily orders probation services to conduct a PSI. Once the report is completed, usually within a period of twenty-one to twenty-eight days, copies are sent to the attorneys as well as to the judge. Either side can question the report's accuracy at a sentencing hearing. The PSI is confidential. Its findings and recommendations may become the basis of the judge's sentencing decision, but they do not become part of the trial record.

The usual procedure for initiating a PSI is for the clerk's office to forward the judge's order to a probation intake officer, who assigns a probation officer to investigate the case. The investigation entails taking statements from people such as the defendant, the victim, the arresting officer, the prosecuting attorney, the defense attorney, the defendant's employer, and members of the defendant's family. These statements either become data in the PSI report or a means to verify such data. For example, the defendant may volunteer information in response to the investigator's questions about school or work. The probation officer verifies these statements by interviewing school authorities or the defendant's employer.

Interviewees provide information on a variety of topics, including loss or injury to the victim, **aggravating circumstances, mitigating circumstances,** and the defendant's socioeconomic status, family history, marital history, physical and mental health, and residential history. Socioeconomic status refers to the defendant's education, employment, and financial condition.

The law may require that the investigator inquire about any damage or loss the victim may have sustained.[1] If any loss has been sustained, the judge must order the defendant to pay restitution.[2] If the prosecution and defense disagree about the amount of the damage or loss, they may air their disagreement at a hearing.

The investigator's interview with the arresting officer can be a source of mitigating as well as aggravating information. For example, the officer might say that the defendant was cooperative at the time of arrest, was helpful in the recovery of the stolen property, or provided leads that culminated in the arrest of a co-defendant.

The investigator also collects information from sources other than interviewees, such as the offense report, the charging document, court records, and computerized data from such agencies as the National Crime Information Center. These sources provide information concerning the circumstances of the defendant's arrest, the offense as charged, whether the defendant pleaded or was found guilty by a judge or jury, the defendant's prior criminal history, the names of the judge and attorneys involved in the case, the number of days the defendant spent in custody, and the disposition of co-defendants.

Based on the PSI, the investigator recommends a disposition within the limits established by the sentencing laws. For example, if the laws allow for a choice between incarceration and community control, the probation officer might recommend community control with alcohol treatment and periodic urinalysis for a man, convicted of aggravated battery with a deadly weapon, who has had a drinking problem, no prior record, and the same job for twenty years.

Sentences

A sentence is the punishment given a person convicted of a criminal offense. The responsibility for determining that punishment is shared by the three branches of government. Legislators classify offenses and their penalties in the criminal codes. Within the codes, felonies are usually classified into categories, such as capital felony, life felony, felony of the first degree, and felony of the second degree. The penalty of an offense varies in severity, depending on the category to which it is assigned. If it is a felony of the first degree, for example, the sentence might be a term of imprisonment not exceeding thirty years or a fixed or flat sentence of exactly thirty years. If the sentence stipulates an indefinite or indeterminate term of imprisonment, usually the court or officials of the executive branch (parole board members or correction officials) have discretion in determining when a prisoner is to be released. Practices vary widely. Where the sentence is definite or determinate, there is no discretion, except for the awarding of **gain time** for good behavior or for participation in treatment or educational programs. In some states, release of prisoners is mandated by a federal court when the prison population comes close to exceeding its capacity. Correction officials then must exercise discretion in deciding which prisoners get released before their sentences end.

Sentences may run concurrently or consecutively. If sentences are **concurrent** and the terms of imprisonment are the same, the defendant serves the sentences simultaneously. If the terms are of different length, the defendant serves until the end of the longest sentence. If the sentences are **consecutive,** the defendant must serve one sentence before the next can begin. When a defendant is convicted of two or more offenses charged in the same information or indictment, the sentences usually run concurrently.[3] When the offenses are not charged in the same information or indictment, the sentences usually run consecutively. However, often the trial judge can order that the sentences be served either concurrently or consecutively.[4]

Mandatory minimum sentences have been established for certain offenses. In some cases, statutes simply set minimum terms of imprisonment that must be served. For example, people convicted of drug trafficking in Florida who have in their possession a semiautomatic firearm with a magazine capable of holding twenty cartridges must serve a minimum sentence of eight years in prison before they are eligible for gain time or release.[5] In other cases, statutes require an increase in penalty by reclassifying the offense charged. For example, if a man commits a felony of the second degree with a firearm that he has taken from a law enforcement officer without authorization, the offense charged might be reclassified to a felony of the first degree.

Those offenses for which mandatory minimum sentences have been established might include:

- A violent offense committed against a law enforcement officer, correctional officer, or prosecutor acting in the line of duty;[6]

- An attempt to murder a law enforcement officer;[7]

- A combination of two or more felonies, provided the felony for which the defendant is currently sentenced was committed within five years of the conviction for the last prior felony or within five years of the defendant's release from prison;[8]

- One or more of such violent felonies as murder, sexual battery, aggravated battery, kidnapping, arson, and robbery, and having been convicted previously of a felony or an attempt or conspiracy to commit a felony;[9]

- Carrying, displaying, using, threatening or attempting to use a weapon while committing a felony, except where the use of a weapon is an essential element of the offense;[10]

- Wearing a hood or mask while committing an offense;[11]

- Committing an offense that evidences prejudice toward the victim based on race, color, ancestry, ethnicity, or national origin.[12]

Several states as well as the federal government have adopted sentencing guidelines. They are standards, based on a point system, that guide the judge in sentencing defendants who are found or plead guilty. Sentencing guidelines stipulate a term of imprisonment, depending on the number of points the defendant has accumulated. In Florida, for example, points are assigned on the basis of primary offense at conviction, additional offenses at conviction, prior record, legal status at time of offense, and victim injury.[13] If the defendant is convicted of more than one offense, the prosecutor completes separate scoresheets for each offense. The scoresheet recommending the most severe sentence is the one that is used for sentencing. Other offenses committed at the time of the primary offense are considered additional offenses at conviction. Prior record refers to past offenses for which the defendant was convicted and includes juvenile offenses committed within three years of the commission of the primary offense. Legal status at time of offense refers to whether the defendant was under legal constraint when the primary offense was committed. An escapee, an offender on probation, or a fugitive fleeing to avoid prosecution would be considered to be under legal constraint. If the victim is hurt physically during the course of a criminal transaction, the defendant is scored points for victim injury (see Exhibit 6-1). The guidelines do not apply to misdemeanors or capital offenses.

Once the points are assigned, the prosecutor totals them and refers to the guideline grids in order to determine the prescriptive sentence. For example, in Exhibit 6-2, the defendant's composite score of fifty-four points calls for a sentence of either community control or incarceration for a period of twelve to thirty months. In the case of John Wesley Peavy, this sentence would be the defendant's only sanction were "shooting into a dwelling" and "use of a firearm in commission of a felony" the only offenses, provided that the judge did not depart from the sentencing guidelines.

Judges are allowed to depart from the sentencing guidelines upon reasonable justification.[14] A written statement explaining those reasons must accompany the recommendation if the sentence departs from the guidelines. Approved reasons for upward departure include excessive use of force, inducing others to participate in the commission of crime, and committing a crime in which the victim is a law enforcement officer.[15] Approved reasons for downward departure include cooperation with law enforcement officers, provocation by the victim, and the defendant's intoxication at the time of the offense or record of substance abuse. Of course, just because the defendant used excessive force or has a record of substance abuse does not mean that the court automatically departs from the sentencing guidelines. Whether or not the court departs is a matter of judicial discretion. If the sentence imposed is outside the recommended range, the defendant may appeal it.[16] The state may also appeal it.[17]

8

Rule 3.988(h)
Category 8: Weapons
Chapter 790 and 944.40

1. DOCKET NO. (PRIMARY OFFENSE)	3. COUNTY	4. JUDGE	5. DATE OF SENTENCE
85CF4810	Leon	Charles D. McClure	4-22-87

2. DOCKET NO. (ADDITIONAL CASES)	6. NAME		
	John Wesley Peavy, Sr.	7. DATE OF BIRTH 11-15-46	8. SEX ☒M ☐F

9. DATE OF OFFENSE	10. PRIMARY OFFENSE AT CONVICTION	11. DEGREE
10-31-85	Shooting Into Dwelling	F-2

12. ☐ PROBATION VIOLATION ☐ COMMUNITY CONTROL VIOLATION	13. ☐ PLEA ☒ TRIAL	14. ☐ GUIDELINE SENTENCE IMPOSED ☐ DEPARTURE FROM GUIDELINE

I. Primary offense at conviction

Degree	Number of Counts 1	2	3	4	Points
1st	70	84	91	98	
2nd	45	54	58	63	45 (Ct.3)
3rd	15	18	20	21	

Primary offense counts in excess of four (from back) _____

Guideline Sentence:
Community Control or 12-30
Months Incarceration

Sentence imposed, indicating length and type
(Please print or type)
Cts. 1 & 2-- Life in Prison
each count to run
consecutive
Cts 3 & 4-- Prison, 30 months
each count to run
consecutive

II. Additional offense at conviction

Degree	Number of Counts 1	2	3	4	Points
1st	14	17	18	19	
2nd	9	11	12	13	9 (Ct.4)
3rd	3	4	5	6	
MM	1	2	3	4	

Additional offense counts in excess of four (from back) _____

FOR OFFICE USE ONLY

Offense Code _____

T.S. _____

S.P. _____

Prob. _____

III. Prior record

Degree	Number of Prior Convictions 1	2	3	4	Points
Life	10	20	40	60	
1st pbl	8	16	32	48	
1st	6	12	24	36	
2nd	3	6	12	18	
3rd	1	2	4	6	
MM	1	2	3	4	

Prior convictions in excess of four (from back) _____

C.C. _____

C.J. _____

IV. Legal status at time of offense
No restrictions   0
Legal constraint   12 _____

Charles D. McClure
Sentencing Judge

Anthony Guarisco
State Attorney

Anthony Bajoczky
Defendant/Defense Counsel

V. Victim injury (physical)
None   0
Slight   4
Moderate   8
Death or severe   12 _____

Brian Engles
Scoresheet Preparer

Reasons for departure: Total 54 _____

NOTE: Sentencing guidelines not applicable pertaining to Counts
1 & 2, First Degree Murder.

8

SG8 - effective 7/1/84

DISTRIBUTION:
White.......Court File
Green.......Sentencing Guidelines Commission

Canary.......State Attorney
Pink.......Defendant Defense Counsel
Goldenrod.......Scoresheet Preparer

Exhibit 6-1 Scoresheet used in the sentencing of John Wesley Peavy for weapons offense.

Category 8
Weapons

Points	Recommended Range
15–49	any nonstate prison sanction
50–75	Community Control or 12–30 mos. incarceration
76–91	3 yrs. incarceration (2½–3½)
92–105	4 years (3½–4½)
106–115	5 (4½–5½)
116–133	6 (5½–7)
134–157	8 (7–9)
158–193	10 (9–12)
194–253	15 (12–17)
254–313	20 (17–22)
314–373	25 (22–27)
374+	30 (27–40)

Exhibit 6-2 Guideline grids, showing recommended ranges of sanctions for weapons offense.

Sentencing Hearing

The sentencing hearing in a noncapital case is held as soon as practicable following the determination of guilt and the judge's examination of the PSI report. Defendants are usually required to be present.[18] The judge informs them of the charges and asks whether there is any reason why sentence should not be pronounced. Legal grounds for not pronouncing sentence might include that the defendant is insane, has been pardoned already, or is not the same person who was found guilty.[19] If there is no reason for not pronouncing sentence, the judge pronounces sentence after the defendant has had an opportunity to make a statement to the court. A record of the proceedings is made so that it can be transcribed if the case is appealed. For identification purposes, the defendant may be fingerprinted at the conclusion of the proceedings if adjudicated guilty.

Both the defense and prosecution may call witnesses to testify at a sentencing hearing. If they do, as is frequently the case, the proceedings are usually conducted informally. The defense might have a friend of the defendant's family talk about the defendant's character. The prosecution, instead of cross-examining that witness, might ask the victim to make a statement.

In some jurisdictions, the judge is required to allow the victim of a noncapital crime to appear and make a statement or submit a sworn statement.[20] The statement may mention the facts involved in the case, the extent of physical injury suffered, or the financial loss incurred because of the crime. The judge is obliged to review this statement before imposing any sentence. The victim's statement in the PSI report frequently substitutes for the courtroom appearance.

It is rare for witnesses to testify when the defendant pleads guilty or no contest. The defendant usually signs a plea form, often referred to as a **Boykin form** (see Exhibit 6-3). The judge then may ask the defendant a series of questions, such as:

- Did you read the form?

- Do you understand everything in the form, including the information about the rights you have in this proceeding and what it means to enter a plea?

- Do you understand that the maximum penalty for the crime of [name of crime] is [description of punishment]?

- At some point during the course of this case, did your lawyer review your rights with you and explain them to you?

- Do you understand that by pleading you are giving up your rights; there will not be a trial in your case; all that will be left is for me to sentence you?

- Is this the sentence you agreed to? [Judge reads sentence from plea form.]

- Is this your signature?

At this point, the judge determines the factual basis of the charge from the probable cause affidavit or a presentation by the prosecution, makes a finding that the plea is voluntary, and formally accepts the plea on the record.[21]

Sentencing in a capital case is different. In a 1972 decision, *Furman v. Georgia,* the Supreme Court held that the indiscriminate manner in which the death penalty had been applied made it cruel and unusual punishment.[22] In *Gregg v. Georgia,* it later ruled that, to be constitutional, a death penalty law must provide for a bifurcated trial.[23] The first phase, in which the jury finds the defendant guilty, must be followed by a penalty phase. It is during the latter phase that the jury

IN THE CIRCUIT COURT OF THE
SECOND JUDICIAL CIRCUIT IN
AND FOR LEON COUNTY, FLORIDA

STATE OF FLORIDA

vs.   CASE NUMBER _____

_____,

PLEA AND ACKNOWLEDGEMENT OF RIGHTS

I hereby enter a plea of ( ) no contest, ( ) guilty to the following criminal offense(s), withdrawing any previous plea of not guilty.

Count ____ *Offense* _____ *Max/Min Penalty* _____

Count ____ *Offense* _____ *Max/Min Penalty* _____

Count ____ *Offense* _____ *Max/Min Penalty* _____

Count ____ *Offense* _____ *Max/Min Penalty* _____

My plea is entered with the understanding that the state has agreed or does not object to the following disposition of my case:

_____

_____

_____

My plea is entered with the acknowledgment and understanding of the following:

(1) I understand that the judge will place me under oath to question me about this plea. I must answer the judge's questions truthfully, and if I make a false statement while under oath I could be prosecuted for perjury.

(2) I understand that a plea of not guilty denies my guilt, a plea of guilty admits my guilt, and a plea of no contest means that I will not contest the evidence against me. I also understand that if the Judge accepts this plea of guilty or no contest, there will be no trial and that I will be sentenced based on my plea.

(3) I understand the nature of the charges to which I am pleading and I am aware of the maximum and minimum penalties. My lawyer has informed me of the facts the State would have to prove before I could be found guilty, and discussed with me any possible defenses that could be raised in my case. I am satisfied with my lawyer's advice and help.

(Sign on Reverse Side After Reading Both Sides Carefully)

Exhibit 6-3 Plea form, or Boykin form, signed by defendants entering a plea of guilty or no contest.

decides the appropriateness of the death penalty after receiving additional evidence regarding aggravation and mitigation of the punishment. The death penalty is currently authorized in thirty-seven states.

The sentencing hearing in a capital case usually is conducted immediately following the determination of guilt. Typically, it begins with the judge and attorneys discussing a variety of matters out of hearing of the jurors. The following scenario illustrates the matters they are likely to discuss. The defense moves that the death penalty is an inappropriate sentence because there is insufficient evidence of aggravation. The prosecution responds, countering the defense's arguments. The judge rules. Matters of procedure are taken up next. The two sides decide what kind of opening statement each will make. The

(4) I understand that if the Judge accepts this plea, I give up the right to a trial, the right to require the State to prove the charge against me beyond a reasonable doubt, the right to have a jury decide whether I am guilty or not guilty, the right to see and hear the witnesses against me and to have my lawyer question them, the right to subpoena and present witnesses or other evidence or any defenses I may have, and to testify or remain silent as I choose.

(5) I understand that by pleading guilty or no contest I am giving up the right to appeal all matters relating to the final judgment, including the issue of my guilt or innocence. If the judge accepts this plea, the only issues I will be able to appeal are those relating to my sentence and the judge's authority to hear my case. I understand that I have 30 days to appeal the court's judgment and sentence, and if I cannot afford a lawyer, one will be appointed for me.

(6) I understand that if I am not a United States citizen, a plea of guilty or no contest could result in my deportation.

(7) I understand that the judge may assess court costs against me under the Florida statute governing my case, and that the judge will impose court costs in the amount of $200.00 ($50.00 for misdemeanors) under F.S. §27.3455; in the amount of $20.00 under F.S. §960.20; and in the amount of $5.00 under F.S. §943.25.

(8) I have read this entire form carefully, front and back, and I understand all of the rights and duties explained in this form.

I state to the Court that I am not under the influence of drugs or alcohol, that no one forced or threatened me to enter this plea, and that I am entering this plea freely and voluntarily. I acknowledge that I am entering this plea because I believe it is in my best interest.

SWORN TO AND FILED in open court in the presence of my lawyer and the Judge this _____ day of _____ 19_____.

_____
DEFENDANT

I hereby certify that I am counsel for the defendant and that I have informed the defendant of the nature of each charge against him, the maximum penalty, any applicable minimum penalty, the required elements of proof, and any possible defenses. I believe the defendant understands the rights and duties explained in this plea form and that the defendant is entering this plea freely and voluntarily with a full and complete understanding of the consequences.

_____
COUNSEL FOR THE DEFENDANT

Plea Accepted and Plea Form Filed by: _____
CIRCUIT JUDGE

Exhibit 6-3 Continued.

---

defense then moves to continue the proceedings. The judge denies the motion. Finally, the deputy court clerk swears in witnesses. It is decided that witnesses will be sequestered. The judge asks the bailiff to bring in the jurors once these preliminary matters have been completed. The court then instructs the jurors regarding the penalty phase of the trial (see Excerpt 26).

EXCERPT 26

THE COURT: Ladies and gentlemen, this phase of the trial is divided into certain portions also. You have found the Defendant guilty of two counts of first-degree murder. The punishment for this crime is either death or life in prison without possibility of parole for 25 years.

The final decision as to what punishment shall be imposed rests solely with the judge of this Court. However, the law requires [that] you, the jury, render to the Court an advisory sentence as to what punishment should be imposed upon this Defendant.

The State and the Defendant may now present evidence relative to the nature of the crime and the character of the Defendant. You are instructed that this evidence, when considered with all the evidence that you have already heard, is presented in order that you might determine first whether sufficient aggravating circumstances exist that would justify the imposition of the death penalty; second, whether there are mitigating circumstances sufficient to outweigh the aggravating circumstances, if any. At the conclusion of the taking of the evidence and after argument of counsel, you will be instructed on the factors in aggravation and mitigation that you may consider.

Following the judge's instructions, each attorney makes an opening statement. The prosecution goes first. Opening statement during the penalty phase is similar to opening statement during the determination-of-guilt phase. It previews what the attorney expects to show during the upcoming taking of evidence and sets the mood for the remainder of the proceeding (see Excerpt 27). If no evidence is to be presented, the attorney may be noncommital, saving forceful arguments until closing statement.

EXCERPT 27

MR. HARPER [a defense attorney]: Ladies and gentlemen, my name is Bob Harper. I'm going to handle this portion of the case. I invite your attention to the seriousness and the solemn responsibility we all have at this stage of the proceeding.

You have played the role of judge. Today, you play the role of God. Today, we are here to decide whether John Peavy is worth living or not. We're not here to defend John Peavy's trial or the acts that you found him guilty of. We're here to determine whether he should die because of those [acts].

In the taking of evidence, the prosecution presents testimony establishing circumstances that it argues aggravate the crime (see Exhibit 6-4). The defense is given an opportunity to cross-examine the prosecution's witnesses. The defense then presents evidence establishing circumstances that it argues mitigate the crime, after which the prosecution cross-examines the defense's witnesses (see Excerpt 28).

EXCERPT 28
Direct Examination

BY MR. HARPER [a defense attorney]:

Q: Ms. Peavy, state your name, please, ma'am.

A: Gloria Archer Peavy.

Q: Where do you reside?

Aggravating Circumstances

1. The capital felony was committed by a person under sentence of imprisonment;
2. The defendant was previously convicted of another capital felony or felony involving the use of threat or violence to the person;
3. The defendant knowingly created a great risk of death to many persons;
4. The capital felony was committed while the defendant was engaged or was an accomplice in the commission of or attempt to commit flight after committing or attempting to commit a robbery, sexual battery, arson, burglary, kidnapping, aircraft piracy, or unlawful throwing, placing or discharging of an obstructive device or bomb;
5. The capital felony was committed for the purpose of avoiding or preventing a lawful arrest or affecting an escape from custody;
6. The capital felony was committed for pecuniary gain;
7. The capital felony was committed to disrupt or hinder the lawful exercise of any government function or the enforcement of laws;
8. The capital felony was especially heinous, atrocious, or cruel;
9. The capital felony was a homicide committed in a cold, calculated, and premeditated manner without any pretense of moral or legal justification;
10. The victim of the capital felony was a law enforcement officer engaged in the performance of official duties;
11. The victim of the capital felony was an elected or appointed public official engaged in the performance of his official duties if the motive for capital felony was related, in whole or in part, to the victim's official capacity.[24]

Mitigating Circumstances

1. The defendant has no significant history of prior criminal activity;
2. The capital felony was committed while the defendant was under the influence of extreme mental or emotional disturbance;
3. The victim was a participant in the defendant's conduct or consented to the act;
4. The defendant was an accomplice in the capital felony committed by another person, and the defendant's participation was relatively minor;
5. The defendant acted under extreme duress or under the substantial domination of another person;
6. The capacity of the defendant to appreciate the criminality of his conduct or to conform his conduct to the requirements of law was substantially impaired;
7. Age of defendant at time of the crime;
8. Any other aspect of the defendant's character or record, and any other circumstance of the offense. Mitigating circumstance Number Eight includes such conditions as having been abused as a child, being an alcoholic, having experienced religious conversion, expressing genuine remorse, having been a model prisoner while awaiting trial, and having experienced extreme mental or emotional disturbance at the time the offense was committed.[25]

Exhibit 6-4 Attendant Circumstances.

A: [Witness gave address.]

Q: Are you related to John Wesley Peavy?

A: Yes, sir.

Q: How are you related to him?

A: John Peavy is my husband.

Q: And how long have you been married?

A: Twenty-one years.

Q: Do you have children of that marriage?

A: Yes, we do.

Q: How many children do you have?

A: We have two children.

Q: What are their ages?

A: John, Jr., is thirteen; and Page is seven.

Q: And do they reside at home?

A: Yes.

Q: Are they in school?

A: Yes, sir.

Q: Is your family unit close or not close?

A: We are a very close family unit.

Q: Have you had occasion to visit John Peavy since he's been in custody?

A: I visited Johnny every weekend that he's been in custody.

Q: And that's been since when?

A: They arrested Johnny December 23, 1985.

Q: Would you continue to visit with John Peavy if his life was spared and he was given a life sentence in lieu of the electric chair?

A: Wherever Johnny is, I'll visit Johnny.

MR. HARPER: That's all I have of Ms. Peavy, Your Honor.

THE COURT: Any questions?

MR. GUARISCO: Yes.

Cross-Examination

BY MR. GUARISCO [a prosecutor]:

Q: Ms. Peavy, you've just testified that your family unit is very close.

A: Yes, sir.

Q: Have you had any problems with Johnny in the past?

A: Would you state what kind of problems you mean, Mr. Guarisco, please?

Q: Yes, ma'am. When he's been drinking, have you had problems with him?

A: When he's been drinking. What are you talking about? Problems? I don't understand. Sure. He's had—

Q: Ms. Peavy, I'm asking you a question. Have you ever had problems with him in the past?

A: No, sir, no problems.

Q: Has he ever struck you before?

A: After I struck him.

Q: I see. And you call that a close family unit.

A: If you want to go back, this was when we first got married, Mr. Guarisco. This has not been in the past few years.

Q: Has he left you in the past?

A: Leave me? Are you talking about overnight?

Q: Left you and went with another woman?

A: Yes, my husband had gone with other women; but I have forgiven him for that. I don't think that's up to you to judge whether that makes me—

Q: Well, I understand what you are getting at, Ms. Peavy; but you have testified that this was a close family unit.

A: It is a close family unit. I love my husband regardless of what he has done in the past.

MR. GUARISCO: I have no further questions, Your Honor.

THE COURT: [To the witness.] You may step down.

Although the judge may be required to allow the victim to make a statement in a non-capital case, relatives of the victim in a capital case are not permitted to testify regarding the impact of the crime on them. In *Booth v. Maryland,* John Booth and Willie Reid broke into the home of Irvin and Rose Bronstein to steal money for drugs. They bound and gagged the seventy-year-old victims, then stabbed them repeatedly. Their bodies were found two days later by their son, who testified that his parents were "butchered like animals" and that he "doesn't think anyone like that should be able to do something like that and get away with it." The Supreme Court held that such testimony tends "to inflame the jury and divert it from deciding the case on the relevant evidence concerning the crime and the defendant."[26]

As in the determination-of-guilt phase of the trial, closing state-ments are preceded by a conference at which judge and attorneys dis-cuss what the judge will say to the jury before it retires to deliberate (see Excerpt 29). This conference is held out of hearing of the jurors.

EXCERPT 29

THE COURT: Number Nine [referring to the ninth aggravating circumstance].

MR. BAJOCZKY [a defense attorney]: We believe that Number Nine is not applicable, Your Honor.

MR. GUARISCO [a prosecutor]: We believe that it is.

THE COURT: Let's hear the argument from the Defense as to why it is not applicable. You submitted a memo covering this?

MR. HARPER [a defense attorney]: Yes.

THE COURT: Are you going to argue from that memorandum?

MR. HARPER: Initially, I am, Your Honor.

THE COURT: OK.

MR. HARPER: The heightened premeditation which this aggravating cir-cumstance requires, commonly referred to as cold, calculated, is a type of premeditation above and beyond the premeditation to commit the offense itself.
    In other words, there must be something in the nature of a period of time of reflection, and it's been typically held that this type of aggravating circumstance is applicable only in execution-style slaying where victims are tied and systematically eliminated as in *Combs v. State,* which I cited in the memo.
    I believe it was in *Combs* where the victims, six in number, were tied up and the defendant went from one to the other and executed the victims in the presence of the others. There was sufficient evidence for the Su-preme Court to hold that the capital felony was a cold, calculated, ag-gravating circumstance.
    In this case, the evidence is to the contrary. In fact, the evidence is that these victims were unaware of any impending doom—that they were shot while they were sitting and had virtually no time for any reaction, reflection, or realization even of what was going on. . . .

[Judge McClure addressed the prosecution:]

THE COURT: What says the State?

MR. POITINGER [a prosecutor]: Your Honor, we believe that this does, in fact, apply . . .

[The prosecutor proceeded with his argument:]

    I think the facts of this case [show that the jury] believed the testimony of the persons to whom the Defendant gave a confession that he followed them home, parked his truck, got his gun out of the car or truck where he kept it, walked over to the window, looked into it, stepped back and started firing. And that he fired at one victim, as their own defense expert admitted, and turned the weapon on the other victim, which would be almost synonymous with reloading the weapon.

I think in this particular situation there was no sign of a struggle. They were inside the home. They were shot to death. I don't know how [much] more execution-style that can be. . . .

[Judge McClure deliberates on the arguments:]

THE COURT: It's my opinion that aggravating circumstance Number Nine is an appropriate matter for . . . the jury to consider.

Closing statements sum and rebut testimony presented during the taking of evidence. The prosecution usually speaks first, asserting the presence of aggravating circumstances and arguing the absence of mitigating circumstances (see Excerpt 30). In arguing the latter, the prosecution may employ tactics used in the earlier phase of the trial. For example, it may attack the credibility of the defense's witness. The defense follows, using similar tactics and asserting the presence of mitigating circumstances and the absence of aggravating circumstances.

EXCERPT 30

MR. POITINGER [a prosecutor]: The crime for which the Defendant is to be sentenced was committed in a cold, calculated and premeditated manner without any pretense of moral or legal justification. . . .

[Mr. Poitinger then detailed the aggravating circumstance:]

Now, what have we done to establish that [aggravating circumstance]? You've heard testimony from a number of witnesses that on October 31, 1985, this Defendant, by your verdict and the findings that you have already made beyond a reasonable doubt, was at the Shady Rest [tavern]. That during the evening hours, he encountered Bobby Harrison and Mary Lee Driggers therein.

You recall the comments to Sam Castle regarding this Defendant and the victim Bobby Harrison. That after Bobby Harrison and Mary Lee Driggers left, he followed shortly thereafter.

[There is] further testimony that he followed them to their home, parked his truck, got out of his truck, reached behind the seat, pulled out that semiautomatic nine-millimeter Tech 9 weapon, and proceeded to their trailer without any announcement, without any notice to anybody therein.

He looked into the window, located his intended victims, stepped back and ended their lives.

He shot Bobby Harrison first. At least five bullets ripped through his body. He then without any remorse, without any pity, without any mercy, turned the gun on Mary Lee Driggers and took her life, sent three bullets ripping through her body.

Where in the evidence have you heard of any enemies of Mary Lee Driggers? Where in the evidence have you heard of any bad blood between Mary Lee Driggers and this Defendant? To the contrary, there is an absence of that.

Where is any moral or legal justification for the taking of either life?

Bobby Harrison or Mary Lee Driggers? I submit to you that it is devoid of justification. What we have is the act of a person bent on taking human life.

Finally, the judge instructs the jurors in their duty as advisers to the court. Although instructions vary among states employing capital punishment, those described here are illustrative of the procedure in general. Jurors are told that their advisory sentence should be based on the evidence presented in both phases of the trial. The judge informs them which of the aggravating and mitigating circumstances they may consider in making their decision. They are told that if they find any aggravating circumstances, they must determine whether there are mitigating circumstances that outweigh them. An aggravating circumstance must be proved beyond a reasonable doubt before jurors may consider it, but jurors may consider a mitigating circumstance as established if they are reasonably convinced that it exists. It takes a majority of the jurors to decide that the defendant should be sentenced to death. If six or more of them decide otherwise, they recommend to the court that it impose a sentence of life imprisonment.

After the judge has instructed the jurors, the bailiff escorts them to the jury room and provides them with verdict forms. When they have completed their deliberations and filled in the forms, the bailiff escorts them back into the courtroom, where the judge asks the deputy court clerk to publish the jury's decision. Finally, the judge thanks the jurors and discharges them from further jury duty.

The defendant is given an opportunity to make a statement, usually at a later hearing. It is then that the judge may be asked to rule on the motion for a new trial. Those proceedings end with the judge passing sentence and the bailiff taking the defendant's fingerprints (see Exhibit 6-5 and Excerpt 31).

EXCERPT 31

THE DEFENDANT: Your Honor, if I may, on December 23, 1985, I was arrested for a crime that I did not commit. Before going to trial I was incarcerated in Leon County Jail for fifteen months for a crime I did not commit. I was tried in a court of law, this court, for a crime that I did not commit. In this same court I was wrongfully found guilty by twelve jurors for a crime that I did not commit.

Your Honor, in the eyes of the law I stand before this Court a convicted man, wrongfully convicted of the murders of Robert Lester Harrison and Mary Lee Driggers. But, Your Honor, in the eyes of God I stand before this Court an innocent man wrongfully convicted of a crime I did not commit.

Your Honor, I honestly believe that if the verdict had been given by you and you alone, I think that I would have walked out of this Court a free man; but that was not the case.

Your Honor, I worked for this system in law enforcement for six years and I know it has its faults; but, thank God, it has its safeguards for miscarriages of justice; and [those are] the appellate courts.

I want to thank all of you, the Bailiffs, the Prosecutor, and you, Your

□ PROBATION VIOLATOR
(Check if Applicable)

1

IN THE CIRCUIT COURT, <u>SECOND</u>
JUDICIAL CIRCUIT, IN AND FOR

<u>LEON</u> COUNTY, FLORIDA

DIVISION <u>FELONY</u>

STATE OF FLORIDA

CASE NUMBER <u>85-4810</u>

—vs—

<u>JOHN WESLEY PEAVY</u>
Defendant

FILED
PAUL F. HARTSFIELD
CLERK CIRCUIT COURT
LEON COUNTY, FLORIDA
APR 23 1 44 PH '87

4/23/87

JUDGMENT

The Defendant, <u>JOHN WESLEY PEAVY</u>
_____ , being personally before this

Court represented by <u>ANTHONY BAJOCZKY</u>
_____ , his attorney of record, and having:

XXXXXBeen tried and found guilty of the following crime(s)

(Check Applicable Provision)
    □ Entered a plea of guilty to the following crime(s)
    □ Entered a plea of nolo contendere to the following crime(s)

COUNT	CRIME	OFFENSE STATUTE NUMBER(S)	DEGREE OF CRIME	CASE NUMBER
1	FIRST DEGREE MURDER	782.04	LIFE FEL.	85-4810
2	FIRST DEGREE MURDER	782.04	LIFE FEL.	85-4810
3	SHOOTING INTO DWELLING	790.19	FEL 2	85-4810
4	USE OF FIREARM IN COMMISSION OF A FELONY	790.07(2)	FEL 2	85-4810

and no cause having been shown why the Defendant should not be adjudicated guilty, IT IS ORDERED THAT the Defendant is hereby ADJUDICATED GUILTY of the above crime(s).

•••••••••••••••••••••

The Defendant is hereby ordered to pay the sum of $20.00 pursuant to F.S. 960.20 (Crimes Compensation Trust Fund). The Defendant is further ordered to pay the sum of $3:00 as a court cost pursuant to F.S. 943.25(4).

    □ The Defendant is ordered to pay an additional sum of two dollars ($2.00) pursuant to F.S. 943.25(8).
    (This provision is optional; not applicable unless checked).

(Check if Applicable)
    □ The Defendant is further ordered to pay a fine in the sum of $_____
    pursuant to F.S. 775.0835.
    (This provision refers to the optional fine for the Crimes Compensation Trust Fund, and is not applicable unless checked and completed. Fines imposed as part of a sentence pursuant to F.S. 775.083 are to be recorded on the Sentence page(s)).

    □ The Court hereby imposes additional court costs in the sum of $_____.

Exhibit 6-5 Judgment made against Peavy. These documents show the charges of which he was convicted, the fingerprints taken from him, his sentence, and his placement in custody.

1a

Imposition of Sentence Stayed and Withheld (Check if Applicable)	☐ The Court hereby stays and withholds the imposition of sentence as to count(s) _____ and places the Defendant on probation for a period of _____ under the supervision of the Department of Corrections (conditions of probation set forth in separate order.)
Sentence Deferred Until Later Date (Check if Applicable)	☐ The Court hereby defers imposition of sentence until _____. (date)

The Defendant in Open Court was advised of his right to appeal from this Judgment by filing notice of appeal with the Clerk of Court within thirty days following the date sentence is imposed or probation is ordered pursuant to this adjudication. The Defendant was also advised of his right to the assistance of counsel in taking said appeal at the expense of the State upon showing of indigency.

JUDGE

FINGERPRINTS OF DEFENDANT

1. R. Thumb	2. R. Index	3. R. Middle	4. R. Ring	5. R. Little

6. L. Thumb	7. L. Index	8. L. Middle	9. L. Ring	10. L. Little

Fingerprints taken by:

George Granger LCSD   _John Wesley Peavy Sr._

Name and Title   JOHN WESLEY PEAVY

DONE AND ORDERED in Open Court at _____LEON_____ County, Florida, this __23rd__ day of __Apr.__ A.D. 19__87__. I HEREBY CERTIFY that the above and foregoing fingerprints are the fingerprints of the Defendant, _JOHN WESLEY PEAVY_ and that they were placed thereon by said Defendant in my presence in Open Court this date.

JUDGE

Exhibit 6-5 Continued.

Honor, for all the consideration you have shown my family throughout this trial.

Your Honor, I want you to know that, whatever this sentence is that you are about to give me, I still will hold you in the highest esteem.

To the Jury: I hold no malice nor any anger toward any one of you, just disappointment. I guess my wife best summed it up in her letter to the paper; and I quote: "You, the jury, have made a decision you must live with the rest of your life, and that is beyond a reasonable doubt, beyond

Defendant JOHN WESLEY PEAVY

Case Number _____ 85-4810 _____

SENTENCE

(As to Count _____ 1 _____)

The Defendant, being personally before this Court, accompanied by his attorney, ANTHONY BAJOCZKY

_____, and having been adjudicated guilty herein, and the Court having given the Defendant an opportunity to be heard and to offer matters in mitigation of sentence, and to show cause why he should not be sentenced as provided by law, and no cause being shown,

☐ and the Court having on _____ deferred imposition of sentence
until this date.   (date)

*(Check either provision
if applicable)*

☐ and the Court having placed the Defendant on probation and having subsequently revoked the Defendant's probation by separate order entered herein.

IT IS THE SENTENCE OF THE LAW that:

☐ The Defendant pay a fine of $ _____, plus $ _____ as the 5% surcharge required by F.S. 960.25.

☒ The Defendant is hereby committed to the custody of the Department of Corrections
☐ The Defendant is hereby committed to the custody of the Sheriff* of _____ County, Florida
(Name of local corrections authority to be inserted at printing, if other than Sheriff)

To be imprisoned (check one; unmarked sections are inapplicable)

☒ For a term of Natural Life
☐ For a term of _____
☐ For an indeterminate period of 6 months to _____ years.

☐ Followed by a period of _____ on probation under the supervision of the Department of Corrections according to the terms and conditions of probation set forth in a separate order entered herein.

*If "split" sentence
complete either of
these two paragraphs*

☐ However, after serving a period of _____ imprisonment in _____ the balance of such sentence shall be suspended and the Defendant shall be placed on probation for a period of _____ under supervision of the Department of Corrections according to the terms and conditions of probation set forth in a separate order entered herein.

SPECIAL PROVISIONS

By appropriate notation, the following provisions apply to the sentence imposed in this section:

*Firearm — 3 year
mandatory minimum*

☐ It is further ordered that the 3 year minimum provisions of F.S. 775.087(2) are hereby imposed for the sentence specified in this count, as the Defendant possessed a firearm.

*Drug Trafficking —
mandatory minimum*

☐ It is further ordered that the _____ year minimum provisions of F.S. 893.135(1)( )( ) are hereby imposed for the sentence specified in this count.

*Retention of
Jurisdiction*

☒ The Court pursuant to F.S. 947.16(3) retains jurisdiction over the defendant for review of any Parole Commission release order for the period of *2.5 years.* The requisite findings by the Court are set forth in a separate order or stated on the record in open court.

Habitual Offender

☐ The Defendant is adjudged a habitual offender and has been sentenced to an extended term in this sentence in accordance with the provisions of F.S. 775.084(4)(a). The requisite findings by the court are set forth in a separate order or stated on the record in open court.

Jail Credit

☒ It is further ordered that the Defendant shall be allowed a total of *486 days* credit for such time as he has been incarcerated prior to imposition of this sentence. Such credit reflects the following periods of incarceration (optional):

Consecutive/Concurrent

It is further ordered that the sentence imposed for this count shall run ☐ consecutive to ☐ concurrent with (check one) the sentence set forth in count _____ above.

Exhibit 6-5 Continued.

any assumption. And if it is any consolation to the jury, you are not the first jury to convict an innocent man, nor will you be the last."
     Thank you.

THE COURT: Are you prepared for sentencing?

MR. BAJOCZKY [a defense attorney]: Yes, sir.

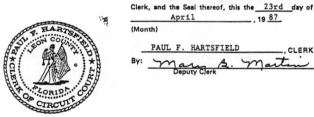

CASE NO: 85-4810
STATE OF FLORIDA

UNIFORM COMMITMENT TO CUSTODY
OF DEPARTMENT OF CORRECTIONS

The Circuit Court of _____ LEON _____ County
in the _____ Fall _____ Term, 19_87_, in the case of

State of Florida

vs

_____ JOHN WESLEY PEAVY _____
Defendant

IN THE NAME AND BY THE AUTHORITY OF THE STATE OF FLORIDA, TO THE SHERIFF OF SAID COUNTY AND THE DEPARTMENT OF CORRECTIONS OF SAID STATE, GREETING:

The above named defendant having been duly charged with the offense specified herein in the above styled Court, and he having been duly convicted and adjudged guilty of and sentenced for said offense by said Court, as appears from the attached certified copies of Indictment/Information, Judgement and Sentence, and Felony Disposition and Sentence Data form which are hereby made parts hereof;

Now therefore, this is to command you, the said Sheriff, to take and keep and, within a reasonable time after receiving this commitment, safely deliver the said defendant, together with any pertinent Investigation Report prepared in this case, into the custody of the Department of Corrections of the State of Florida: and this is to command you, the said Department of Corrections, by and through your Secretary, Regional Directors, Superintendents, and other officials, to keep and safely imprison the said defendant for the term of said sentence in the institution in the state correctional system to which you, the said Department of Corrections, may cause the said defendant to be conveyed or thereafter transferred. And these presents shall be your authority for the same. Herein fail not.

WITNESS the Honorable _CHARLES D. MCCLURE_
Judge of said Court, as also _PAUL F. HARTSFIELD_
Clerk, and the Seal thereof, this the _23rd_ day of
_____ April _____ , 19_87_
(Month)

PAUL F. HARTSFIELD , CLERK
By: _Mary B. Martin_
    Deputy Clerk

Exhibit 6-5 Continued.

THE COURT: Mr. Peavy, you have just been convicted by a jury of your peers on two counts of murder in the first degree, shooting into an occupied dwelling, and use of a firearm in the commission of a felony. The jury has recommended life in prison. The State has asked for the death penalty. I am going to accept the recommendation of the jury.

I do adjudicate you guilty in Count One of murder in the first degree and sentence you to life imprisonment with a mandatory twenty-five years before you are eligible for parole.

As to Count Two, I adjudicate you guilty of murder in the first degree and sentence you to life imprisonment with a mandatory twenty-five years before you are eligible for parole, to run consecutive with the sentence now imposed in Count One.

As to Count Three, shooting into an occupied dwelling, I adjudicate you guilty of that offense. I sentence you to thirty months in the Department of Corrections, to run concurrent with any and all other sentences imposed in this case.

As to Count Four, I adjudicate you guilty of the use of a firearm in the commission of a felony and sentence you to thirty months in the Department of Corrections, to run concurrent with any and all of the sentences imposed herein.

You have thirty days to file a notice of appeal if you wish. A lawyer will be appointed and court costs waived if necessary.

Do you understand?

THE DEFENDANT: Right.

MR. BAJOCZKY: We understand, Your Honor.

THE COURT: All right, sir.
We'll stand in recess. . . .

(Whereupon, the defendant was fingerprinted in open court and the proceedings adjourned.)

Study Questions

1. Why do you suppose they had to hold a special hearing when Peavy did not want to return to the courtroom for the penalty phase? What would have happened if he had not taken his seat at the defense table? How would such an action have mattered?

2. Why do you suppose it took twelve people only fifteen minutes to render a life-or-death decision in the penalty phase?

3. Are there any reasons for downward departure from the guidelines in sentencing Peavy?

Endnotes

1. See Florida Statutes 921.231 (1989).

2. See Florida Statutes 775.089 (1989).

3. See Florida Statutes 921.16 (1) (1989).

4. See Algia R. Cooper, Stephan L. Gorman, and Leonard J. Holton, "Sentences," in *Florida Rules and Practices* (Tallahassee, FL: Florida Bar, 1986), 291.

5. Florida Statutes 775.087 (1989).

6. For example, see Florida Statutes 775.0823 (1989).

7. For example, see Florida Statutes 775.0825 (1989).

8. For example, see Florida Statutes 775.084 (1989).

9. For example, see Florida Statutes 775.084 (1989).

10. For example, see Florida Statutes 775.087 (1989).

11. For example, see Florida Statutes 775.0845 (1989).

12. For example, see Florida Statutes 775.085 (1989).

13. *Florida Rules of Criminal Procedure*, rule 3.701 (1987).

14. Florida Statutes 921.001 (5); for a discussion of reasons for departure from the guidelines for recommended sentences, see Algia R. Cooper, Stephen L. Gorman, and Leonard J. Holton, "Sentences," in *Florida Criminal Rules and Practices* (Tallahassee, FL: Florida Bar, 1986), 290c–290e.

15. Leonard J. Holton, director, Sentencing Guidelines Commission, Florida Supreme Court, Tallahassee, FL, personal communication, 29 March 1990.

16. Florida Statutes 924.06 (1989).

17. Florida Statutes 924.07 (1989).

18. *Neering v. State*, 164 So.2d 29 (Fla. 1st DCA 1964).

19. *Florida Rules of Criminal Procedure*, rule 3.720 (1987).

20. For example, see Florida Statutes 921.143 (1989).

21. Philip J. Padovano, circuit judge, Second Judicial Circuit of Florida, Tallahassee, FL, personal communication, 8 May 1990.

22. *Furman v. Georgia*, 408 U.S. 238 (1972).

23. *Gregg v. Georgia*, 428 U.S. 153 (1976).

24. Florida Statutes 921.141 (5) (1989). Aggravating circumstances 10 and 11 were added after 1987.

25. Florida Statutes 921.141 (6) (1989).

26. *Booth v. Maryland*, 482 U.S. 496, 508 (1987).

7

Legal Remedies

Controversy Still Churns

In most murder trials, the jury speaks, the losing side sheds a few tears, the winning side shakes a few hands, and an appeal quietly cranks into action. It's usually the end of the story, but not so with this case.

Weeks after the verdict, controversy still churned about whether the right man had been investigated, arrested, jailed, tried, convicted, and locked in prison for two life terms.

At the helm of the controversy were the Peavys. The guilty verdicts only caused them to proclaim even more loudly that Johnny was innocent. Someone else, they insisted, killed Bobby Harrison and Mary Lee Driggers.

They went public, pouring our their story to a newspaper reporter who had covered the trial. The Peavys accused investigators of lazily probing drug-related leads, which the Peavys believed would have led to the real killer.

They named suspects, some of whom investigators had already probed and dismissed. They found reports connecting guns, drugs, and motives to kill. They continued their search to make the names of suspects fit the evidence.

Petitions began circulating in the communities of Tallahassee, Havana, and the surrounding area, with members of Harrison's own family joining more than 4,000 people signing their names to ask for a new trial for Peavy or a governor-appointed investigation if an appeal failed.

Even the Peavys admitted that such actions were long shots. But they pressed on, offering a $25,000 reward to anyone coming forward with new information that would clear Johnny's name.

While Peavy wrote a letter to the judge, Peavy's family and friends sent letters to the *Tallahassee Democrat* questioning the IQs of the jurors at Peavy's trial and blasted coin-toss justice (see Exhibit 7-1). One was signed by a "burdened citizen of our judicial system:"

"Circumstantial evidence and small talk at a local tavern does not make a man guilty. How can the jurors sleep at night? I can't."

179

April 1, 1987

Dear Judge McClure,

Mr. Brian Engles, from D.O.C. Prob. & Parole, told me if I wanted I could write you concerning my trial which was recently concluded in your court. I have certain views & feelings that I wish to share with you.

To start out let me tell you about Bobby Harrison's and our relationship. Regarding Mary Lee Driggers, I did not know her therefore can not relate any information concerning her. Bobby & I have known each other since approximately 1965. This was when he started dating my sister whom he married. Bobby & I were always good friends.

Exhibit 7-1 Letter written by John Wesley Peavy to Judge Charles McClure, April 1, 1987.

Larry Stephens, who said he had known both Peavy and Harrison for many years, wrote to the newspaper: "I have tried to figure out what the jury heard that I didn't. And the only thing in my wildest imagination would be the testimony of the two jailbirds presented by the state attorney. In my opinion, it would take a total imbecile to believe one word either of these people had to say. It was obvious that their testimony resulted in dropped charges, reduced sentences, and was completely self-serving to their future."

Just as vigorously as the Peavys and their supporters proclaimed Johnny innocent, the police and prosecutors on the case insisted they had nailed the right man. They praised the jurors' wisdom, congratulated themselves on a job well done, and resented all the second-guessing. There may be two sides to a controversy, but only one side wins. And, the prosecutors said, they won in a courtroom, fair and square.

"I've been a prosecutor for sixteen years," said Deputy State Attorney Tony Guarisco, "and I've never had this aggravation. I think this jury did a great job, and they were very conscientious. They took notes, pad after pad after pad. We appreciate their service, and we're sorry they've had to go through this abuse."

But private investigator Ronnie Boyce, who used to do his sleuthing for the law, said he was so jolted by the verdict that he stayed up thinking until dawn.

"I've been a deputy and a bailiff, and I've watched lots of trials," Boyce said. "In my opinion, that's one jury in over a thousand that would ever have

I would like to say though that our relationship was probably more like brothers. We each had some friends in common and also had our separate friends. Bobby was the type of friend that would do almost anything for me and I must say my feelings toward him were likewise. Over the years, Bobby and I hung around with each other a lot, but I also must say that he and I spent more time with our other friends than we did with each other.

At this time let me say that I respected Bobby and also loved him like a brother. I respected him because he was the type of man that would not talk about you behind your back. If he had anything to say about someone, he would say it directly to them. I know, because I have seen him do this on several occasions. I also respected Bobby because he was good at every task he set out to do. Bobby was the type of person that you could say would always complete what he started.

Bobby and I had only two verbal arguments in the almost twenty years that we knew each other. Once, in approx. 1976 or 77, while my son and I were at Bobby's place, having a cook-out, I had had too much to drink. Bobby did not want me to drive home in the condition I was in. I smarted off at Bobby and told him it was none of his business what I did. Words were exchanged between Bobby and I. Bobby finally stated that he was just telling me this because he loved me and my son and didn't want anything to happen to us. I apologized and told him I understood his concern. My son and I ended up staying overnight. The only other time Bobby and I had words was I believe in 1982. While Gloria and I were separated, a female friend and myself rode to Bobby's house. While we all were standing outside talking, one of Bobby's dogs sniffed a certain part of my female friend's body. Bobby made the comment that "you must be in heat." The remark should not have been made and I told Bobby so. We had words and me and my friend left. I saw Bobby the next day at his service station and nothing about the incident of the night before was mentioned then nor was it ever mentioned again.

Even after Bobby's and my sister's divorce, Bobby and I remained friends. Bobby and Sandra's divorce hurt me and the whole family. We all knew that Bobby and Sandra loved each other but fussed a great deal. Sandra told Bobby that if he would change some of his ways she would not file for a divorce. After their divorce, I felt like one day they might get back together.

After their divorce, I saw Bobby often. I also hung around his service station. My whole family continued to buy gas from Bobby. On one occasion several months after the divorce, me, my wife, and kids went to Bobby's to a cook-out. On several occasions me and my kids went to Bobby's. My kids loved Bobby and he also loved my kids.

I guess it was around the time that Martha Monroe was charged with trying to buy cocaine that me and other people begin to notice a change in Bobby. I saw him on several occasions during this time but you could tell that something was wrong. It was like his personality had changed. For the last few months of Bobby's life, I saw him only a few times.

On the night of Oct. 31, 85, the last time I saw Bobby at the Shady Rest, he was the same Bobby that he had been for the past several months. We exchanged greetings and that was about it. My comments to Mr. Sam Castle, the bar tender, were taken out of context and worded to mean what the prosecution wanted them to mean. My statements to Mr. Castle were more informative than anything else because he had stated to me that he did not know Bobby Harrison. I merely was telling him who Bobby was, and during the conversation told him that he and my sister had lost their house. Sir, my statement to Mr. Castle was in no way intended to be vindictive toward Bobby. As to when I left the bar, the only thing I can tell you is that I went straight to the farm. I at no time went to Bobby's house that night nor have I since.

In regards to my Tec-9, the last time it was fired it was shot by my son and the gun was jamming. This was the second time it had done so in the previous two or three weeks. On the day it jammed on my son, I took the gun into the house and cleaned and oiled it. Later that day, or the next, my wife told me to put it up. I put

Exhibit 7-1 Continued.

the gun behind the seat of my truck. This was either one or two weeks prior to Oct. 31, 85. My reason for putting the gun in my truck was to take it to Kevin Gun Shop and have him check it out.

Sir, I did not find out that my gun was missing until the latter part of November while I was at Twelve Oaks near Fort Walton. At this time I have no idea who stole the gun, nor do I have any idea where it could be. As far as my Tec-9 being used to commit the crime, deep in my heart I don't believe and can't accept that it was used to commit the crime. As for my Tec-9 coming from the factory without rifling, it would be almost impossible. I know my Tec-9 had rifling because I could see it when I cleaned my gun.

I am a veteran police officer. Why would I bore out the rifling of a gun, use it to commit a crime and then leave the shell casing at the scene of the crime? From my police training, I know that shell casings can be matched to other shell casings to prove they were fired from the same weapon.

As for the shell casings found at the scene, I don't believe they were in anyway connected to the crime. If you remember what was called hole #1, the hole in the shutter, one of the holes that both Lt. Gunter and Dale Nute used to get the trajectory of the bullets. If as the state maintained that this shot was fired from several feet back from the trailer, then the gunman moved toward the trailer and fired the remaining shots, then why were there no shell casings found away from the spot where the 12 were originally found?

There are so many "If And or Buts" about this case. Did the shell casing come from the murder weapon? Were they fired from a gun that someone was using for target practice? This is a question that never will be answered unless my weapon or the murder weapon can be found.

Now, I would like to express to you some of my feelings and views of the trial. After picking the jury the first week, I felt we had a jury that would be fair to both sides. During the first week of the trial I got bad vibes from the jury. I never at any time tried to stare anyone down. All I know is that during that first week and the weeks that followed, none of the fifteen jurors would hold or make eye contact with me. If I happened to look up at one of them and they were looking at me, they would turn their head. I know that eye contact with someone may not necessarily mean they think you're guilty but it did give me bad vibes. I honestly believe that those twelve jurors were the type of citizens that believed if the law arrested you for a crime, then you must be guilty.

This case is a prime example of a miscarriage of Justice. My family, friends and many other people in the surrounding communities cannot believe the verdict rendered in my case in view of the evidence presented. I myself know that the wrong verdict was given.

If it were possible, which I know it's not, I would like to be able to ask each juror what their reasons were for rendering a guilty verdict.

Judge McClure, I do not have nor do I hold any malice toward anyone involved in this case. I know that the twelve that rendered their verdict are only human. As you know, on Friday the 27th, I showed a lot of emotions and anger toward the jury. This past Tuesday night a friend of mine handed me his Bible. He told me to read Ephesians 4:26, 27. After reading it and praying, I must say I felt better and the anger is now gone. I must say though, I still have disappointment toward our Judicial system. I know it is supposed to work, but there are faults in it. I guess that is the reason we have our appellate courts. Its also hard for me to accept the fact that I have lost my freedom for a crime I did not commit.

Sincerely,

John Wesley Peavy, Sr.

Exhibit 7-1 Continued.

found that man guilty. If John Peavy could be convicted, so could I and so could you."

It was hardly easy being a juror in the Peavy case. Rendering the verdict may have technically ended their job at the courthouse, but it didn't end the upheaval in their lives. After weeks of living in that tense otherworld of justice, shut off from their families and jobs, they returned home. At last, they slept in their own beds. But every morning, another acidic letter to the editor about the verdict stared up at them from the paper.

"It's not pleasant being called an idiot," one juror said.

Going back to work meant a desk piled high and questions from everyone. The aftermath of holding a man's life in their hands was so intense that jurors gathered for lunch, and it felt more like a support group.

It wasn't that anyone on the jury wanted to change their guilty vote. If any juror felt indecision or regret, they never said so publicly. Summing up the jury's feelings about the verdict, one juror said, "We felt good about it. Otherwise, we wouldn't have left the [deliberations] room."

They were a collection of blacks and whites, of men and women, with jobs ranging from custodian to college professor. Their first vote had split the jurors down the middle: six to six. Within three hours, though, the unconvinced had joined the convinced. Some jurors were willing to explain their deliberations, as long as they were not named.

"The tough part was the absence of evidence on either side," said one juror.

Though the prosecution and the defense had presented no motive, no gun, and no eyewitness, the jury, on the other hand, had heard no alibi or explanation for how the gun was missing. While the jurors wished they had had more to consider, what they did have in the matching shell casings and in bullets without rifling was enough. They concluded that Peavy's gun, with Peavy at the trigger, had killed Harrison and Driggers.

"The only way he could have been innocent is if somebody had stolen his gun," said another juror. "But why would an ex-police officer not report his gun stolen? That didn't make sense."

Once they agreed on the guilty verdict, a juror recalled, "We sat back, took a deep breath, and said, 'OK, now let's figure out how he was innocent.'"

"We were dreaming up alibis for him," said one juror. "That was the frustrating part. We knew we couldn't do that."

As for the testimony of Osborn and Johnson, the convicts, one juror said, "Honestly, those were not the most credible witnesses. That's kind of obvious. They only way we could grant them credibility was because the things they said weren't in the newspaper."

Gloria Peavy had searched for credibility, sympathy, or hostility in the face of each and every juror. Picturing their faces, she tried to figure out which ones might have been leaning toward Johnny's side. She got upset when she heard that one of the alternate jurors made it known that he could not believe the jury's verdict.

"I heard he refused to ride the bus back to the motel with the other jurors," Gloria said.

But that was only rumor. In the legal scheme of things, the alternate juror's opinion did not matter.

Two weeks after the verdict, Gloria and Sandra, Peavy's sister, took a newspaper reporter to the murder scene. They studied the bullet holes in the windows and walls. No longer did they have to rely on the plywood mock-up in the courtroom. They stood on the front porch of Harrison's trailer, peered into the window, and saw the kitchen where bullets had sprayed and blood had flowed. They could almost hear the long-winded experts testifying about trajectory. Like the lawyers pacing before the courtroom prop, they stood where the killer must have stood.

Staring at the shattered kitchen window, they hoisted an imaginary Tec 9 and aimed at bullet holes. They tried to see how far back someone five feet eight inches tall, like Johnny, would have had to stand to shoot a bullet hole at that height. The newspaper reporter happened to be five-foot-eight, but it didn't make estimating the killer's height any more scientific.

Sandra stood within spitting distance of where the killer must have stood and shook her head, saying that her brother would never kill a man. She had buried her ex-husband sixteen months ago, and she reminisced about Bobby aloud: "Gambling. Drinking. Jukes. Bobby loved those three things, and that's why I left him."

Looking toward the meandering Ochlockonee River, Sandra said she believed its dark waters delivered the killer and helped him quietly escape. Sandra said she thought Bobby's murder was drug-related. She remembered her husband bringing home huge sacks of cash and helping him count it. She remembered when a convicted cocaine trafficker, Martha Munroe, had leased Bobby land to farm. Martha had called Bobby several times, Sandra said, at two and three in the morning, to tell him, "The cows are out."

Sandra never made a fuss back then, but she was now convinced that the fences were fine and that Martha's messages were some kind of drug code.

"Big Delacy," Johnny's older brother and Bobby's good friend and former boss, said he had no reason to believe Harrison was involved with drugs.

"But let me say this," he said. "Bobby lost money farming every year. But if I needed $25,000, he always had it. Cash."

But, according to the prosecution, this was just family talking after the trial, after their kin had been found guilty under the law, after the good Peavy name of Gadsden County pioneer stock had been sullied by murder. Tony Guarisco fumed on a couch in State Attorney Willie Meggs's office, not pleased about explaining his case—again.

"You ask why I'm so aggravated? I pick up the paper and see all these letters to the editor—from Peavy family members!"

His blood boiled when people blasted the jury verdict, Guarisco said, because he believed the criticism resulted from Peavy family orchestration and slanted media coverage of the trial.

It was a case hinging on the jury's interpretation of circumstantial evidence, a case that could go either way; but it was a case in which Guarisco believed so strongly that he argued for the death penalty over the jury's recommendation for mercy.

All anyone had to believe, Guarisco said, was the key evidence, the shell casings that had convinced the jury that the murder weapon was Peavy's gun. Casings found at the crime scene matched those found at three other locations Peavy had shot his Tec 9, Guarisco said.

The defense had emphasized that the Tec 9 semiautomatic comes from the manufacturer with rifling, grooves in the barrel that cause fired bullets to spiral out. Yet, said the defense, the bullets in the dead people had had no rifling; and the state provided no evidence that the rifling had been removed from Peavy's Tec 9.

"That didn't bother us," Guarisco said. "Little Delacy," Peavy's nephew, told investigators he was with Uncle Johnny shooting the Tec 9 a few days after Peavy first bought it, around Christmas 1984. One of the bullets landed in an old radiator in the Peavy company shop, and when investigators dug it out, there was no rifling. That, Guarisco said, established that Peavy's Tec 9 had no rifling. How the gun got that way didn't matter.

To place Peavy at the murder scene holding the gun, prosecutors had been forced to depend on the word of two convicted felons, who gave different versions of Peavy's confession.

Defense attorney Tony Bajoczky had called them lowlife jailbirds willing to lie to help themselves, but they had passed polygraphs, a fact important to the prosecutors in weighing their credibility and a fact the jury never heard.

Given the limited evidence and the shaky credibility of Johnson and Osborn, some in the state attorney's office had predicted the case was a loser. Even the jury heard Assistant State Attorney Jack Poitinger say in his closing arguments, "This has not been the greatest case in the world."

"We knew we might lose going in," Willie Meggs said. "The real question the whole time was, 'Was it enough?' It was enough for us. We knew we were prosecuting the right person. But would it be enough for the jury?"

After the trial, Tony Bajoczky said the jury's verdict sent shocked "Oh, my God!"'s rushing through his brain. When the guilty verdicts rang out, the always-confident defense lawyer slumped in his chair. This case, he said, rattled his faith in the jury system.

"This trial was just like a heavyweight fight where the decision is announced and everybody booed," Bajoczky said. "They can't believe what happened. They're wondering who fixed the damn fight."

Leaning back in his leather chair, beside the scales of justice resting on his credenza, Bajoczky admitted he despised losing. But he said he was more concerned that an innocent man had lost his freedom.

Mickey Watson, who worked for the Florida Department of Law Enforcement, smiled when he heard what Bajoczky had said, and commented, "I think we have to remember Mr. Bajoczky's livelihood. In this case, there's a client with money. As long as he can keep the emotions of the family aroused, he can continue to collect their money. And he loves it."

"Malarkey!" was Bajoczky's blunt response. "I don't have the power to stir up four or five thousand people who signed those petitions."

Once a prosecutor himself, Bajoczky said he knew too well the pressure on the law enforcement to solve a case. He likened the investigators in Peavy's case to a pack of wolves chasing caribou.

"Old drunk Johnny starts lagging behind the pack," Bajoczky said, then he slapped his hand. "And, all of a sudden, one of 'em grabs Johnny. And that caribou goes down. And then all the wolves come in and get Johnny.

"The minute John Peavy got hit and went down, all the rest of those caribou can stop and eat grass. And no one bothers to stop and look whether any of those other caribou are wounded."

He did not let the jury hear Peavy's alibi, he conceded, because Queen Jackson's could have sounded like bought testimony. Jackson, Bajoczky said, was a humble black woman dependent on the Peavys for a place to live, the recipient of their hand-me-down clothes and discarded furniture.

But the alibi had other problems. While Jackson insisted Peavy was at her trailer that Halloween night close to ten o'clock, one of her daughters, who worked as a data processor at the Florida Department of Law Enforcement, testified at a deposition that he wasn't. The other children who had been at the trailer were young, and their testimony all sounded alike and memorized, a sheriff's investigator said. It was an alibi rife with inconsistency, and prosecutors and investigators delighted in saying they could tear it to shreds.

But Bajoczky was so confident in the lack of evidence against Peavy that he didn't think it necessary to put him on the witness stand, either, where character assassination about his drinking, womanizing, and temper flare-ups—including the time, authorities said, when Peavy got drunk and fired his gun—might damage Peavy in the eyes of the jury.

All the reports of suspected drug connections that pointed to Harrison were not admissible in the trial, Bajoczky said, unless the defense had enough evidence to focus on one suspect and prove he or she committed the murders.

After the trial was over, Bajoczky and private eye Boyce studied hints and allegations; and they said they had narrowed the field down to a few key suspects. Though they believed their work might lead nowhere, they insisted they weren't giving up.

"I'm positive the killer is still out there," Bajoczky said. "No doubt about it." Leaning low over his desk, he said, "The defense is not going to rest."

The judge signed an order to keep Peavy locked up until he was ninety years old. But the Peavys intended to speed up the homecoming.

Big Delacy, Johnny's older brother, said the case made him view justice as a crapshoot and law enforcement as deceitful. Sitting behind his desk at Peavy & Son Construction, Big Delacy got fired up and said, "We Peavys are tough people. This land you're sitting on was part of the family before Florida was even a state. And we're not going anywhere. We've got to prove who did this thing. As long as our resources hold out, we'll fight this. And if Larry Campbell thinks this is the end of it, he's just never dealt with a Peavy!"

Weeks after Peavy had bunked down in his prison bed, a woman who had known his family for more than thirty years and who belonged to the same Havana Baptist church, sat down with a tape recorder and revealed a secret. In case anything ever happened to her, Thelma Nalls said, the truth would be preserved.

Then Nalls visited Gloria Peavy on Memorial Day weekend 1987, saying she had something to get off her chest, something she just couldn't hold in any longer. What she blurted to Gloria on that hot May day would soon be transcribed as an official sworn statement. Nalls would submit to a polygraph test to show she was telling the truth. And her testimony would become part of a three-volume appeal to try to get Johnny a new trial.

Waiting until Peavy was tried, convicted, and sentenced to two life terms, Thelma Nalls finally came forward as Johnny's alibi witness.

"You know he's innocent and you sit mum for months and months?" Bajoczky boomed at Nalls, a fifty-eight-year-old administrator at a hospital not far over the state line in Georgia.

Nalls, blinking behind thick eyeglasses tinted blue, tried to explain why she waited so long to come forward. With rapid-fire speech, she said that because she knew Peavy had been with her on Halloween night, she assumed he would be found not guilty.

"I have sworn, so help me God, I knew where Johnny was somewhere around ten o'clock to eleven o'clock. And I knew that there was no way that Johnny could be put on the scene of the murders at that time, that night," Nalls said. "There was no way that they could put him there. There was no way they could have any evidence such as fingerprints, or his tire tracks, or anything else, because he wasn't there. And knowing this, I thought, 'There is no way that a jury can convict that man.'

"So, therefore, I thought, why should I expose my life? The killer is still out there. And I tell you now, I am very afraid since I have come forward," she said. "And even, me being afraid, if I had seen any way possible that he could have been convicted, I would have come forth. But I saw no way possible."

Because she said, she believed Peavy had been framed, she thought it was safer for him to sit in jail until the trial. And having witnessed Peavy completely intoxicated, Nalls rationalized, jail would be a good time for him to dry out. And she also thought it would be safer for her if she kept her mouth shut.

So, how was it that this matronly woman, married to Havana, Florida's retired postmaster, a woman with a doctorate in nursing, was with Johnny Peavy that Halloween night?

The night of the murders, Nalls said, Peavy called her at 9:45 P.M. to ask her to meet with him. Outside of her work at the hospital, Nalls said, she counseled people with alcohol problems, as part of her religious stewardship as a good Baptist. Peavy was one of the alcoholics, Nalls said, with whom she regularly met.

"I got to know Johnny more when we were in a Soul-Winning Class in church," Nalls told the defense lawyers. "I suppose Johnny probably got to know a lot about some of the things that I did more or less in private, [that I was] the helping hand, that I tried to help."

About a year before his arrest, Nalls said, Johnny first called her and asked her to meet with him.

"After then, Johnny would call me kind of on a regular basis. And when people call me, I make a little private note on my calendar [so] that I know, so I can watch a cycle [in their behavior]." Johnny, Nalls said, "had a pattern of calling me about every three to six weeks. He would just want to talk. He was looking for, you know, somebody to just talk with and be supportive, or try to help him in some way.

"And he would talk about his drinking problem. He knew he wanted to do something about it. And I would try. My role was to be a good listener and try to find something that—some incentive for Johnny that would motivate Johnny to stop drinking. And I will tell you this. The last three or four months that I worked with Johnny before he was arrested, Johnny was drinking worse. And he was, in my professional opinion, having mental blackouts at times."

On the night of the killings, at the very time of the shooting, Nalls insisted she and Johnny were having one of their private, alcohol-counseling chats. She didn't live far from Peavy's house and when he called, Nalls said, she got ready right away. She met him at the gate to his driveway "in the neighborhood of ten P.M." They sat talking in Johnny's truck for about fifteen minutes, then ended with a prayer because, as Nalls said, "I always put the spiritual part to it."

Only after his arrest, Nalls said, did she remember that she had met him around the end of October. Her calendar, the one on which she charted the patterns of the alcoholics she counseled, showed that Johnny had called on the night of October 31 to ask, "Miss Thelma, can you meet me at the gate?"

The time was crucial. Nalls said it was "somewhere about 9:45. And it may be a minute or two, two or three minutes off; but that's pretty close, about 9:45. Johnny called me. And so I did meet him at the gate. I left home shortly after ten. Now, the gate: it doesn't take but a very short time [to get there]. I would say five minutes at the most to get from my house to the gate. When I pulled in, behind the little building, I saw Johnny come out of a road to my left, in his truck. And he pulled up beside my car."

She got into his truck, Nalls said. Johnny was swigging booze from a bottle.

"He was real sluggish as far as his speech or movement," Nalls said. "This time he just, you know, thought he had a problem, a bad physical problem, which he never [specified]; but I have an idea what he was referring to. He wanted me to see about, you know, connecting him up with a doctor in Georgia."

After their private talk, Nalls said, she got back in her car and watched Peavy's truck wind down the long lane to his house. Then she waited another five minutes at the highway, to make sure Peavy didn't get back on the road.

By the time Nalls got back home, she estimated, it was shortly before eleven P.M. At the trial, prosecutors estimated the killings had occurred between 10:25 and 10:30 P.M. If Johnny was with Thelma when she said he was, he could not be the killer. Nalls said she knew he was innocent, and she called the guilty verdict "the greatest shock of my life."

Thelma Nalls told her story to the defense lawyers, while a court reporter took down every word. When it was all out, Nalls leaned close and told Bajoczky, "Keep my name as quiet as possible for as long as possible."

But the lawyer matter-of-factly replied, "You realize that I'm going to have to divulge your name when we file these papers."

Nalls looked startled. "Not in the newspaper!" she said.

"It may very well be in the newspaper," Bajoczky said firmly, "once it gets filed in the public records in the courthouse."

"Well," Nalls said, "I told you [to do] whatever you had to do."

The defense attorney asked, "And everything you have testified to today before this court reporter is the truth, the whole truth, and nothing but the truth, so help you God?"

"So help me God," Nalls said, nodding her head and pressing her lips together.

Her neatly typed statement, dated May 29, 1987, and a transcript of her testimony to the court reporter, dated August 19, 1987, became part of the 557 pages of documents the defense attorneys gathered to file in the First District Court of Appeal. But the defense lawyers kept secret their latecomer alibi witness. First, they had to document, transcribe, and argue the new information convincingly.

Part of the documentation backing Nalls's testimony was a report written by C. Vincent Dix, a psychologist, on November 23, 1987, detailing Peavy's chronic alcoholism: "Mr. Peavy has a long, full history of alcohol problems. His use of beverage alcohol began at the age of twelve, with the first known episode of drinking to intoxication occurring at age fourteen. His first alcoholic blackout was associated with this episode" (see Exhibit 7-2).

In his report, Dr. Dix described a blackout: "Contrary to what the name implies, a blackout does not mean passing out or losing consciousness." Rather, he said, a blackout is "an amnesia-like period that is often associated with heavy drinking. Someone who is or has been drinking may appear perfectly natural, and [may] function quite normally at the task at hand. Yet later, the person has no memory of what has transpired. A better term might be 'blankout.'"

The report said there had been drinking problems in the Peavy family for generations, making Peavy "a prime candidate for alcohol addiction before he ever graduated from adolescence."

The defense lawyers wanted Dix to answer a question: Could Peavy have suffered one of those alcoholic "blankouts" on the night of the killings?

The psychologist scrutinized Peavy's alcohol-dependent routine on October 31, 1985. Breakfast had been two to four twelve-ounce cans of

Psychological Evaluation

NAME: John W. Peavy
DOB: 11/15/46
REGARDING: Evaluation of Alcoholic Condition
EXAMINER: C. Vincent Dix, Ph.D.
                   Psychologist
DATE: 11/23/87

The following report represents an evaluation of John W. Peavy regarding his disease of alcoholism and the facts and circumstances surrounding October 31, 1985. This review is comprised of a review of all pertinent medical and psychological history for John Peavy, including the medical records and prior testimony of Dr. Peter A. Macaluso, a family history, and a clinical interview with Mr. Peavy. I furthermore reviewed the sworn statement of Dr. Thelma Nalls, and statements of Ms. Winessa "Queen" Jackson, Barbara Ann Jackson, Lawrence Herring, Quanisha Roberts, Deron Robinson, and Joyce Ann Jackson regarding the evening events on October 31, 1985.

Mr. Peavy has a long, full history of alcohol problems. His use of beverage alcohol began at the age of 12 with the first known episode of drinking to intoxication occurring at age 14. His first alcoholic blackout was associated with this episode. Contrary to what the name implies, a blackout does not mean passing out or losing consciousness. Nor does it mean psychological blocking of events, or repression. A blackout is an amnesia-like period that is often associated with heavy drinking. Someone who is or has been drinking may appear perfectly natural, and function quite normally at the task at hand. Yet later, the person has no memory of what has transpired. A better term might be "blankout." The blank spaces in the memory may be total or partial. A person who has been drinking and who experiences a blackout will not be able to recall how he got home, who he saw or spoke with, the importance of a given decision, his thoughts or feelings. During the blackout, the alcoholic is entirely conscious and capable of a full range of volitional behavior; after the blood alcohol level diminishes and the brain clears, the individual will not remember aspects (crucial or trivial) of his behavior.

Research indicates that after a period varying from months to a few years of alcohol abuse, an individual enters a phase of prodromal (precursory) signs that foreshadows the shape of future behavior. Among the prodromal signs are blackouts. Coupled with Mr. Peavy's multigenerational family history of alcoholism, another highly weighted factor in predicting alcoholism, he was a prime candidate for alcohol addiction before he ever graduated from adolescence.

Mr. Peavy first acknowledged having a problem with alcohol at the age of 22. His first formal hospital treatment was in 1975 when he was 28 years old. His drinking history from that time reveals increasing frequency of alcohol consumption and increased tolerance. This refers to how the body handles alcohol as a result of repeated exposures. There becomes a drive for higher blood alcohol levels to be held in the body. When this happens, the individual feels "normal." During a period after completing his treatment in 1975, Mr. Peavy was hospitalized for alcohol detoxification in 1976, and again in December 1982, for a seizure, secondary to alcohol withdrawal and alcoholic hepatitis. He was diagnosed as being alcohol dependent at this time.

Mr. Peavy's drinking consumption continued after his hospitalization in 1982 until he was admitted to an in-patient chemical dependency treatment program in August 1984. Mr. Peavy's alcohol consumption prior to this hospitalization was approximately one-fifth of Vodka per day. At this time he was medically treated for dehydration and for being malnourished. It was documented that Mr. Peavy had been experiencing blackouts several times a week, and in the attending physician's statements, "We found the patient was in a blackout during the first several days of treatment."

Upon completion of this program (September 1984), Mr. Peavy began drinking immediately. His consumption rapidly returned to pretreatment levels. In July 1985, Mr. Peavy was admitted to another detoxification program, but refused to

Exhibit 7-2 Report, written by C. Vincent Dix in November 1987, chronicling Peavy's history of alcoholism.

stay and complete treatment and was discharged. His drinking became close to constant for a two-month period prior to November 6, 1985, when he was again admitted to an in-patient treatment program for Pathological Intoxification, Alcohol Dependency, and detoxification. Pathological intoxication implies subsequent amnesia for the period of intoxication. A blood alcohol level of .375 was drawn on Mr. Peavy on November 6, 1985. This level is known to be lethal. Mr. Peavy was having difficulty with detoxification and mental orientation during this seven-day hospitalization. Records indicate "he continues to appear toxic through his stay" and ". . . unaware of his surroundings, evidence of both recent and remote memory impairment." On November 11, 1985, Mr. Peavy was transferred to Twelve Oaks in Navarre, Florida, for on-going treatment. He completed that program December 9, 1985.

Clearly, Mr. Peavy has as severe problems with alcohol as one can have. His diagnosis as of December 9, 1985, was: (1) Alcohol Dependency, Chronic and Continuous, and (2) Pathological Intoxication (upon admission).

On October 31, 1985, Mr. Peavy was accused of shooting and killing two people. He has subsequently been found guilty and is in prison. The question posed, what is the likelihood of Mr. Peavy's being in an alcoholic blackout on this day? Mr. Peavy began the day of October 31, 1985, consuming two to four 12-ounce cans of beer in order to function normally. He consumed a minimum of one pint of Vodka during the day and may have consumed a second pint. He recalls being unable to eat for some days. He knows he had some beer at a local tavern that night after taking the kids out for Halloween. His memory of the events of that day are incomplete. With the documented clinical history and the above subjective date, one other piece of information must be acknowledged. The heavier the drinking and the greater number of years over which it has occurred, the more likely the occurrence of blackouts. Several other factors are positively associated with the occurrence of blackouts. These include out-of-control drinking, poor diet, ability to consume large quantities (tolerance), history of a prior head injury (bullet wound to the head in 1958), and gulping drinks—all of which pertain to Mr. Peavy.

After reviewing the medical and alcohol history of John W. Peavy, the medical records and prior testimony of Dr. Peter A. Macaluso, the sworn statement of Dr. Thelma Nalls, Ms. Winessa "Queen" Jackson, Barbara Ann Jackson, Lawrence Herring, Quanisha Roberts, Deron Robinson, and Joyce Ann Jackson, witnesses regarding the evening events on October 31, 1985, and after having personally conducted a clinical interview of John W. Peavy on November 6, 1987, it is my opinion that Mr. Peavy was in and out of alcoholic blackouts on the day and evening of October 31, 1985. It is further my opinion that Mr. Peavy saw and spoke with persons on that date of whom he has no recollection whatsoever. Similarly, there are behaviors on other dates of which he has no recollection. A similar pattern of alcoholic blackouts are equally predictable for a period of time before and after the day of October 31, 1985.

Exhibit 7-2 Continued.

---

beer, just for Johnny to feel good enough to function normally. Then came a minimum of one pint of vodka during the day, and perhaps a second pint. Peavy remembered being unable to eat for days after October 31.

"He knows he had some beer at a local tavern that night, after taking the kids out for Halloween," Dix wrote. "His memory of the events of that day are incomplete."

The psychologist reviewed the history of John Wesley Peavy's medical treatment and alcohol abuse, noting an injury involving a bullet wound to the head in 1958; and he studied the testimony of witnesses. He came to this conclusion:

"It is my opinion that Mr. Peavy was in and out of alcoholic blackouts on the day and evening of October 31, 1985. It is further my opinion that Mr. Peavy saw and spoke with persons on that date of whom he has no recollection whatsoever."

The blackout testimony, the defense insisted, explained why Peavy never volunteered Nalls as his alibi. He had no alibi available for his trial, the defense argued, because Peavy had memory gaps he could not fill.

But when Nalls came forth as Peavy's alibi witness, the prosecution pounced on her testimony. They investigated her reputation in the Havana community. They insisted she was wrong. The time gap that Peavy could not explain, the time gap a psychologist called a "blankout," was, to prosecutors, a stretch of time in which Peavy crept up to Bobby Harrison's window and ended two lives. The gap was filled with murder, the prosecutors insisted; and the jury's verdict had supported the prosecutors' belief.

On February 15, 1988, Peavy's lawyers filed a motion for a new trial at the First District Court of Appeal, making public for the first time the alibi of Thelma Nalls.

"Her testimony, I feel, proves Johnny Peavy innocent," Bajoczky said on the day the papers were filed at the appellate court. "I certainly hope justice will be done and we get a new trial."

When he learned of the new alibi witness, State Attorney Willie Meggs said, "All I can say is, 'File your motion.' It'll be an interesting hearing."

Asked if he believed he prosecuted the right man for murder, Tony Guarisco, the prosecutor, answered, "Absolutely!"

"We just thank God that she's come forward," Gloria Peavy said on the night the alibi was publicly unveiled. "We're putting a lot of hope on this. The whole family is."

The appeals court granted the motion, and the matter was returned to the trial court level for a hearing, in which Leon Circuit Judge Charles McClure would decide if there was enough new evidence to warrant a new trial. On April 20, 1988, it was time for the judge to decide whether a man convicted of murdering two people should get an extraordinary second chance.

The courtroom was packed. Nalls sat tensely with Peavy's family and supporters, who buzzed with anticipation of publicly proclaiming Johnny's innocence. Florida Department of Law Enforcement agents sat behind the prosecutors, dreading another rehashing of the case that would not end.

The air was thick with tension by the time Judge McClure, in his black robe, swished up the steps to his bench. Gloria whispered, "I am so scared something is going to go wrong."

First, the judge examined the defense's "extraordinary motion for a new trial." According to the Florida Rules of Criminal Procedure, the defense must file a motion for a new trial within ten days of the jury's verdict. And Peavy's defense had met the time limits: the verdict was rendered March 25, 1987; the defense filed a motion for a new trial on April 3; and the judge denied it on April 28, on Peavy's sentencing day.

Now, on April 21, 1988, more than a year after Peavy's conviction, de-

fense attorney Robert Harper told the judge he was asking for either an
"extraordinary motion for new trial," because of the newly discovered evidence, or a motion for postconviction relief, under the argument that Peavy's
Sixth Amendment right to counsel had been damaged because his lawyers
had lacked critical alibi testimony.

But there is no such thing as an extraordinary motion for a new trial,
argued Assistant State Attorney Ray Marky. Pointing toward Harper, the
prosecutor said, "He knows that the burden in a 'coram nobis' [where relief for a mistake at trial is brought straight to the trial court judge, rather
than being reviewed first by the appeals court] is that with the new evidence, the jury couldn't have returned the guilty verdict. And he can't beat
that." And, Marky argued, the defense could not exceed the ten-day deadline for filing motions for new trials.

"Strike this horse he calls a cow, but still won't give milk," Marky said.

Harper replied by saying that he had asked the First District Court of
Appeal for permission to file his extraordinary motion for a new trial and
that he had been granted his wish.

"In your discretion, you can deny [the request] or grant it," Harper told
the judge. He tried to bypass the ten-day deadline for new trial motions by
saying, "When leave is granted by the appellate court, the jurisdictional
time frame problem is deleted."

Harper suggested that McClure's choice was simple: "If it meets the
standard for a motion for new trial [on the basis] of newly discovered evidence, it's granted. If it doesn't [meet the standard], it's denied. That's all
there is to it."

Marky jumped up to reiterate: "Counsel's motion is untimely, and there
is no right for an extraordinary motion for new trial."

"I'm not trying to say there is a right. I said there is a proper case,"
Harper replied. The defense attorney said that Marky only wanted to argue "the technical point of timeliness" because "the state is trying to avoid
getting to substantive arguments."

"I don't think the time limit on filing is the issue," Harper again told the
judge. This time, his voice was more pleading than demanding. "The issue is that the appellate court gave you jurisdiction. It's [up to] your discretion to consider it [the motion] or not."

Marky interjected: "They gave you the power to look at these motions,
nothing more. You don't have the discretion to extend the time. The appellate court doesn't have the discretion to extend the time. The motion for a
new trial must come within ten days. If you miss that, you've got coram
nobis. That's why this man can't prevail on an extraordinary motion for
new trial."

The spectators watching this legal Ping-Pong match were relieved
when Judge McClure finally spoke. "It appears the First District Court of
Appeal sent this back to me," McClure began. "They did not say any motion had any merit or demerit. In looking at the jurisdictional question of
the trial court, it appears a timely motion for a new trial was filed. It appears that this is nothing more than a second motion for a new trial, and

this court feels it does not have jurisdiction for a motion for a new trial because it was not timely filed. So I strike the motion for a new trial."

The Peavys and Nalls exchanged devastated expressions. Shoulders tensed. Gloria looked ready to cry. Johnny's chances were now sliced in half, and everything depended on the second and final motion, the one arguing ineffective assistance of counsel, on the grounds that Peavy's defense lawyers did not use crucial evidence discovered after the trial.

"Frivolous!" was Marky's emphatic word for that defense bid. How could Bajoczky have been expected to know about the new evidence before trial, he argued, when "Ms. Nalls didn't come forward and didn't tell a soul"? Sarcastically, Marky muttered, "I guess God knew about it."

It was Nalls who had failed to come forward, Marky argued. "I want to know what deficiency Mr. Bajoczky is guilty of! Nowhere did they allege that Mr. Bajoczky failed to investigate or call witnesses."

Proving ineffective assistance of counsel, Marky argued, was a two-part test. First, evidence must show a deficiency on the part of counsel. Second, evidence must show that, because of this deficiency, prejudice to the defendant resulted.

"But Mr. Bajoczky, in his own affidavit, said he hired investigators and explored alibis," Marky said. "Mr. Bajoczky said he conferred with the defendant extensively about the alibi. They had alibi witnesses they chose not to use. Now we're told the alibi was not presented because of this gap [in Peavy's memory]. I want to know how the attorney is defective when he can't find what is not known. A lawyer can only do the best he can do. We don't require he pull out a miracle!"

Harper rose slowly from his seat at the defense table and, with the tone of a professor explaining a problem to a classroom of students, said that there are two kinds of argument to prove ineffective assistance of counsel. One is that a lawyer did not do the job out of a failure to use what testimony or evidence was available. The second is the argument, applicable to this situation, of "intervening causes and acts."

Bajoczky did not forget or fail to do anything crucial to the defense, Harper argued. He simply could not have provided the key evidence of an alibi because he did not know about it. Therein lay the flaw in the defense, the ineffective assistance of counsel: Peavy could not tell his lawyers where he had been because he really did not know himself.

"Because we've found new evidence," Harper told the judge, "Mr. Peavy's Sixth Amendment right to effective assistance of counsel has been violated. To what extent requires a hearing. I think we've triggered the necessity of an evidentiary hearing." He asked for, at the very least, a hearing to question Peavy about his relationship with Nalls.

Marky responded: "Mr. Harper [may have] classified this as an act of God. But just to say the counselor didn't find her [Mrs. Nalls] isn't enough. Mr. Bajoczky simply couldn't find her, though he found all the other alibi witnesses." The prosecutor turned and waved toward Nalls. "She'll have to carry the burden the remainder of her time, that she didn't bring forth her testimony at a time Mr. Bajoczky could have considered it and perhaps used it. But the burden is hers, and hers alone. Not the state of Florida's. And certainly not Mr. Bajoczky's, who did all he could do." Until Harper pointed out what Bajoczky failed to do, Marky argued, the motion must fail.

The lawyers stopped talking, and the judge looked up from behind his reading glasses.

"I've been a judge for fifteen years," McClure said, as the Peavy clan clasped hands. "And I've never seen a more competently tried case, both by the state and defense. Extra efforts were made to find witnesses; a private investigator was hired. I find that there was very effective counsel in this case. I find Mr. Bajoczky to be a premier defense counsel. I find no deficiency. I find he exercised extra due diligence and did all he could."

McClure also praised the prosecution's competency, and added, "I find there was no government misconduct. I don't believe I can go any further. I would deny the motion to vacate."

With those words, McClure struck down the motion for a new trial, also denying the second motion based on ineffective assistance of counsel, and dashing the Peavy's hopes. His ruling also silenced Nalls, who desperately wanted to publicly tell her story.

Not everyone was disappointed by the decision. "It appears terminated," Guarisco said after the hearing, looking relieved.

The Peavy family hurried by the prosecutor, who stood in the courthouse hallway, ducked into a small witness waiting room with Bajoczky, and closed the door. Harper, carrying a fat briefcase of failed legal strategy, waited for the elevator. Asked if Nalls would have another chance to give her testimony, Harper said, "Apparently not, unless we win something on appeal. I'm just extremely disappointed that there will be no chance to air Ms. Nalls's testimony. I'm sure she's feeling terribly guilty right now."

Later that evening, on the phone, Nalls said that the judge's ruling gave her "grave concern" about the criminal justice system and that she planned to write him a letter telling him so.

"As I was driving home, I could still hear that state attorney making those remarks about me, that 'Ms. Nalls will have to live with it all her life.' Well, it's just not fair!" Nalls said. "I did not make the right decision in not coming forward. But listen to me now! If anybody could find evidence that puts Johnny Peavy on the scene, from now till eternity, they will not find it. Johnny was with me.

"Johnny Peavy and his family should not have to pay for my failure of not coming forward. The public ought to do something, because tomorrow it may be their loved one. I raise the question: Why is that judge and state attorney's office so bound and determined not to hear evidence from a person who is a trustworthy and honest and upright and law-abiding citizen, when they were willing to take evidence from persons in jail? I can swear that Johnny's innocent!"

While the Peavys again put their hope in a higher court, Nalls tried to make her testimony public. When the *Tallahassee Democrat* wouldn't print her lengthy statement verbatim, Nalls, on June 19, 1988, took out an ad that filled three-quarters of a page. In bold headlines, the ad proclaimed

MESSAGE FROM PEAVY'S ALIBI

By: Thelma Nalls

Prior to my experience with the Johnny Peavy case, I had confidence in our judicial system and in our State Attorney's Office. Now, I am urging everyone to become concerned about what apparently is going on in our judicial system and how our State Attorney's Office really operates behind the scene. Until anyone personally experiences what apparently is going on in our State Attorney's Office and with certain judges, it is difficult to believe and/or understand. I believe that it is my obligation to share with the public, opinions from my experience, of some of the most unjust, cruel and brutal actions being carried out by the State Attorney's Office and Judge Charles McClure known to mankind. I will start by sharing content from a statement I wrote to Tony Bajorsky, (Johnny Peavy's attorney) dated May 28, 1987. I also gave this same information in a sworn deposition at a later date.

For approximately 20 years, I have worked at a mental institution. For four years of this time, I received outstanding training and instructions from a psychoanalyst. I have also spent a considerable amount of time doing counseling, one-to-one therapy, and group therapy. My academic preparation, my professional experience, and my christianity have prepared me well to effectively do some of the things I am continuously involved with.

One of the things I do continuously (over and above my regular job) is to try to help individuals with problems, especially in the physical, mental and spiritual areas. I spend a considerable amount of time working with individuals of all types, who have all types of problems, including alcohol and drug (substance) abuse. When I am at home, I am called for help at all times of the day and night.

Johnny Peavy is one of the many I have worked with and have tried to help. While Johnny and I were attending soul winning classes at the First Baptist Church, Havana, Florida, he learned that I often try to help those with problems. About a year before Johnny was arrested, he called me and asked could I talk with him. I arranged to meet him in front of the Recreation Hall, Havana Baptist Church. After this meeting, Johnny called me many times for counseling. Sometimes, he would be drinking and sometimes, apparently, he was not drinking. It was apparent to me that sometimes when I met Johnny to counsel with (at a later time) he would not have any recall of the previous meeting and at other times, he remembered about the previous meeting.

OCTOBER 31, 1985, was one of the times Johnny Peavy called me. He called me about 9:45 p.m., and said he wanted to talk with me. I asked him where he was. he said he was close to home. I asked him where should I meet him, and he said at the gate going up to his house. I told him that as soon as I finished with what I was doing I would be there. I met Johnny at the gate between 10:10 and 10:15 P.M. As I was turning in toward the gate, behind a small building, I saw Johnny pull out of a drive from a trailer (house) on the left side of the road. He drove up beside me, I got out of my car and got into his truck. It was obvious that Johnny had drunk a lot during the evening. He told me the reason he wanted to see me was he thought he had some kind of a physical problem and he wanted me to help get him an appointment with a good doctor in Georgia - one he could trust and would not just think his physical problem was caused by drinking. We talked for about 15 minutes, then I got in my car and Johnny went down the lane to his house. To make sure he didn't turn around, I waited about 5 or so minutes, then I drove very slowly home watching to see if he was coming down the road. A few days before he was arrested, he called me one morning (he didn't sound like he was drinking) and he told me that he thought he had a physical problem and he wanted to talk to me about helping him see a doctor. As I talked with Johnny, it was obvious he had NO RECALL of seeing me on October 31st.

When Johhny was arrested, I thought it was the most shameful thing I had ever heard of. It wasn't long before I became firmly convinced that he had been framed, and if he had been framed, he was in the safest place at the time being, until his trial.

I never came forth and told anyone about me trying to help Johnny and one of these times was October 31, 1985. My reason for this was MAINLY fear. I knew there was no way POSSIBLE that he could have committed the crime during the time that the State had determined the crime took place, because I was with him. I also knew that regardless as to how anyone tried, there was no way possible to find any evidence whatsoever that he was even at the scene of the crime. Knowing this, and feeling that if it were known that I could attest to his whereabouts, I felt very strongly that my life could be in danger. I felt that the same thing that happened to Bobby Harrison, who was supposed to be a witness for Martha Munroe, could happen to me. It is also my understanding that the jury is to make a decision ONLY on the evidence which is beyond a reasonable doubt, given from the witness stand.

When Johnny was sentenced, I knew that I had to come forth with what I knew about him. Even though I felt very strongly that my life could possibly be in danger, I knew it was my Christian responsibility, my duty to him, the Peavy family and the public, and I could not live with myself if I did not come forth. In trying to decide on who I should go to, I did a lot of praying and thinking about my safety. April 22, 1987, I made an audio tape regarding my knowledge about Johnny Peavy. I made the tape so if anything happened to me before I decided on who to talk with, there would be some type of a record giving information evidencing that Johnny Peavy could not have committed the crime as the State Attorney's Office was accusing him. I finally decided to go to Gloria (Johhny's wife). May 15, 1987, I went to see Gloria. I explained my reason for staying quiet and gave her a tape to listen to. I asked her to return the tape to me the next Monday and not mention my coming to her to anyone (except to Johnny's parents - if she wanted to). I also asked Gloria what I should do. She told me that I should go to talk with Johnny's attorney and she agreed to make the appointment.

On the afternoon of May 25, 1987, I went to see Tony Bajorsky and gave him the information as I have stated above. May 28, 1987, I put this information in a written statement. PLEASE NOTE: I came forth to Gloria about 8 weeks after Johnny's trial and I came forth to his attorney exactly 10 weeks after the trial.

April 20, 1988, I sat in the court room along with many other citizens and witnessed what I consider the most cruel, brutal, unfair action imaginable, by our State Attorney's Office and Judge Charles McClure. Raymond Markey (from State Attorney's Office) compared MY coming forth with new evidence with cases where new evidence had come forth 10 and 12 years later. Remember, I came forth no later than 10 WEEKS. Mr. Markey also made the request to the judge, something to effect of - "Your honor, I ask that you deny the motion for new evidence to be heard. Let us suppose that Mrs. Nalls is telling the truth - Just let her live with herself."

Considering what has actually taken place in the courtroom during Johnny Peavy's trial and during the hearing for new evidence to be heard from a reliable, trustworthy, law-abiding and competent citizen, it is my very strong OPINION that something is going on with Judge McClure and our State Attorney's Office that is NOT above-board - there has to be a snake in the grass. Remember, two "jail-birds" with records were used as witnesses for the State, and their reward was a lesser sentence. I urge citizens in North Florida who care anything about fairness and justice to become concerned and take some type of action regarding the issues of: Why don't the State Attorney's Office and Judge McClure want new evidence to be heard from a reliable, trustworthy, law-abiding citizen? Is the real reason that they are being paid off? Or is it for political gain? Public, please remember that you or your loved one could be the next victim of such cruelty and unjustness. It is my understanding that the State Attorney's Office is basing its stand on some rule that prevents new evidence from being heard after 10 days of a trial. Therefore, regardless as to what new evidence is discovered, even if it were from Jesus himself, it should not be heard. Apparently, Judge McClure agrees. If there is such a rule which disallows new evidence within a reasonable length of time - I urge the public to band together and get such rule changed. Furthermore, a motion for a new trial within 10 days was filed, but no new evidence was available. It is my opinion that a decision to deny new evidence of any kind (from anyone - even a sworn statement by someone other than Johnny, saying that they committed the crime) to be heard, was already made before the hearing for Johnny Peavy on April 20, 1988. I believe that the vast majority of those in the courtroom on April 20th will also agree. I want to stress my opinion is based on what I saw and heard taking place in the courtroom. Another opinion is that out State Attorney's Office is in cahoots with certain judges, and works to get certain cases heard before these judges. Therefore, it is my further opinion that until some "cleaning house" takes place in our State Attorney's Office and with Judge McClure, Johnny Peavy will never get a new trial.

It is no fault of Johnny Peavy or his family that I did not come forth before his trial. Why should Johnny and his family have to pay by him spending the rest of his life in prison? Why should the taxpayers have to pay for someone to spend his life in prison for a crime that he could not have possibly committed at the time the State has determined the crime took place? I am certainly willing to pay the penalty or whatever necessary for not coming forth before Johnny's trial, even though I feel that I had justifiable reasons. Everyone who kept up with the case knows that no evidence beyond a reasonable doubt was presented during the trial from the witness stand that proved Johnny committed the crimes or that he was even on the scene of the crime. I urge the members of the jury for his trial to closely examine the rationale behind the decision they made. Should any of them have any doubt whatsoever about the decision, or any questionable information that influenced their vote (such as, was the case discussed among them during the time they were out of the court room, etc.) to please come forth. I also urge anyone who may have heard a jury member express any concern about the verdict to please encourage that person to come forth with these concerns. Please remember, I can identify with and certainly understand the fear about doing such. However, a person's life and his family's well-being is at stake. And this could easily happen to you or your loved ones.

I urge everyone, including the families of Bobby Harrison and Mary Driggers, to take a stand regarding what is really going on with the State Attorney's Office and with Judge McClure, and what the real reason is that they are so very much against new evidence to be heard regarding Johnny Peavy's case. I recommend that they contact the Governor and the other state offices regarding such injustice and ask for their intervention and that a concerted investigation be made as to what is going on. Is there a pay off involved? Is there political gain involved? My opinion (from my observations) is that something undercover is going on.

Grapevine talk is that the State Attorney's Office has lead some persons to believe that it has some "inside information" which proves that Johnny Peavy murdered Bobby Harrison and Mary Driggers. One thing I know for sure - they DO NOT have any kind of information and never will have such that Johnny Peavy did the murdering during the time they have determined the crime took place. We know that if they had any kind of information that could prove he actually committed the crime, they would have used it during his trial.

Another point, I want to make is that in my opinion, if the State Attorney's Office had spent as much time in trying to get RELIABLE evidence beyond a reasonable doubt regarding who actually committed the crime, as it spent trying to discredit me and my statement, the real murderer could have been found; taxpayers' money would be better spent; families could have been together and there would have been a demonstration of fairness and justice, rather than cruelty and injustice.

I, Thelma Nalls, thank you for reading this article, and hope you will become concerned about the situation.

If you are concerned about the injustice in this case, please clip article, sign & send to Governor Martinez, State Capitol, Tallahassee, FL 32301.

Publication of the article written by Thelma Nalls is paid for by friends of John Wesley Peavy and Thelma Nalls.

Exhibit 7-3 Thelma Nalls took out a three-quarter page newspaper ad to make known her alibi for John Wesley Peavy.

"Message from Peavy's Alibi, by Thelma Nalls." Nalls explained in great detail how she happened to be with Johnny at the time of the murders. She also included heavy doses of self-justification and hurled at the state attorney's office and the judge accusations that were just shy of slanderous (see Exhibit 7-3). She ended the ad with a plea for help: "If you are concerned about the injustice in this case, please clip [this] article, sign and send to Governor Martinez, State Capitol, Tallahassee, Fla. 32301."

But her appeal, like the efforts of Harper and the defense, had no effect. On January 12, 1989, the First District Court of Appeal ruled. And all it said was "Per Curiam. Affirmed." Those three words simply meant that Peavy's conviction and sentence were upheld and that the appellate judges were not offering any reasons or comments for or about their decision. Lawyers call per curiam affirmed rulings "PCA"s, and when they say it, they spit it out like an obscenity. After all the lawyers' work and research, the appellate court would offer not even a speck of feedback, leaving the attorneys to wonder which arguments had merit and which had no chance. All was lost in appellate silence.

Over at the state attorney's office, the prosecutors breathed sighs of relief. Guarisco said that the appellate court's decision should conclude Peavy's attempts to seek a new trial, adding "Unless they seek a rehearing."

But Bajoczky promised that it was far from over. "I can assure you that this will not end Johnny Peavy's recourse," he said, still true to his bulldog spark, as soon as he learned of the appellate court's three-word ruling.

He said he had yet to settle what the recourse would be. He listed Peavy's options: asking for a rehearing, appealing to the Florida Supreme Court, or asking Governor Bob Martinez or the Florida Cabinet for a reduction of sentence or a pardon. Politics would have to be involved. And, as always in politics, there were no guarantees. The defense tried to decide which Cabinet member to court. The Peavys visited Agriculture Commissioner Doyle Conner and LeRoy Collins, former governor of Florida.

"I felt very good talking with them," Gloria said in the summer of 1989. "I even got a handwritten thank-you note from Governor Collins."

Governor Bob Martinez was preparing to run for re-election in 1990. When their favored candidate, Agriculture Commissioner Conner, announced he would resign, the Peavys resigned themselves to another disappointment.

When politics and the courts failed, Gloria Peavy kept searching for a way to keep attention focused on her Johnny, locked away in prison. She found a taker: the world of television. Her tragedy would be late-night entertainment, but at least there was a chance, however slight, that someone who knew something might see the program and come forward. This way, she thought, there was a chance that Johnny's missing gun would turn up and that firearms experts would perform tests showing, once and for all, beyond a reasonable doubt, that her husband was no murderer.

On a steamy Tallahassee day in August 1989, a Dallas television producer and film crew checked into a cheap motel near Interstate 10. They auditioned local actors to play Bobby, Mary Lee, and Johnny in a recreation of the murders on the river. Some, like Queen, Gloria, and Thelma, played themselves.

The crew brought a camera into prison and filmed Johnny, behind bars for nearly four years, proclaiming his innocence. They beamed spotlights on the old, weathered Shady Rest, closed since the murders, and recreated the exchange between Bobby, Mary Lee, and Johnny during the crap game in the back room. Then, in the dramatization, the actor playing Johnny swigs a beer at the bar and talks to Sam, the owner. In this dramatization, Johnny does not seem that angry, certainly not out of control.

Gloria, who gathered together all the newspaper stories and her own file and sent the material to the producer, said she had to resort to television tactics.

"We're backed into a corner. It can't hurt Johnny. He's already sitting in jail," Gloria said during the week the film crew came to Havana. That the Peavys continued to offer a $25,000 reward for additional information fit right in with the show's format. "You can't get back into court. What else are you going to do?" she said.

She hoped the TV show would stir things up enough to produce new evidence. "If this will get us back into court, that's all we ask. I know out there somewhere, there's somebody who knows something. It could be the smallest detail, and that could be the piece of the puzzle we're looking for. There's somebody who knows where that gun is."

Tommy Lee Johnson, the convict who acted as a witness in Johnny's trial, would co-star in the TV show, Gloria said. Serving a life term in Florida State Prison for attempted murder, Johnson was willing to tell the Peavys' private investigator that he had lied at the trial and that he had never really heard Johnny confess. He said the other convict, Ricky Osborn, was lying, too. But only Johnson would say so now, on tape. He passed a polygraph. But, then again, he had passed one testing the truth of his testimony concerning Peavy's supposed confession. To Gloria, it was gripping, convincing drama. She prayed the show's airing would bring Johnny his break. "I still think it [the killing] was a paid hit," she said. "But we've taken rabbit trail after rabbit trail. Yeah, I get tired. But if we go nationwide, we might find that little piece [of evidence] we need."

On a September night in 1989, Johnny's story was aired nationwide. Tough-guy actor Stacy Keach, best known for playing private investigator Mike Hammer on TV, narrated.

No one ever interviewed the law enforcement side, Assistant State Attorney Jack Poitinger complained a few days after the show aired. No doubt about it: the show's tone was sympathetic to Johnny.

"It's our premier show," said Michael Cerny, an independent director working on the episode for "Missing: Reward."

"I believe John Peavy is innocent," he said. "Well, I shouldn't say that, but it [the case] deserves a re-examination. We're just bringing it up and letting the viewer decide."

The segment aired nationwide on September 23, with the $25,000 reward offered by the Peavy family, adding to the drama. But even with all that money dangling out there, time slips by and no one has yet come forward. There has been no change in the status of Johnny's case, except that the passing days shorten his two life sentences totaling fifty years minimum. He still lives in the state prison, in Jackson County, less than an hour's drive for the family on Sundays.

The prosecutors, investigators, and agents have moved on to other cases. But at Havana's feed and hardware stores, folks might still bring up Johnny Peavy and wonder aloud if he is really guilty. The Shady Rest shut down soon after the murders, looks more weathered and hollow than ever. No longer do the windows glow, signaling a haven for rednecks to shoot pool and swig beer. Driving past the deserted tavern, knowing that this is the place where ill will or bad luck began, depending on which side one believes, leads one to think that on that Halloween night in 1985, spookiness and treachery were real, real enough to send two robust lives crashing to a trailer floor during a dark rainstorm.

The mind traces the path Peavy said he took that night: up the highway toward Havana, curving around the back way past Thelma Nalls's red brick house near the lumber company, then left on the four-lane highway, and left up the long driveway home. There, one can see Johnny's tree. He hasn't been drinking under its branches, or anywhere else, since late 1985.

Up at the house, Gloria Peavy raises their two children alone. She has been on her own since her husband was arrested on December 23, 1985; and she never took down the Christmas tree of that aborted holiday.

"I'll take it down when Johnny's home," Gloria said. "It's a symbol of support."

Under its artificial branches, Johnny's unopened gifts remain, along with a mound of other gifts from the next Christmas and every Father's Day and birthday in between. On top of the tree is an angel. Gloria said that the angel is waiting for her angel to return.

The wait will last until the year 2035 or later, because Peavy has at least forty-six years left to serve on his life sentence. Nearly half a century is plenty of time to think about how to fill in the blank of missing time during that murderous Halloween night. Choose Thelma Nalls, and Peavy is just a drunk whose luck ran out.

Choose the jury, and he crept up to Harrison's trailer with killing in his heart.

Choose neither.

Or choose all of the above.

══════════ PROCEDURAL DESCRIPTION ══════════

A remedy is a legal procedure to redress a wrong or enforce a right. For the person convicted of a crime and sentenced to prison, it is a means of **vacating** the conviction or reducing the sentence. **Relief** is deliverance from a wrong. Remedies are authorized by both federal and state law and are available from the three branches of government. Executive remedies include **pardons, commutations,** and **reprieves.** Legislative remedies include granting **amnesty** and compensating an innocent person mistakenly convicted of a crime.

Judicial remedies are available in the courts. They include **direct remedies** and **postconviction remedies.** In a direct remedy, the defendant files a motion or takes an appeal claiming that a legal error was committed before, during, or after the trial. Postconviction remedies are available once direct remedies have been attempted or the time for seeking them has expired. They are sought on grounds of newly discovered evidence of innocence, jurisdictional error, or denial of constitutional rights.

Direct Remedies

Trial Remedies

There are several remedies available in the trial court as part of the original proceedings. The defense may move for a judgment of acquittal before the jury even returns the verdict. Failing that, the defense may appeal later, arguing that the trial court erred in not granting the motion for a judgment of acquittal. If persuaded, the appellate court will order an acquittal or dismiss the indictment. This motion is used commonly to challenge the sufficiency of the state's evidence.[1]

Another type of trial remedy is the motion for a new trial in which the defense argues that the court should set aside the guilty verdict and grant a new trial (see Exhibit 7-4). The court, on motion of the defense or on its own motion, may grant a new trial in Florida, for example, if:

- There is newly discovered evidence of innocence;

- The verdict is contrary to the weight of the evidence;

- The court erred in instructing the jury;

- The prosecuting attorney was guilty of misconduct;

- The jury received evidence out of court.[2]

Granting a new trial and declaring a mistrial are not the same thing. The court can grant a motion for a new trial only when the jury has rendered a verdict of guilty. It can declare a mistrial at any time during the proceedings when there is misconduct so prejudicial as to deny the defendant or the state a fair trial.

After the jury has rendered its verdict but before the judge pronounces the judgment, the defense may move to **arrest the judgment.** A **judgment** is a court order finalizing a trial by setting forth the defendant's plea, verdict, and, if guilty, sentence. In arresting the judgment, the court stays it. In the federal courts, the judge, on motion of the defendant, should arrest judgment if the indictment or information does not charge an offense for which the defendant was tried.[3] In *Sutton v. United States,* for example, the Fifth Circuit Court of Appeals

IN THE SECOND JUDICIAL CIRCUIT COURT

LEON COUNTY, FLORIDA

4/3/87

STATE OF FLORIDA   :

v.   :   CASE NO. 85-4810-CF

JOHN WESLEY PEAVY   :   FL BAR NO. 0127600

MOTION FOR NEW TRIAL

Defendant, JOHN WESLEY PEAVY, by and through undersigned counsel, and pursuant to Rule 3.590, Fla. R. Crim. P., moves the Court to order a new trial herein, and alleges:

1. The jurors decided the verdict by lot.

2. The verdict is contrary to law.

3. The verdict is contrary to the weight of the evidence.

4. The Court erred in the decision as a matter of law arising during the course of the trial which is more fully set forth below.   *JURORS 2/3 11, 101*

5. Through no fault of the Defendant, the Defendant did not receive a fair and impartial trial.   *SHACKLES*

6. The Court erred in allowing the admission into evidence of State's Exhibits 75, 76, 77, 78, 79, 80, 81, 82, 83, 84, 85, 86, 87, 88, 89 and 90.

7. The Court erred in allowing into evidence the alleged "jailhouse confessions" of JOHN WESLEY PEAVY.

WHEREFORE, Defendant prays the Court to enter its order granting a new trial.

CERTIFICATE OF SERVICE

I HEREBY CERTIFY that a true and correct copy of the foregoing instrument has been furnished to Assistant State Attorney Anthony S. Guarisco, Jr., Esquire, Office of the State Attorney, Suite 500, First

Exhibit 7-4 Motion for a new trial for John Wesley Peavy, submitted by Robert Harper and Anthony Bajoczky.

Florida Bank Building, Tallahassee, FL 32301, by hand/~~mail~~ this _03_ day

of April, 1987.

Respectfully submitted,

ANTHONY BAJOCZKY
131 North Gadsden Street
Post Office Box 1501
Tallahassee, FL 32302
(904) 222-9000

ROBERT AUGUSTUS HARPER
Law Firm
317 East Park Avenue
Post Office Box 10132
Tallahassee, FL 32302-0132
(904) 224-5900

Counsel for PEAVY

RAHff50

Exhibit 7-4 Continued.

held that judgment should have been arrested when the information failed to charge an essential element of the offense.[4]

Appellate Remedies

Appellants are defendants who are seeking review of their convictions and sentences in an appellate court. The **appellee** is the government, represented in a state court usually by a lawyer from the office of the attorney general. The **petitioner** is the person who seeks further discretionary review or postconviction relief. The person who contends against an appeal or responds to a petitioner's claim in a postconviction proceeding is the **respondent.**

Although there is no federal constitutional right to appeal, federal and states statutes permit it. Defendants who pleaded not guilty in the trial court are entitled to seek review of their convictions as a matter of right. They have a right to one appeal. Should their convictions be affirmed, they may seek review by a higher court, but that review is usually discretionary. In discretionary review, the appellate court must first decide whether it will accept or deny the petitioner's application. If it accepts, then it orders the petitioner and respondent to submit a written response.

In most cases that the appellate court reviews, the trial court has made a final judgment. Occasionally, though, the appellate court will take an **interlocutory appeal,** meaning that the trial court has entered an order that does not necessarily end the case. For example, a trial judge might order the prosecution to disclose the identity of a confidential informant. If the prosecution thinks the trial judge is wrong in making such an order, there is no way to continue the case until the appellate court has reviewed the trial judge's finding.

What appellants or petitioners may challenge on appeal depends on what they pleaded in the trial court. The issues that those who pleaded guilty may raise include the trial court's jurisdiction, the voluntariness of the plea, and the state's failure to abide by a plea agreement. In some states, defendants who pleaded no contest can reserve the right to appeal a specific ruling of the trial court. For example, if the trial judge denies a pretrial motion to suppress evidence, the defendant can plead no contest while reserving the right to appeal the judge's ruling on that motion. Defendants who pleaded not guilty may challenge on appeal the trial court's jurisdiction, fundamental error, and any issue that has been raised previously in the trial court.

It is important to preserve the record by motion or objection in earlier phases of a case because an appeal may be taken on issues raised in the trial court. As a rule, attorneys should object at the time of the act that is the target of their objection. The exclusion of illegally seized evidence, for example, should be raised on motion in the pretrial phase of the case as well as during the trial when the evidence is introduced.

Many of the errors brought on appeal are **harmless errors.** An appellate court will not review a judgment just because an error was made in the trial court. The reversal of a judgment is likely to occur only if the appellant can show that the error was so prejudicial as to invalidate the entire trial. In this case, it might be argued that (1) the outcome of the trial probably would have been different in the absence of the error; (2) there was a miscarriage of justice; or (3) the defendant was denied a fair trial. When the error involves provisions of the Constitution, an appellate court must find beyond a reasonable doubt that the error was harmless.[5] A fundamental error, such as right to counsel, cannot be treated as harmless under any circumstances. It may be challenged even if no objection was made to the court's failure to appoint counsel.

The grounds frequently alleged by appellants include:

- Failure to suppress evidence obtained by illegal search and seizure;

- Evidence insufficient to support finding the defendant guilty beyond a reasonable doubt;

- Misconduct on the part of the prosecutor or jurors;

- Failure by the court to give pertinent instructions to the jury;

- A ruling by the trial court interpreting a statute;

- The legality of the sentence imposed.

The prosecution's right of appeal is limited. Some states permit the state to take an appeal, but only when such an appeal does not violate the prohibition against double jeopardy. In Florida, for example, grounds for state appeal include:

- An order dismissing an indictment or information;

- An order suppressing evidence obtained by search and seizure or an order suppressing a confession;

- An order granting a new trial;

- An order adjudicating the defendant incompetent.[6]

Rules governing post-trial release vary widely. In one state, for example, it is mandated that "no person may be admitted to bail upon appeal unless the defendant establishes that the appeal is taken in good faith, on grounds fairly debatable, and not frivolous."[7] Trial courts usually have discretion whether to release defendants on bail pending appeal. The factors they consider in exercising their discretion include community and family ties, respect for the law, and severity of the punishment.

The government must provide indigent felons with counsel if they have a statutory right to appeal. Although some states provide counsel for those seeking discretionary review, others do not.

The procedure for taking an appeal consists of (1) filing a notice of appeal, (2) preparing the record on appeal, (3) preparing and filing the appellate briefs, (4) filing a request for oral argument, and (5) making the presentation. In some instances, the appellant can file a motion for rehearing.

An appeal is initiated when the appellant files a notice of appeal with the court clerk and pays the filing fee (see Exhibit 7-5). The notice of appeal must be filed by the appellant usually within a period of thirty days from the time the judgment was pronounced. The state may be required to file a notice of appeal in even less time.

The record on appeal consists of the formal allegations made by the parties regarding their respective claims and counterclaims (called **pleadings**) and a transcript of trial hearings. The record must support the points the attorney is raising on appeal, or the appellate court cannot consider their merit. Although it is the attorney's responsibility to ensure that the record is complete and transmitted to the appellate court, the court clerk actually prepares and transmits it. When the ap-

```
                    IN THE CIRCUIT COURT OF THE
                    SECOND JUDICIAL CIRCUIT, IN
                    AND FOR LEON COUNTY, FLORIDA.

                    CASE NO. 85-4810

JOHN WESLEY PEAVY,

         Defendant/Appellant,

    -vs-

STATE OF FLORIDA,

         Plaintiff/Appellee.

_____/
```

NOTICE OF APPEAL

NOTICE IS HEREBY given that JOHN WESLEY PEAVY, Defendant/
Appellant, appeals to the District Court of Appeal, First District
of Florida, the order of this Court rendered in Open Court on
April 23, 1987.

The nature of the order is a final judgment adjudicating
guilt and imposing sentence on the Defendant/Appellant.

```
ROBERT AUGUSTUS HARPER              ANTHONY L. BAJOCZKY
Law Firm
317 East Park Avenue
Post Office Box 10132               BARRETT AND BAJOCZKY
Tallahassee, Florida  32302        131 North Gadsden Street
(904) 224-5900                     Post Office Box 1501
                                   Tallahassee, Florida  32302
                                   (904) 222-9000

Lawyer for Defendant/Appellant     Lawyer for Defendant/Appellant
```

CERTIFICATE OF SERVICE

I HEREBY CERTIFY that a true and correct copy of the fore-
going Notice of Appeal has been furnished this ___ day of
May, 1987, to Mr. Anthony S. Guarisco, Assistant State Attorney,
Suite 500, First Florida Bank Building, Tallahassee, Florida 32301;
and to Department of Legal Affairs, Criminal Division, The Capitol,
Tallahassee, Florida 32399.

```
                    ANTHONY L. BAJOCZKY
```

Exhibit 7-5 Notice of appeal filed by the defense for John Wesley Peavy.

pellant is adjudged insolvent, the court pays the cost of the appeal
and appoints an attorney (see Exhibit 7-6).

Briefs, usually supported by court decisions and other citations,
are the principal vehicle attorneys use in the appellate court to present the points of law they want to argue. Generally, any point that
can be raised but is not argued on appeal is abandoned and may not
be used as the basis for further **appellate remedies**. There are several
types of briefs, including the initial brief of the appellant, the answer

IN THE CIRCUIT COURT OF THE
SECOND JUDICIAL CIRCUIT, IN
AND FOR LEON COUNTY, FLORIDA

CASE NO. 85-4810

JOHN WESLEY PEAVY,   :

    Defendant/Appellant,   :

vs.   :

STATE OF FLORIDA,   :

    Plaintiff/Appellee.   :

_____   :

ORDER OF INSOLVENCY

This cause coming on before me upon motion of the defendant, JOHN WESLEY PEAVY, for the appointment of counsel to represent him on appeal from the following final orders: Order Denying Motion for Post Conviction Relief, dated May 9, 1988; Order Denying Petition for Writ of Error Coram Nobis, dated May 9, 1988; and Order Striking Motion for New Trial, dated May 9, 1988 (all orders appealed from being rendered May 9, 1988), and this Court having been advised in the premises and having previously made inquiry of the defendant and having found him so insolvent that he was incapable of hiring his own attorney, it is hereby

ORDERED AND ADJUDGED that the Public Defender, Second Judicial Circuit, in the State of Florida, be and he is hereby appointed to represent the defendant on his appeal in this cause.

It is further ORDERED AND ADJUDGED that the defendant, JOHN WESLEY PEAVY, is without funds to pay the cost of his appeal and that Leon County, Florida, shall bear any and all costs necessary and incident to the prosecution of this appeal for the defendant.

DONE AND ORDERED THIS 25th day of _____ May _____,
19 88

_____
Circuit Judge

cc: District Court of Appeal   State Attorney
    Attorney General   Public Defender

Exhibit 7-6 Order of insolvency appointing counsel to represent Peavy and covering the cost of his appeal.

brief of the appellee, and the reply brief of the appellant. In both the brief of the appellant and the brief of the appellee, each point on appeal should be made in a concise statement, followed by an appropriate argument.

Each side may file a request for oral argument. The court grants oral argument if the judges decide that it would be useful. The time allotted for oral argument varies from one jurisdiction to another. Thirty minutes to a side is not uncommon. Attorneys appearing before the court for oral argument usually limit themselves to arguing only a few points, relying on briefs for other points, and spend the rest of their time answering the judges' questions. Appellants go first and may reserve part of their time to rebut appellees. In contrast, appellees are not permitted to rebut appellants.

The court usually does not rule immediately after oral argument. The members first take a vote at a judicial conference. Then one judge writes an opinion to which the other judges respond. Some may agree. Others may dissent. The dissent may be so persuasive that other judges will change their stand, thus altering the outcome of the case. Except for the judges and their staffs, nobody knows about this give-and-take because the opinion of the court is not officially released until each judge has decided. The vote may be unanimous, or one or more judges may dissent. Sometimes although judges agree with the outcome, they prefer to state separately their reasons for concurring. The court may affirm or reverse the lower court or criticize its errors without finding that such errors had any impact on the outcome of the case.

The amount of preparation required for an opinion varies, depending on whether the court simply announces a decision or discusses its reasons. There are two types of opinion: **per curiam** and signed. A per curiam opinion represents the court as a whole. Most decisions are signed by the judge who writes the opinion. In some courts, the senior judge or the senior judge voting with the majority decides at conference who will write the opinion. In other courts, the clerk's office assigns cases to judges at random.[8] Judges who disagree with the majority can write dissenting opinions. Opinions are published in books known as **reporters,** available in law libraries.

An appellant may file a motion for rehearing in some appellate courts. It is limited to stating those points that the court may have failed to consider. Reargument is not permitted. Cases in intermediate courts of appeal are usually decided by three-judge panels. A rehearing **en banc** may be requested. If the motion is granted, the case is heard by all the judges in the court.

Postconviction Remedies

The purpose of applying for a postconviction remedy is to obtain relief. Relief, though, is usually granted only if petitioners can prove their claims by an appropriate standard of proof. Relief is denied if the application fails to state a claim that is recognized as grounds for relief in that jurisdiction or if certain obstacles block relief. For example, failing to have exhausted all of the state remedies can block an application for the federal habeas corpus remedy extending to persons convicted in state courts. The relief granted in federal and state courts depends basically on two things: the remedy invoked and the grounds for ruling in favor of the petitioner.[9]

Habeas Corpus Remedies

In habeas corpus proceedings, petitioners may win either conditional or absolute discharge from custody, depending on their claims. Petitioners who claim that their conditions of confinement violate a constitutional right may be granted conditional discharge. The court may order their release at a future time unless government officials have taken a certain action to correct the violation. Prisoners are released unconditionally when the discharge is absolute.

Although grounds for habeas corpus relief vary from one jurisdiction to another, the most common are jurisdictional and constitutional. If Manuel Noriega, the ex-president of Panama, were convicted and sentenced to prison in a federal district court, for example, he might argue that the court did not have jurisdiction to try him because he committed no crime in the United States. For state prisoners, for example, constitutional grounds for relief in the federal courts are twofold:

1. A petitioner's conviction for committing an offense is unconstitutional if the state law defining the offense is unconstitutional;

2. Even if the law is constitutional, the conviction is unconstitutional if it resulted from a denial of the petitioner's procedural rights under the federal constitution.

A writ of habeas corpus is the principal method of postconviction relief in ten states.[10] It may be sought in a major trial court or in an appellate court. When the writ is sought in an appellate court, certain problems can arise. For example, if a prisoner petitions an appellate court, alleging improper treatment by correctional officers, the court is likely to **remand** the case to a major trial court for an evidentiary hearing. This sort of case requires fact-finding, a task for which an appellate court is ill suited. Other habeas corpus petitions, however, are best litigated before an appellate court. For example, if a prisoner complains that the attorney who represented him at trial was ineffective, this matter would be decided by an interpretation of the law, based on the already existing record of the trial.

Coram Nobis Remedies

Coram nobis, like habeas corpus, has its roots in English tradition. In this country, the writ of error coram nobis, as it is known, is authorized by common law. It is not recognized today as the principal postconviction remedy in any jurisdiction. Nevertheless, it is available in several states as an alternate remedy that may be used under certain circumstances. The remedy *in the nature of* the writ of error coram nobis, a statutory spin-off from the common law writ, is currently the principal remedy in thirty-nine states.[11]

In coram nobis proceedings, convictions are usually vacated or sentences are corrected. When a conviction is vacated, the defendant is usually retried. A successful coram nobis attack, however, may preclude retrial if the state is unable to use crucial evidence because doing so would violate the defendant's constitutional rights. A sentence can be corrected in a number of ways. It can be vacated, the offender can be resentenced, or months or years can be stricken from the sentence.

Grounds for coram nobis relief are usually jurisdictional or constitutional. Other grounds, including newly discovered evidence of innocence, are permitted in some jurisdictions (see Exhibit 7-7 and Exhibit 7-8). Constitutional grounds include:

- Ineffective assistance of counsel;

- Improprieties in jury selection procedures;

- Withholding of material testimony or evidence by the prosecutor;

- Incompetence of the defendant at the time of the trial or guilty plea;

- Knowing use of prejudiced testimony by the prosecutor.[12]

Procedure for Postconviction Relief

The procedure for petitioning the court for postconviction relief, like the procedure for taking an appeal, consists of several steps. The specific steps depend on the remedy and jurisdiction. A state prisoner, for example, could apply for postconviction relief in a federal district court by filing a **petition** for a writ of habeas corpus, a so-called section 2254 remedy.[13] The petition should state the grounds for relief and name the respondent, the person who has custody of the prisoner, usually the prison warden or the official in charge of state penal institutions. In addition, the petitioner should specify the pertinent facts supporting each of the grounds. The petition, though, is not a place for legal arguments. They may be included in a memorandum filed in support of the petition.

Although the Sixth Amendment does not extend the right to counsel to an indigent prisoner in a federal habeas corpus proceeding, the district court has statutory as well as discretionary power to appoint

IN THE SECOND JUDICIAL CIRCUIT COURT
LEON COUNTY, FLORIDA

STATE OF FLORIDA   :

                     :   CRIMINAL DIVISION

       vs.   :   CASE NUMBER: 85-4810

JOHN WESLEY PEAVY   :

MOTION FOR POST CONVICTION RELIEF

1.   Name and location of the court which entered the judgment of conviction under attack: <u>Second Judicial Circuit, Leon County, Florida</u>

2.   Date of judgment of conviction: <u>23 April 1987</u>

3.   Length of sentence: <u>Life & consecutive life (minimum mandatory 25 years) & 30 months concurrent & 30 months concurrent.</u>

4.   Nature of offense(s) involved (all counts): <u>Count 1, First Degree Murder; Count 2, First Degree Murder; Count 3, Shooting into a dwelling, Count 4, Use of firearm during commission of a felony.</u>

5.   What was your plea? (check only one)

     (a) Not Guilty <u> X </u>

     (b) Guilty <u>   </u>

     (c) Nolo Contendere <u>   </u>

     (d) Not Guilty for reason of insanity <u>   </u>

     If you entered one plea to one count, and a different plea to another count, give details:

Exhibit 7-7 Motion for postconviction relief filed by Robert Harper and Anthony Bajoczky for Peavy.

counsel. Appointment is mandatory, for example, if the court decides an evidentiary hearing is required. The federal government pays the fees of lawyers appointed to represent indigent petitioners. The prisoner who cannot afford to pay court costs and fees may proceed **in forma pauperis** by submitting a declaration of poverty.

Although a district court can release a state prisoner on bail pending disposition of a case, it rarely does. Federalism requires that the federal court use its power sparingly.

The court examines the petition. If it appears that the petitioner is not entitled to relief, the court summarily dismisses the petition.

(f)   In any post-conviction proceeding: <u>Anthony L. Bajoczky and Robert Augustus</u>
<u>Harper.</u>

(g)   On appeal from any adverse ruling in a post-conviction proceeding: <u>David P.</u>
<u>Gauldin, 301 South Monroe Street, Tallahassee, Florida   32301</u>

WHEREFORE, Movant prays that the Court grant all relief to which he may be
entitled in this proceeding, including but not limited to (here list the nature of the relief
sought):

1.   <u>Vacation of judgment and sentence and new trial.</u>

STATE OF FLORIDA   )
COUNTY OF GADSDEN   )

Before me, the undersigned authority, this day personally appeared John Wesley
Peavy, who first being duly sworn, says that he is the Defendant in the above-styled cause,
that he has read the foregoing Motion for Post-Conviction Relief and has personal
knowledge of the facts and matters therein set forth and alleged; and that each and all of
these facts and matters are true and correct.

John Wesley Peavy
JOHN WESLEY PEAVY

SWORN AND SUBSCRIBED
TO before me this ___8___
day of June, 1990.

Peacock
NOTARY PUBLIC, or other person
authorized to administer an oath.
NOTARY PUBLIC, STATE OF FLORIDA.
MY COMMISSION EXPIRES: JULY 9, 1993.
BONDED THRU NOTARY PUBLIC UNDERWRITERS.

Exhibit 7-7 Continued.

Otherwise, it orders the respondent to file an answer to the petitioner's allegations or to take some other action that the court orders.
In addition, the respondent is required to indicate whether the petitioner has exhausted all state appeals and to ensure that transcripts of
all proceedings are available.

After the pleadings have been filed, the court may do one of several things. If the facts are not in dispute, the court may grant or deny
relief without an evidentiary hearing. If the facts are in dispute, the
court may hold an evidentiary hearing, designate a federal magistrate
to conduct a hearing, or order that a hearing be held in a state court.
Basically, an evidentiary hearing is one in which both sides are given
a chance to prove or disprove certain facts by introducing evidence or
testimony. A district court has inherent power to conduct this sort of

B. GENERAL STATEMENT OF FACTS

The evidence at trial showed 31 October 1985 at 10:30 - 11:00 p.m. (A 322; R-7489) as the time of the shooting deaths of Mary Lee Driggers and Bobby Harrison. A gun owned by the Defendant was circumstantially linked to the offense by virtue of the similarity of calibre and similarity of *no* rifling marks. The murder weapon was never recovered. Two jail cellmates testified that JOHN WESLEY PEAVY made admissions in their presence. JOHN WESLEY PEAVY was convicted of first degree murder (R-142-246) and sentenced to life imprisonment with no possibility of parole for twenty-five (25) years (R-289-297) pursuant to jury recommendation (R-278-279).

C. NEWLY DISCOVERED EVIDENCE

1. New Evidence Has Been Discovered Which Closes the Gap in Time at the Time of the Offense Which Conclusively Proves JOHN WESLEY PEAVY Innocent

New evidence of a compelling nature has been discovered which together with previously known evidence completely exonerates the Defendant, JOHN WESLEY PEAVY. Dr. Thelma Nalls of Havana, Florida, has come forward with sworn testimony which proves that JOHN WESLEY PEAVY could not have and in fact, as maintained at trial, did not commit the crimes in question (A 1-41). Dr Thelma Nalls is the Administrator of Staff Development and Training for the Southwestern Georgia State Hospital of Thomasville, Georgia (A 3). She has been employed for more than twenty (20) years at the Georgia State Hospital (A 3) which treats meatal health patients for metal illness and substance abuse (A 4). Dr. Nalls has received a B.S. degree in nursing from

It was the usual practice for Dr. Nalls to go and meet her patients, including JOHN WESLEY PEAVY, for counseling sessions rather than allow them to drive, possibly intoxicated, to meet her (A 36). The usual meeting places for counseling with Mr. Peavy were at the First Baptist Church in Havana and the gate going into the driveway of the JOHN WESLEY PEAVY residence (A 13).

On 31 October 1985, Halloween night (A 19), Dr. Nalls was called on the telephone at her home at 9:45 p.m. by JOHN WESLEY PEAVY (A 19). Mr. Peavy told Dr. Nalls he was near his home (A 19), and asked her to meet with him. Dr. Nalls lives a mile from JOHN WESLEY PEAVY (A 20). She agreed to meet Mr. Peavy at the gate of his residence (A 20), and she arrived at that location within a few minutes of 10:00 p.m. (A 20). At 10:15 p.m. (A 21), within two or three minutes (A 21), Mr. Peavy, driving his pickup truck, came out of the roadway from the left which roadway is a drive to a mobile home (A 20).[2] Dr. Nalls exited her vehicle and got into Mr. Peavy's truck where they sat

Exhibit 7-8 Memorandum supporting the motion for postconviction relief for Peavy, written by the defense.

and talked (A 21). JOHN WESLEY PEAVY was drinking (A 21-22). He evidenced symptoms of memory loss by failing to recall the last counseling session with Dr. Nalls some days prior. Mr. Peavy discussed a physical problem (A 23) with Dr. Nalls for some fifteen minutes (A 22) after which time Dr. Nalls got back into her automobile. Mr. Peavy drove down the driveway to his residence. Dr. Nalls waited several minutes to make sure Mr. Peavy did not turn around (A 24-25), and then she drove home arriving just before 11:00 p.m.

    2.   <u>The New Evidence is Corroborated by Subsequent Known Events</u>

    In deposition on 23 February 1987, Gloria Peavy (A 42-105, R-2576-2639), the wife of JOHN WESLEY PEAVY, testified that on Halloween evening she and her husband had taken their two children trick-or-treating (A 49; R-2583). Mrs. Peavy was recovering from surgery (A 48; R-2582), and when the family returned at 8:00 - 8:15 p.m. (A 50; R-2584), Mrs. Peavy lay down on the couch (A 51; R-2585). The children occupied themselves with their Halloween treats (A 51; R-2585). JOHN WESLEY PEAVY left the home before "Simon and Simon"[3] after having built a fire (A 51; R-2585). Mr. Peavy said he would be back in a little bit and in fact about halfway through "Knots Landing"[4] he arrived at home (A 52; R-2586), whereupon he carried his sleeping daughter to her bed and then went to bed himself (A 83; R-2617).

    3.   <u>The New Evidence Substantiates and Corroborates</u>
           <u>Known Alibi Evidence and Witnesses</u>

    a.   <u>Winessa "Queen" Jackson.</u> On 08 January 1986, the State Attorney took the sworn statement of Winessa "Queen" Jackson of Route 4, Box 2185, Havana, Florida, (A 106-150) where she lives with her children, Agnes Jackson (A 108) and Barbara Jackson (A 109), and two grandchildren (A 122). The home is located on the driveway entrance, the gate, to the residence of JOHN WESLEY PEAVY. Ms. Jackson recalled Halloween night, 1985, as a rainy night (A 118). She and her family were eating hotdogs when JOHN WESLEY PEAVY came to her house (A 123). Her daughter, Agnes Laquita Jackson, was in the yard in the automobile of her boyfriend, Lawrence Herring (A 127). A conversation followed.

    JOHN WESLEY PEAVY said, "Queenie, how you doing?"

    Ms. Jackson responded, "I'm doing all right, Johnny. How you doing?"

    Mr. Peavy then turned to the children and asked, "Did y'all have a good trick-or-treating?"

    The children answered, "Yeah."

    JOHN WESLEY PEAVY began to give them more candy and said, "I brought you some trick-or-treat candy. Y'all look good in your costume suits, you got some pretty good costume suits." Mr. Peavy turned to Ms. Jackson and said, "Well, Queen, you know

Exhibit 7-8 Continued.

what? They look so nice. You know when we was growing up we didn't have those." (A 127)

Ms. Jackson replied, "No we sure didn't, Johnny, we didn't have those. Kids got'em.

Mr. Peavy repeated, "They sure look nice." Then Ms. Jackson got a beer for herself and Mr. Peavy which they each drank. (A 128)

Mr. Peavy stayed 25 to 30 minutes (A 130) before going to his pickup truck (A 130-131), getting in, cranking up, and driving off. He "drove out [and] went straight down the road towards [his] home." (A 131)

    b.   <u>Barbara Ann Jackson</u>. The State Attorney also took the sworn statement of Barbara Ann Jackson on or about 08 January 1986 (A 151-200). Barbara Jackson, date

    g.   <u>Joyce Ann Jackson</u>. On 27 February 1987, the State took the deposition of Joyce Ann Jackson (A 301-317; R-2559-2575) who lives with her mother, Willie Queen Jackson (A 307). On 31 October 1985, Halloween night, she was in the back room doing her homework when John Peavy arrived at their residence (A 304). She heard his truck drive up (A 305), saw his truck (A 312) and shortly later heard his voice (A 305). JOHN WESLEY PEAVY arrived at "about 10:00." (A 305). He left about 10:20 (A 306). She was aware of the time because "Knots Landing" was on the television, a program the family watches regularly (A 306,308).

    4.   <u>New Evidence Reflects John Wesley Peavy Was Convicted by the Use of Perjured Testimony</u>.

One of the key pieces of evidence in the trial was the testimony of a jail inmate, Tommy Lee Johnson. Tommy Lee Johnson has been interviewed post trial. See attached interview. While under oath, Tommy Lee Johnson stated that all the information he testified to at trial relative to Johnny Peavy was false (Exhibit attached). Mr. Johnson has stated under oath that, his testimony was not based on the "jailhouse confession" of John Peavy. Rather, he has stated that the source of his testimony was the newspaper accounts of the case. Mr. Johnson has admitted that he lied at the trial of John Wesley Peavy. Mr. Johnson has also subsequently testified that the second "jailhouse confession" of John Wesley Peavy was also the product of false testimony by Ricky Osborn. The office of the State Attorney knew the testimony of Ricky Osborn was false.

D. MEMORANDUM OF LAW

A new trial based on newly discovered evidence is addressed to the sound discretion of the trial court, and only very rarely will its determination be disturbed. *Baker v. State*, 336 So.2d 364 (Fla. 1976); *Bell v. State*, 90 So.2d 704 (Fla. 1956). A new trial will not be awarded on the basis of newly discovered evidence unless the evidence was (a)

Exhibit 7-8 Continued.

discovered after trial, unless (b) due diligence was exercised to have such evidence at the former trial, (c) unless the evidence goes to the merits of the cause and not merely to impeach a witness who testified, unless (d) the evidence is not cumulative, and unless (e) it is such that it probably would have changed the verdict. *Harvey v. State*, 87 So.2d 582 (Fla. 1956): *McVeigh v. State*, 87 So.2d 694 (Fla. 1954); *Branch v. State*, 96 Fla. 307, 118 So. 13 (1928); *Hudson v. State*, 353 So.2d 633 (Fla. 3d D.C.A. 1977).

Applying these principles the Third District reversed the conviction under review because the trial court was in manifest error in denying the defendant's motion for new trial

CONCLUSION

Petitioner prays the Court to set aside and vacate its judgment and sentence in this cause and grant a new trial. It is submitted that the factual allegations, if rebutted, trigger an evidentiary hearing on the claims made.

Exhibit 7-8 Continued.

hearing.[14] The court may direct that the prisoner be present at a hearing in which the facts are in dispute.

The court may conduct a law hearing once the evidentiary hearing is held or deemed unnecessary. The court hears legal arguments at this hearing. No evidence or testimony is presented.

In its final order, the court grants or denies relief (see Exhibit 7-9). The order is usually accompanied by findings of fact and conclusions of law. Habeas corpus relief is granted only to those who can prove their case by a **preponderance of evidence**. The standard of proof for a habeas corpus remedy is different from that of the trial because a habeas corpus remedy is a civil action and the rules of civil procedure apply. The final order of a district court may be appealed, but the notice of appeal must be filed within thirty days.

Non-Judicial Remedies

If all efforts at judicial relief fail, the convicted innocent can resort to non-judicial remedies, including pardons, commutations, reprieves, and amnesty. A pardon is an act of clemency by the president or governor, exempting from punishment a person convicted of a crime. It can be full or partial. A commutation is a reduction in an offender's sentence. For example, in some states governors can commute a death sentence to life imprisonment. A reprieve is a postponement of punishment. It is used in capital cases, for example, to give prisoners time to pursue other remedies. Amnesty is an act of foregiveness

IN THE CIRCUIT COURT OF THE SECOND JUDICIAL
CIRCUIT, IN AND FOR LEON COUNTY, FLORIDA.

CASE NUMBER: 85CF4810

STATE OF FLORIDA,

vs.

JOHN WESLEY PEAVY,

Defendant.

_____/

ORDER DENYING POST CONVICTION RELIEF

THIS CAUSE is before the Court on the Defendant's Motion for Post Conviction Relief and the Court having considered the Motion and the State of Florida's Answer and Motion to Summarily Deny Motion for Post Conviction Relief, and the respective exhibits and attachments thereto, and otherwise being fully advised finds as follows:

The Court finds that Defendant's Motion is inadequate to support relief under F. R. C. P. Rule 3.850. Defendant asserts that newly discovered evidence of a compelling nature has been discovered, which if presented at trial, would have resulted in a not guilty verdict. Defendant alleges that he is entitled to an evidentiary hearing or new trial because the newly discovered evidence "probably" would have changed the verdict. Defendant is mistaken as to the legal test required for this Court to entertain a 3.850 Motion.

In Richardson v. State, 546 So2d 1037 (Fla 1989), the Supreme Court held that claims of newly discovered evidence that were previously considered only by writ of error coram nobis should be brought pursuant to Rule 3.850. The Supreme Court, however, did not alter or modify the rigorous test required in a coram nobis proceeding. The conclusivity test is still utilized in determining whether a defendant is entitled to Post Conviction Relief based on a new evidence ground; Wilson v. State, 561 So2d 1295 (Fla. 1st DCA 1990); Preston v. State, 564 So2d 120 (Fla. 1990). Were this Court to use the same legal test as when considering a timely Motion for a new trial under Rule 3.590(a), Fla. R. Crim. P., it would render the time limits of Rule 3.590

Exhibit 7-9 On December 3, 1990, Circuit Judge Charles McClure denies Peavy's second request for post-conviction relief.

meaningless. A fact which was noted by this Court in its May 9, 1988, Order Striking Motion for New Trial.

The Court concludes that the newly discovered evidence does not conclusively show that it would have precluded the verdict of guilt and the imposition of the judgment. Accordingly, the Motion is hereby denied for the reason that it fails to state grounds for relief as a matter of law.

DONE AND ORDERED in Chambers, at Tallahassee, Leon County, Florida, this 3rd day of December 1988.

CHARLES O. McCLURE
CIRCUIT JUDGE

cc: Raymond L. Marky
State Attorney's Office

Robert A. Harper, Esq.

Exhibit 7-9 Continued.

---

offered to a class of persons as a whole. The power to grant amnesty can be exercised by both the legislative and the executive branches of government. Compensating an innocent person mistakenly convicted of a crime is an additional remedy available to the legislature.

Study Questions

1. If Peavy's lawyers were not arguing that an error was made at trial, what was their basis in asking for a new trial? If no errors were made, why should Peavy be allowed a second trial?

2. Defense attorney Robert Harper tried two arguments in his attempts to get Peavy a new trial. What were they? At the very least, what did Harper want to accomplish with this hearing?

3. How did the state counter the defense's argument of ineffective counsel? According to the prosecution, would the defense have had a difficult time proving its allegations in postconviction proceedings?

Endnotes

1. For example, see *Jackson v. State*, 511 So.2d 1047 (Fla. 2d DCA 1987).

2. *Florida Rules of Criminal Procedure*, rule 3.600 (1987).

3. *Federal Rules of Criminal Procedure*, rule 34 (1990).

4. *Sutton v. United States*, 157 F.2d 661 (1946).

5. *Chapman v. California*, 386 U.S. 18 (1967).

6. Philip J. Padovano, *Florida Appellate Practice* (St. Paul, MN: West Publishing Co., 1988), 405.

7. *Florida Rules of Criminal Procedure*, rule 3.691 (1987).

8. Thomas Duffy, law clerk, Florida Supreme Court, Tallahassee, FL, personal communication, 9 July 1990.

9. Donald E. Wilkes, Jr., *Federal and State Postconviction Remedies and Relief*, 2d ed. (Norcross, GA: The Harrison Co., 1987), 1–14.

10. Donald E. Wilkes, Jr., *Federal and State Postconviction Remedies and Relief*, 2d ed. (Norcross, GA: The Harrison Co., 1987), 268.

11. Donald E. Wilkes, Jr., *Federal and State Postconviction Remedies and Relief*, 2d ed. (Norcross, GA: The Harrison Co., 1987), 270.

12. Robert Popper, *Post-Conviction Remedies in a Nutshell*. (St. Paul, MN: West Publishing Co., 1978), 59–60.

13. 28 U.S.C.A. § 2254.

14. *Townsend v. Sain*, 372 U.S. 293 (1963).

Glossary

Adjudicate   To hear and decide a case judicially.

Adversary system   A system of justice in which prosecution and defense are opponents with an impartial judge umpiring the proceedings.

Adverse witness   Witness presumed to favor the opposition.

Affidavit   Written statement of facts confirmed under oath by the person making the statement to a person having authority to administer the oath.

Aggravating circumstances   Circumstances attending a crime that increase its guilt or enormity (e.g., use of a weapon increases the degree of battery from simple to aggravated).

Allen charge   Judge encouraging a deadlocked jury to reach a verdict.

Amnesty   General pardon or act of forgiveness for a class of people as a whole.

Appellant.   Person who appeals a case to a higher court.

Appellate remedies.   Proceedings in which a higher court reviews the decision or ruling of a lower court.

Appellee.   Person against whom an appeal is taken.

Arraignment   Proceeding in which the defendant is brought before a judge to hear the charge and enter a plea.

Arrest   Form of detention in which a person is taken into custody and deprived of liberty by legal authority.

Arrest the judgment   Court order staying the judgment after the verdict has been given.

Attorney-client privilege   Privilege that permits attorneys to refuse to testify about communications from their clients.

Back-striking   Using a peremptory challenge to exclude a prospective juror who was passed over in previous questioning.

Bail   Surety exchanged for the release of arrested persons as a guarantee of their appearance at court proceedings.

Bench trial   Trial held before a judge sitting without a jury.

Binding over   Act of a lower court in transferring a case to a trial court after finding cause to believe that the accused committed a crime.

Bond   Sum of money paid as bail.

Bond schedule   List of bond amounts for different offenses, making court appearance unnecessary.

Booking   Administrative procedure following arrest in which accused is given Miranda warnings, fingerprinted, photographed, relieved of personal property, and assigned a jail number.

Boykin form   Questionnaire courts use to inquire of defendants pleading guilty whether they understand the nature of the charges and the rights they are waiving.

Briefs   Written statements, containing summaries of facts, pertinent laws, and arguments concerning how laws apply to facts supporting attorneys' positions.

Burden of proof   Responsibility of proving an allegation or disputed charge.

Capias   Writ requiring a law enforcement officer to take the body of the defendant into custody.

Capital case   Case involving a crime for which death is the permissible punishment.

Case in chief   That part of a trial in which the side with the initial burden of proof presents its evidence.

Certiorari   Writ issued by a higher court, granting discretionary review of a case decided in a lower court and requesting the transcript of the proceedings.

Challenge for cause   Request from a party to a criminal proceeding that a certain prospective juror not be allowed to be a member of the jury because of a specified cause.

Challenge to the panel   Challenge regarding the propriety of the drawing, selecting, or impaneling of the whole jury panel or array.

Charging   Formal accusation of a crime made by the prosecution in an information or by the grand jury in an indictment.

Circumstantial evidence   Indirect evidence from which the existence of a fact may be inferred.

Civil law   Body of laws concerned with private rights and remedies.

Common law   Judge-made law.

Commutation   Reduction of a penalty to one less severe.

Complainant   Person who makes a complaint.

Complaint   A charge, preferred before a lower court judge, that a person has committed an offense, coupled with the offer to prove the fact.

Concurrent   Refers to a multiple sentence in which prison terms run simultaneously.

Consecutive   Refers to a sentence in which one prison term begins when the other ends.

Continuance   Adjournment of court proceeding to a subsequent day or time.

Coram nobis   Proceedings to vacate a conviction or sentence brought in trial court and authorized by common law or statutory law.

Criminal law   Body of laws that deal with crime and its punishment.

Cross-examination   Interrogation of a witness called by the opposing side.

Defendant   Person formally charged with an offense.

Deponents   Persons who are deposed.

Depose   To take down sworn statements in writing from a person, to be used in court or as a discovery device.

Direct evidence   Testimonial evidence from a witness who actually saw, heard, or touched the subject of interrogation.

Direct examination   First interrogation of a witness by the side that called the witness.

Direct remedies   Remedies available in trial court as part of the original proceedings or an appeal.

Discovery   Pretrial devices used by one side to obtain facts and information about the case from the other side.

Docket sounding   Judicial review of the status of pending cases with attorneys to determine which defendants are going to trial and which are pleading guilty or no contest, so that upcoming needs for jurors, courtrooms, and judges can be assessed.

Double jeapardy The act of putting a person through a second trial for an offense for which that person has already been prosecuted.

Due process Procedural rights protecting citizens from government denial of life, liberty, or property.

Elements of a crime Those constituent parts of a specific crime which must be proved by the prosecution to sustain a conviction.

En banc Refers to session where the entire membership of the appellate court participates in a decision.

Estreated Forfeited.

Evidentiary hearing Hearing in which both sides are given a chance to prove or disprove certain facts by introducing evidence or testimony.

Exclusionary rule Judicial doctrine that illegally seized evidence cannot be admitted at trial.

Exculpatory Tending to clear from a charge.

Exhibits Evidence that is tangible and can be offered to the court for inspection.

Expert witness Person with specialized experience or knowledge who is permitted to testify at trial not only about facts but also about conclusions drawn from these facts.

Felony More serious than a misdemeanor, an offense for which a person can be sentenced to death or to a term of imprisonment in excess of a year.

First appearance Proceeding in lower court at which bail is set and the accused are informed of the charges and their rights.

Gag order Court order banning attorneys or witnesses from discussing the case with reporters or publicly disclosing anything about the case.

Gain time Reduction in a prison sentence, usually as a reward for good behavior or participation in prison programs.

Good faith exception Evidence not excluded during trial because police acted in good faith on a warrant found later to be defective.

Grand jury Jury of persons convened in private to evaluate accusations against a person charged with a crime and to determine whether the evidence warrants an indictment.

Habeas corpus Proceedings to discharge a prisoner from unlawful custody.

Harmless errors Errors made at trial that do not affect its outcome.

Hearsay Evidence based on the reports of others instead of the personal knowledge of a witness or informant.

Hostile witness Witness who unexpectedly exhibits hostility toward the attorney who is doing the questioning.

Hot pursuit Pursuing a fleeing suspect.

Hung jury Jury unable to reach a verdict.

Impeach To call into question the veracity of a witness by introducing contradictory evidence.

Incompetency Inability of a defendant to understand the nature of the court proceedings and to assist counsel in preparing the case because of a lack of mental competency.

Inevitable discovery exception Illegally seized evidence is admissible because it would have been discovered inevitably.

Indigent Too poor to be able to hire an attorney.

In forma pauperis Without liability for court costs and fees.

Information Formal accusation of a crime, made by the prosecution.

Interlocutory appeal Appeal of a matter whose resolution is required before a case can be decided.

Judgment Official decision of the court setting forth the plea, verdict, and, if the defendant is found guilty, sentence.

Judgment of acquittal Court order of acquittal without allowing the jury to consider the case because, as a matter of law, there can be only one verdict in light of the state's failure to present a prima facie case.

Jurisdiction Persons over whom a court has power and subject matter about which a court can make legally binding decisions.

Laying the foundation Showing that an exhibit is what it purports to be.

Leading question Question so worded as to suggest the desired answer.

Lesser included offense Offense composed of some, but not all, of the elements of a more serious offense.

Lower courts Courts of limited jurisdiction which are responsible for the preliminary stage of felony cases and which hold trials in petty cases where the penalty is restricted to imposing sentences of no more than a year in jail.

Major trial courts Courts of general jurisdiction which hold trials in felony cases and which may hear cases on appeal from lower courts.

Mandatory minimum sentences Laws directing that offenders convicted of certain offenses be sentenced to prison terms of not less than a specified period of time.

Master jury list   List of citizens in a jurisdiction from which the venire is chosen at random.

Miranda warnings   Warnings given to persons arrested or taken into custody that they have the right to remain silent; that any statement they make may be used as evidence against them; that they have the right to the presence of an attorney; and that, if they cannot afford an attorney, one will be appointed prior to questioning.

Misdemeanor   Less serious than a felony, an offense for which the maximum punishment is a term of imprisonment not exceeding a year.

Mistrial   Trial terminated without conclusion on the merits of the case because of some error in the proceedings or because the jury could not agree.

Mitigating circumstances   Circumstances attending to a crime that extenuate it (e.g., killing in the heat of passion reduces the degree of homicide from murder to manslaughter).

M'Naghten rule   Rule that defines a person as legally insane when that person cannot distinguish right from wrong.

Motions   Applications made to a court for orders or rulings.

Motion to strike   Motion to a court to strike from the record any statement deemed impertinent, immaterial, or scandalous.

Nolo contendere   No contest, a plea in a criminal case that has a legal effect similar to pleading guilty.

Occurrence witness   Witness who saw, did, or heard something related to the case.

Offer of proof   Person whom the court rules against when an objection to a question is made may answer the question out of presence of the jury to determine for the record the correctness of the ruling.

Opinion   Formal statement summarizing the legal reasons for the conclusions of the judge or majority of judges.

Pardon   Act of clemency by a president or governor, exempting from punishment a person convicted of a crime.

Per curiam   Opinion rendered by the whole court rather than by an individual judge.

Peremptory challenge   Formal objection to the service of a juror by a party to a criminal proceeding; such an objection requires no showing of cause.

Petition   Formal written application to a court seeking discretionary appellate review or postconviction relief.

Petitioner   Person who brings a petition before a court.

Plaintiff   Person who initiates action in a civil case.

Plea negotiations   Prosecution and defense negotiating an agreement that allows a defendant to plead guilty or nolo contendere.

Pleadings   Formal allegations made by the parties regarding their respective claims and counterclaims.

Postconviction remedies   Proceedings to vacate a conviction or discharge a prisoner, invoked usually after the time for appeals has expired or appeals have been exhausted.

Preliminary hearing   Proceeding at which the court determines whether the accused should be held for trial.

Preponderance of evidence   Evidence which is of greater weight than the evidence offered in opposition to it.

Presumption of innocence   Principle that the government has the burden of proving every element of the crime and that the defendant has no burden to prove innocence.

Prima facie case   Case in which the evidence produced, unless rebutted, is sufficient to support a finding by the jury.

Probable cause   Exists where facts would warrant a person of reasonable caution to believe that an offense was being committed or had been committed.

Probative   Tending to prove.

Pro bono   Without charge.

Procedural law   Rules governing the procedures by which substantive law is administered at various stages of the criminal justice process.

Process servers   Persons authorized by law to serve writs, summons, and subpoenas.

Rap sheet   Criminal history of the accused.

Reasonable doubt   The standard of proof required in a criminal case: Such proof as satisfies the judgment of the jury, as reasonable persons, and applying their reason to the evidence, that the crime charged has been committed by the defendant and so satisfies them as to leave no other reasonable conclusion possible.

Recross-examine   To examine witnesses subsequent to redirect examination.

Redirect examination   Examination of witnesses by the side calling them after cross-examination.

Relief   Deliverance from a wrong.

Remand To send back.

Remedies Legal procedures to correct a wrong or enforce a right.

Reporters Published volumes of case decisions of a particular court or group of courts (e.g., *Supreme Court Reporter*).

Reprieves Postponement of punishment.

Respondent Person who contends against an appeal or responds to a petitioner's claim in a postconviction proceeding.

Rule of Four The Supreme Court grants certiorari only on agreement of at least four justices.

Sequestered Isolated or kept separate (e.g., jurors isolated from contact with the public; witnesses not allowed in the courtroom during proceedings, except to give testimony).

Stare decisis Doctrine that principles of law on which a court based a previous decision are authoritative in all future cases in which the facts are substantially the same.

Statute of limitations A statute defining the time limits within which a case must be prosecuted.

Statutory law Law enacted by legislators.

Stop and frisk Temporary detention of a suspect who is subjected to a patdown search for weapons.

Subpoena duces tecum Writ directing a person to appear in court and to bring some document described in the writ.

Subpoena ad testificandum Command to appear in court to give testimony.

Substantial capacity test Test according to which persons are not responsible for a crime if as a result of mental disease they lack substantial capacity to appreciate the criminality of their conduct or to conform their conduct to the requirements of law.

Substantive law Law that creates rights and proscribes wrongs.

Testimony Evidence given orally or in the form of a deposition or affidavit by a witness under oath.

Trial de novo Process by which a trial court conducts a new trial instead of reviewing the record of the original trial in a lower court.

True bill An indictment endorsed by a grand jury.

Vacating Setting aside or rendering void.

Venire   Group of citizens, commanded to be in court, from whom jurors are selected.

Venue   Local area where a case may be tried.

Voir dire   Examination of prospective jurors.

Index